PRESCHOOL

The IDEA MAGAZINE FOR TEACHERS®
MAILBOX®

The Education Center®

2011–2012 YEARBOOK

The Education Center, Inc.
Greensboro, North Carolina

The Mailbox® 2011–2012 Preschool Yearbook

Managing Editor, *The Mailbox* Magazine: Kimberly A. Brugger

Editorial Team: Becky S. Andrews, Diane Badden, Kimberley Bruck, Karen A. Brudnak, Pam Crane, Chris Curry, Brenda Fay, Tazmen Hansen, Marsha Heim, Lori Z. Henry, Troy Lawrence, Kitty Lowrance, Tina Petersen, Gary Phillips (COVER ARTIST), Mark Rainey, Greg D. Rieves, Hope Rodgers-Medina, Rebecca Saunders, Donna K. Teal, Sharon M. Tresino, Zane Williard

ISBN 978-1-61276-242-5
ISSN 1088-5536

Printed in the United States of America.

The Mailbox® Yearbook
P.O. Box 6189
Harlan, IA 51593-1689

Look for *The Mailbox® 2012–2013 Preschool Yearbook* in the summer of 2013. The Education Center, Inc., is the publisher of *The Mailbox*®, *Teacher's Helper*®, and *Learning*® magazines, as well as other fine products. Look for these wherever quality teacher materials are sold, call 1-866-477-4273, or visit www.themailbox.com.

HPS242166

Contents

Math Units

Teacher Resource Units

Thematic Units

Arts & Crafts for Little Hands

Arts & Crafts for Little Hands

Process Art

Out of This World!

To make this celestial artwork, pour white paint in a spray bottle and then dilute it with water. Spritz a sheet of black construction paper with the diluted paint. Glue circles to the paper to represent planets; then decorate the project with foil stars and glitter so it resembles outer space.

Jane Mandia
Little Friends Preschool
Marlboro, NY

Process Art

Color and Paint

This pretty process art gives little fingers a fine-motor workout! To make the artwork, use a thick rubber band to bind a cluster of crayons together. Then draw with the bundled crayons on a sheet of white paper. Finally, use watercolors to paint the paper as desired. How lovely!

Popcorn Prints

This process art results in unique, one-of-a-kind prints! Partially fill several balloons with popcorn kernels. Tie the end of each balloon in a knot. Put paint in shallow containers. To make a print, dip a balloon in paint and then press it on a sheet of paper. Repeat the process until you are satisfied with your work. Be sure to discard the balloons in a safe location.

Sherri McFarland
Morristown-Hamblen Child Care Centers
Morristown, TN

Nothing Left!

Apples sure are tasty! To prepare for this project, cut out a simple white construction paper apple-core shape similar to the one shown. Sponge-paint the top and bottom of the core red. Then attach a stem cutout and seed cutouts. If desired, display the finished artwork with the title "Crunch!"

Paper-Strip Sculpture

This abstract art is easy to make and stunning to look at! Cut a supply of paper strips in desired colors. Fold the ends of each strip to create tabs for gluing. To make a sculpture, glue the strips to a sheet of construction paper, arranging them to give the artwork dimension as shown.

Amber Dingman
Sterling, MI

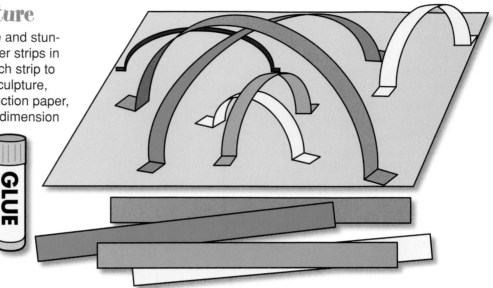

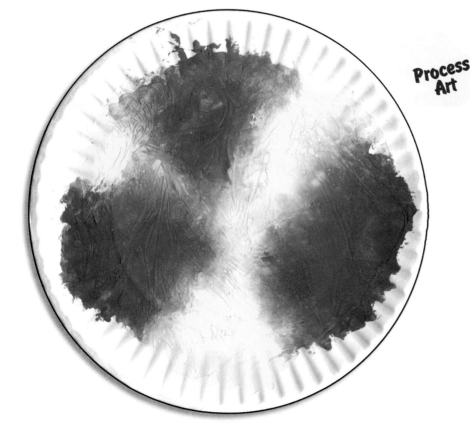

Process Art

No-Mess Fingerpainting

Drop spoonfuls of paint on a paper plate; then wrap the plate with clear plastic wrap and lightly tape it to hold it in place. To paint, gently maneuver your fingers on the covered plate, blending the colors as you work. When the project is complete, remove the wrap. For a textured effect, set the project aside for several hours before removing the wrap.

Ellen Maguire
Little Corner Schoolhouse
Brookline, MA

Arts & Crafts for Little Hands

Intriguing Leaves

These unique leaves would surprise Mother Nature! Draw a tree (minus the foliage) and ground details on a sheet of construction paper. Use a leaf-shaped hole puncher to punch leaves from colorful magazine pages. Glue the leaves to the paper as desired. Then add the poem shown to this lovely autumn artwork.

Sandra Bendickson
Salvation Army Child Care Center
Peoria, IL

Tina Brewer
Fayetteville Creative School
Fayetteville, AZ

Red and yellow,
Orange and brown,
See the leaves
Come tumbling down!

Process Art

Pumpkin Picasso

Obtain several small pumpkins (or gourds) with stems. Place each pumpkin next to a shallow container of paint. Holding onto the stem, dip a pumpkin in paint and press, drag, roll, or twirl it on a sheet of paper. Repeat the process with other pumpkins and colors of paint, overlapping the artwork and blending the colors as you work.

Jesse Scenga
Handprints Christian Early Learning Center
Sterling Heights, MI

Straw Strokes

Looking for a unique paint tool? Bundle lengths of straw together with a rubber band and wrap one end with heavy-duty tape to make a handle. Set out separate containers of paint for each straw bundle. Simply dip the straw bristles in paint and gently stroke them on paper!

Kathie Thornton
Wake Forest, NC

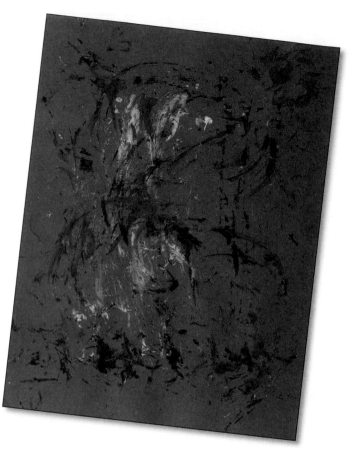

Night Owl

To make this airborne owl, paint one whole coffee filter and two coffee filter halves brown. Glue the filters to a sheet of black paper as shown so they resemble an owl body and wings. Then cut eyes and a beak from paper scraps and glue them in place. Attach star stickers to the page so it resembles the night sky.

Mandi Ellis
Children's Choice Childcare Inc.
Hauppauge, NY

tip → Would you rather make a bat? It's simple to do! Cut notches in the bottoms of the wings and paint the body and wings black. Then mount the bat on dark grey paper. Omit the beak and add a couple of not-so-scary fangs (white triangle cutouts).

Peel, Press, Peel

This process art finely tunes the artist's pincer grasp! Peel sticky dots from their backing and randomly press them onto a sheet of fingerpaint paper. Then fingerpaint the entire page as desired. When the paint is dry, peel the dots off the paper to reveal a polka dot design!

Marie E. Cecchini
West Dundee, IL

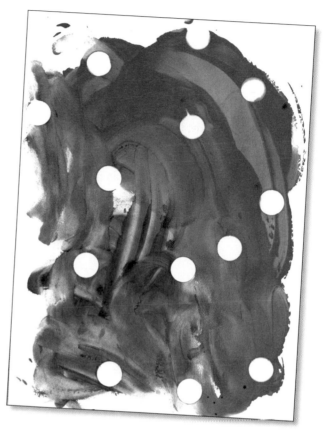

Candy Corn

Cut or tear candy wrappers and glue the pieces to a corncob-shaped cutout. Trim any excess wrappers from the edges of the cutout; then glue torn green construction paper to the corn to resemble husks. To complete the corn, glue pieces of yellow yarn or embroidery thread (corn silk) to the project.

Karen Eiben
The Learning House
LaSalle, IL

 tip → Have parents donate Halloween candy wrappers for this project. (It's healthier than trying to provide them all yourself!)

Arts & Crafts for Little Hands

Spiffy Snowscape

Create the effect of freshly fallen snow with a mixture of shaving cream and glue. Simply apply a thick layer of the mixture to a piece of tagboard. Then stand tree cutouts in the mixture. This project makes a lovely tabletop snowscape!

Sherry Gustafson
YMCA SVCDC
Wilbraham, MA

 tip Consider taking photos of youngsters in their winter wear. Then trim the photos and stand them in the shaving cream mixture as well! You're sure to get compliments on this adorable project!

Process Art

Icy Designs

The forecast calls for oodles of fun when making this chilly process art! Put on a pair of mittens and then dip an ice cube into a shallow pan of powdered tempera paint. Maneuver the ice cube around on a sheet of white paper. Repeat the process with other colors of paint until a desired effect is achieved.

Susan Schoelkopf
Centralia College Children's Lab School
Centralia, WA

Santa's Surprise

This cute craft makes an adorable holiday keepsake! Spread paint thickened with flour (frosting) onto a tagboard cookie with a "bite" torn from the edge. Top off the frosting with holiday-related confetti; then glue the cookie to a small paper plate. To complete the craft, attach a copy of the poem shown to the plate.

Janet Boyce, Cokato, MN

Dear Santa,

Here's a treat
I made just for you.
Although it's missing
a bite or two.
I had to be sure
it tasted just right;
So I nibbled the edge
and then took a bite!

Love,
Olivia

Snowman Snapshot

Here's a no-mess project that emphasizes photography as art! Gather random items and arrange them on a large snowman cutout to make features and accessories. Then take a photo of the finished snowman. Display this artwork with a colorful frame cutout.

Lois Otten
Kingdom Kids Preschool
Sheboygan, WI

 tip → Ask each youngster's family to send random items to school with their child. (Emphasize that the items will be returned.) They might consider natural objects, small toys, scraps of fabric and ribbon, kitchen odds and ends, and jumbo buttons!

Arts & Crafts for Little Hands

Floating Feathers

This process art is simple to make and soothing to watch as it takes shape. Spread colorful tinted glue on the surface of a sheet of white paper. Then drop a craft feather from above the paper and watch as it gently drifts to a resting place on the wet glue. Continue in the same way to create a soft-textured piece of artwork.

Marie E. Cecchini
West Dundee, IL

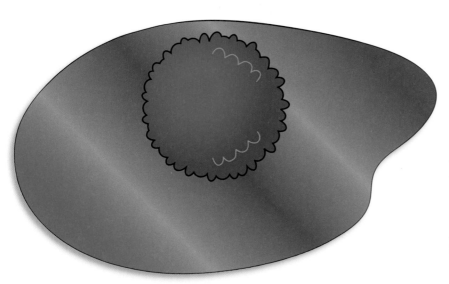

Fried Green Egg

Follow up a read-aloud of Dr. Seuss's *Green Eggs and Ham* with this excellent egg craft! Tint a container of white glue green. (Hint: Tacky glue is thicker and less runny than school glue.) To make a fried-egg shape, use a spoon to drizzle the glue onto a sheet of waxed paper. When you are satisfied with the shape, drop a green pom-pom on the glue. Allow the project to dry for several days and then peel the egg off the waxed paper.

Keely Saunders
Bonney Lake Early Childhood Education and
Assistance Program
Bonney Lake, WA

Conversation Heart

To make a candy heart, spread a layer of glue over the surface of a heart cutout. Then sprinkle ground chalk on the wet glue. After the project is dry, brush a layer of glue on the chalk to kccp if from rubbing off. Then attach a paper strip labeled with a sweet sentiment.

Meghan Zeile
Little Ones On Linwood
Rochester, MI

Valentine Keepsake

For this sweet Valentine's Day memento, wrap a cardboard tube with holiday-themed paper and hot-glue it to a small paper plate to make a vase. Decorate the plate with craft foam hearts and attach a decorative ribbon to the tube. To make a rose, paint the thumb-side of your fist red or pink and press it on white paper. Cut around each dry print and tape it to a green pipe cleaner. Then arrange the roses in the vase. How pretty!

Barbara Romano
St. Joseph Preschool
Hammonton, NJ

Leprechaun's Gold

To make this adorable craft, glue a white paper semicircle to a black pot cutout (pattern on page 109) as shown. Next, dip one end of a cork in a mixture of yellow paint and gold glitter; then press the cork on the semicircle. Repeat the process to make a pile of gold. To complete the project, attach a photo and personalized message as shown.

Meghan Zeile
Little Ones On Linwood
Rochester, MI

Samantha found the leprechaun's gold!

Process Art

Crafty Chopsticks

This process art results in a delicious-looking craft! Tightly bind a pair of chopsticks together with a small sponge between the tips. Then dip the sponge in paint and spread it on a small paper plate. Repeat the process until the plate contains a thick layer of paint. Then sprinkle a generous amount of dyed dry rice on the paint.

adapted from an idea by Nancy Foss
Wee Care Preschool
Galion, OH

 tip → Incorporate the sense of smell with this project by replacing the paint with duck sauce!

Arts & Crafts for Little Hands

Mud Works

Add some potting soil to a mixture of brown paint and glue. Use a spoon (or your fingers) to spread the mixture on a sheet of paper. Then press blades of real grass (or green crinkle shreds) and small sticks into the wet mixture.

Kristy Pulcher
First United Methodist Church Weekday Program
Plano, TX

Best Nest

To make the nest, roll a brown paper lunch bag about three-quarters of the way down; then press down on the bag. Shape the resulting nest as desired and then glue brown paper shreds to it. To make the bird, glue two feathers, two small pom-poms, and a beak cutout to a large pom-pom as shown. Then glue the bird in the nest. Tweet!

Michele Van Buren
Morrison Community Day Care
Morrison, IL

Pull, Push, Spread, and Slide!

For this process art, you'll need a plastic card, such as an expired gift or credit card. To prepare, mix sand into separate containers of different colors of paint. Then scoop dollops of paint onto a sheet of fingerpaint paper. Use the card to pull, push, and spread the paint, blending the colors as you work. Slide the edge of the card through the paint to create interesting designs. For a dazzling effect, sprinkle glitter onto the wet mixture.

Irresistible Resist

This process art fine-tunes the artist's small-motor skills! To make one, smooth out a coffee filter and place it on a tray. Next, use a white crayon to draw marks or designs on the filter. Then use spray bottles filled with tinted water to spritz the filter. If desired, mount the filter on a construction paper square.

Janet Boyce
Cokato, MN

After reading
For about an hour,
Mark your place
With this special flower!
Love, Hailey

Beautiful Bookmark

This adorable keepsake is as practical as it is precious! Paint the palm and fingers of one hand and press it on light-colored construction paper to make a handprint. Trim around the print, and then glue it to a cutout copy of the flower stem pattern below. Laminate the bookmark, if desired. Then hole-punch the top of the bookmark and use yarn to attach a bee cutout (see the bee pattern below). What a lovely Mother's Day gift!

Linda Bille
Riviera United Methodist Preschool
Redondo Beach, CA

Flower Stem and Bee Patterns
Use with "Beautiful Bookmark" on this page.

TEC41060

After reading
For about an hour,
Mark your place
With this special flower!

Arts & Crafts for Little Hands

Aloha Island

Paint the back of a heavy-duty paper plate blue (ocean) and a cardboard tube brown (tree trunk). Cut out several palm-shaped leaves; then cut a slit in each leaf and slide the leaves on the tree trunk as shown. (Hint: Add a touch of glue to secure the leaves in place.) Glue the resulting palm tree to the ocean, surrounding it with extra glue. Then sprinkle a generous amount of sand on the glue so it resembles an island. To complete the craft, glue confetti fish and other sea critters to the ocean!

Sarah Davis
Little Oaks Preschool
Arroyo Grande, CA

Fabulous Foil

This process art adds a whole new dimension to aluminum foil! Place two or more colors of fingerpaint on a sheet of aluminum foil. Spread the paint with your fingertips, blending the colors and creating designs as you work. When you're finished, sprinkle glitter on the wet paint; then attach the dry artwork to a sheet of paper in a contrasting color.

Janet Boyce, Cokato, MN

Lovely Lava

Cut a volcano shape from brown butcher paper or a grocery bag. Crumple the cutout, smooth it out with your hand, and then glue it to a large sheet of construction paper. To create the lava, press your hand in a shallow pan of red paint and then onto the paper, repeating the process so the prints resemble lava spewing from the top of the volcano and flowing down the sides.

Coya Clayton
Kids Inc.
Marion, IA

 Sprinkle red glitter over the handprints for fabulous sparkly lava!

Heavenly Hamburger

This hamburger looks yummy enough to eat! To make one, crumple and shape light brown tissue paper so it resembles a hamburger bun half. Glue the bun to a paper plate; then glue a brown craft foam circle (hamburger) atop the bun. Use plastic squeeze bottles filled with red and yellow paint (ketchup and mustard) to top the hamburger. Then make a second bun half and glue it to the craft as shown.

Helene Vosper
Starbright Childrens Center
Center Moriches, NY

 tip
Looking for some hamburger-themed process art? Encourage students to make brown circular sponge prints on a paper. Then have them squeeze red and yellow paint onto the paper as desired!

Perfectly Patriotic!

Spice up your holiday decor with patriotic decoupage! Brush diluted glue on a large paper plate. Next, cover the plate with a variety of red, white, and blue paper scraps, such as tissue paper, napkins, scrapbook paper, magazine clippings, and gift wrap. Then brush a layer of glue on the surface of the decorated plate. When the glue is dry, trim any excess paper from the edge of the plate; then attach red, white, and blue crepe paper streamers and a string for hanging.

Jan Trautman
Raleigh, NC

Process Art

Drizzle Designs

A colorful abstract masterpiece is the result of this process art! Slightly dilute several colors of paint. Then use individual craft sticks to drizzle each color of paint on a sheet of tagboard, overlapping the drizzled designs as you work.

Natasha Pritchett
University Children's Center
Chicago, IL

BUSY HANDS

Busy Hands

Fine-Motor Explorations for the Season

Off to School!

Draw a schoolhouse, a few houses, and roads on a length of bulletin board paper. Attach the paper to a tabletop. Provide a shallow pan of paint and a toy school bus and car. A student dips the wheels of a vehicle in the paint and then "drives" it from a house to school and then back home.

Tricia Kylene Brown
Bowling Green, KY

Ice-Cold Teddy Bears

Freeze water and a bear counter in each compartment of an ice cube tray. Put the ice cubes in your sensory table along with a spray bottle of warm water and a pair of tongs. A child sprays an ice cube several times with water. Then she uses the tongs to flip it over. She repeats the process, attempting to melt the ice cube and remove the bear. If desired, provide salt shakers to speed the melting process!

Jolee Zehren
Green Bay Head Start
Green Bay, WI

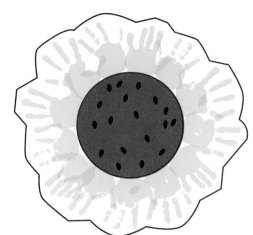

LOVELY SUNFLOWER

Attach a sheet of white bulletin board paper to a tabletop and glue a brown circle cutout to the center of the paper. Have each child paint the palm and fingers of his hand yellow and press it on the outer edge of the circle several times to make flower petals. Then have him glue several craft foam seeds to the center of the flower. After each child has had a chance to contribute, trim the paper and display the flower.

Liz Trujillo
Uno, Dos, Tres Academy
Portland, OR

PLAY DOUGH NAMES

Write youngsters' names (or initials) on individual papers and slide the papers into sheet protectors. Provide play dough. A student rolls play dough between her hands and then places it atop a letter, manipulating the dough to match the letter formation. She continues until she completes her name.

Angie Clark
Tabernacle Christian School
Greenville, SC

DROP AND GLUE

Provide a large tagboard apple and paper scraps in red, yellow, and green. A child places the apple on the floor. He holds a scrap above the apple and then lets it go. If the paper lands on the apple, he glues it in place. If it does not, he continues with other scraps.

Ellen Maguire, Little Corner Schoolhouse,
Brookline, MA

Fine-Motor Explorations for the Season

ideas contributed by Tricia Kylene Brown, Bowling Green, KY

PIGSKIN PRINTS

Place at a table a large white poster board football cutout. Provide a small football and a shallow container of brown paint. Each youngster visits the table, dips the football in the paint, and stamps or rolls it on the cutout to create a unique pigskin design. To complete the project, glue lengths of white yarn to the football so the yarn resembles stitching.

PUMPKIN OR WEB?

Set out a container filled with craft foam seeds and plastic spiders. Provide a pumpkin-shaped pail and a vinyl placemat programmed with a spiderweb (or provide pumpkin and web cutouts) along with a pair of tongs. A youngster uses the tongs to pick up and place each seed in the pail and each spider on the web.

OWL FEATHERS

Scatter around the classroom a supply of brown craft feathers. Provide a large owl body cutout, a glue stick, and a small bag. For added fun, provide a pair of binoculars. A student searches for feathers and places each one he finds in the bag. After collecting several feathers, he glues them to the cutout. Youngsters continue until the owl is covered with feathers.

SALTED SEEDS

Fill a pumpkin pail with lengths of orange yarn, crumpled orange tissue paper, and craft foam seeds. Provide a sheet of newspaper, a large spoon, a tray, and an empty salt shaker. A child scoops the innards onto the paper, picks out the seeds, and arranges them on the tray. Then he pretends to salt and bake them. How fun!

Gobble, gobble, gobble!

PECKING GRAIN

Transform a sock into a turkey puppet. Then spread yellow pom-poms (grain) on the floor and place a container nearby. A child dons the puppet and pretends the turkey says "gobble, gobble, gobble" as it pecks. She picks up a piece of grain with the turkey's "beak" and drops it in the container, continuing until all the grain is collected.

Busy Hands

Fine-Motor Explorations for the Season

ideas contributed by Tricia Kylene Brown, Bowling Green, KY

Ornamental Prints

Place at a table a large Christmas tree cutout, plastic ornaments, and shallow containers of paint. Each youngster visits the table, dips desired ornaments in paint, and presses them on (or drags them across) the tree to make prints. When the paint is dry, attach a star to the top of the tree and display it in the classroom.

It's a Wrap!

Provide several holiday gift boxes and bags, sheets of tissue paper, and play gift items. A child wraps each gift in a sheet of tissue paper and then puts the gift in a box or bag.

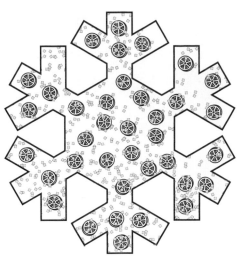

GLISTENING SNOWFLAKE

Have students glue wagon wheel pasta to an oversize snowflake cutout. When the glue is dry, encourage them to help you brush white paint on the pasta and then sprinkle iridescent glitter on the paint.

POLAR PLAY

Freeze water in assorted containers. Put the blocks of ice in your water table along with chunks of white Styrofoam and plastic polar animals. If desired, provide mittens. A youngster uses the ice and props to engage in pretend polar animal play.

DECORATIVE SHAPES

Provide a few holiday-related tagboard shapes, each in a different color. Also provide a collection of gift bows that match the color of each shape. A child places the bows atop the matching shapes.

Fine-Motor Explorations for the Season

*ideas contributed by Tricia Kylene Brown
Bowling Green, KY*

DRIFTING CLOUDS

Attach light blue bulletin board paper (sky) to a tabletop. Provide a few wads of cotton batting (clouds) and a plastic drinking straw for each child. A youngster blows through a straw to maneuver the clouds in the sky.

GOLD DROP

Fill a plastic tub with green paper shreds (grass). Hide a supply of gold plastic coins in the grass. Provide a black pot and plastic tweezers, along with a holiday-related hat, if desired. A child pretends to be a leprechaun who spots gold coins in the grass. Then he uses the tweezers to pick each gold coin out of the grass and drop in the pot.

SOFT WOOLLY LAMB

Attach to a tabletop an oversize clear or white circle of Con-Tact covering (lamb's body), sticky-side up. Provide a supply of white cotton balls (wool). A student visits the center, tears cotton balls, and presses them onto the body. Youngsters continue until the body is covered with wool. To complete the lamb, attach a head cutout and legs as shown.

HEART DESIGNS

Place at a table an oversize heart cutout, a small heart-shaped candy box (top and bottom separated), and disposable plates with paint. A student dips the flat portion of either section in paint and presses it on the cutout to make a solid print. She dips the open portion of either section in paint and presses it on the cutout to make a heart outline.

VALENTINE TUBE PUPPETS

Attach the hook sides of self-adhesive Velcro fastener pieces to the backs of valentine cards that have character designs. Attach the corresponding loop sides to several cardboard tubes. A youngster attaches cards to the tubes and then engages in puppet play. He replaces the characters as desired.

Fine-Motor Explorations for the Season

ideas contributed by Tricia Kylene Brown
Bowling Green, KY

BUNNIES IN THE MEADOW

Attach a length of green bulletin board paper to a tabletop. Provide a marshmallow bunny (or a bunny-shaped sponge) and a container of chocolate pudding. Each youngster visits the table, dips the bunny in the pudding, and stamps it on the paper, sniffing the chocolaty aroma as she works. If desired, have students glue green crinkle shreds (grass) around the prints.

Peep! Peep! Peep!

"PEEPABOO"!

Place a yellow pom-pom (chick) inside each of several plastic eggs; then hide the eggs in a container filled with plastic Easter grass. A child searches through the grass and finds an egg. He opens the egg and says, "Peep, peep, peep!" pretending the chick is hatching from the egg. He continues until each chick has hatched.

SPRINGTIME SPLENDOR

Provide an oversize tree cutout, lengths of thick brown yarn, green paper scraps, and colorful tissue paper scraps. Youngsters visit the area and glue yarn to the tree trunk. Then they glue green paper scraps (leaves) and tissue paper scraps (flowers) to the tree. What a pretty, cooperative project!

RAINBOW STAMPERS

Set out an oversize paper rainbow outline and bingo daubers in rainbow-related colors. Use each dauber to stamp one print on the appropriate arc. A youngster stamps the corresponding color dauber on each arc, using the teacher-made prints as a guide. Youngsters continue until they have all had an opportunity to add to the rainbow.

Rebecca Schumer, Listen and Talk, Seattle, WA

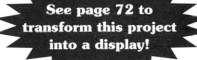

See page 72 to transform this project into a display!

MIX-AND-MATCH KITES

Draw several same-size kite shapes on light blue poster board (sky). For each kite, cut matching triangles from wallpaper samples or scrapbook paper. If desired, add a few cotton batting clouds to the sky. A child arranges triangles on each outline to create her own unique kite designs.

Fine-Motor Explorations for the Season

NIFTY NIGHT SKY

Place at a table black poster board programmed with a moon cutout, a shallow container of glow-in-the-dark paint, and an unsharpened chunky pencil with an eraser. A youngster dips the eraser end of the pencil in the paint and stamps it on the poster board, creating a splattered effect to make stars in the sky. Occasionally, a child drags the eraser across the paper to make a shooting star! Expose the project to direct light; then turn down the lights and watch the stars glow!

Katie Fils, West Point Child Learning Center, Lansdale, PA

LADYBUG INVASION

Place a container of red pom-poms (ladybugs) in your block center. A youngster uses blocks to build structures and homes for the ladybugs.

EXTRA FUN!

Provide pom-poms (ladybugs) in a variety of sizes and provide small green pom-poms (aphids) as well for the ladybugs to eat!

FABULOUS FIREWORKS!

Attach a length of black bulletin board paper to a tabletop; then use a white crayon to draw fireworks designs on the paper. Provide a shallow container of glue, cotton swabs, and glitter. Little ones visit the table, dip cotton swabs in glue and trace the designs, and then sprinkle glitter on the glue. When the glue is dry, simply shake off the excess glitter and mount the display on a board or wall. What fancy fireworks!

Tricia Kylene Brown, Bowling Green, KY

POOL NOODLE PICASSO

Thread small sections of foam pool noodle onto a wooden dowel (paint roller). Set out a tray of paint and large sheets of paper. Holding the ends, a child rolls the paint roller in the paint and then across a sheet of paper, adding more paint to the roller as needed.

Tricia Kylene Brown

CATCHING FIREFLIES

Scatter small yellow pom-poms (fireflies) in an area and provide a clear plastic jar and tweezers. A youngster "catches" a firefly with the tweezers and drops it in the jar, continuing until all the fireflies are caught. If desired, put green crinkle shreds and a small flameless candle (secure the battery casing with duct tape) in the bottom of the jar for a lighted effect!

Tricia Kylene Brown

Kitty's New Backpack

©The Mailbox® • TEC41056 • Aug./Sept. 2011

36 THE MAILBOX

Note to the teacher: Have each child color a copy of this page. Next, have her use a cotton swab to spread glue on the letters and apple. Then have her sprinkle clear glitter on the glue.

Follow the Treat Trail

This Way

©The Mailbox® • TEC41057 • Oct./Nov. 2011

Note to the teacher: Give each child 15 M&M's Minis candies. Encourage her to put one candy piece atop each candy picture along the trail. After completing the candy trail, invite her to nibble her treats and color the page as desired.

Walking to the White House

©The Mailbox® • TEC41059 • Feb./Mar. 2012

Note to the teacher: Give each child a copy of this page for some Presidents' Day fun! Have her press her fingertip on a black ink pad and then onto the path to make a trail of footprints leading from Abraham Lincoln to the White House. Then encourage her to color the page as desired.

Peep! Peep!

Note to the teacher: Have each child trace the egg. Next, have her crumple yellow tissue paper squares and glue them to the chick. Then have her glue an orange triangle beak to the head.

Chatting Over Lunch

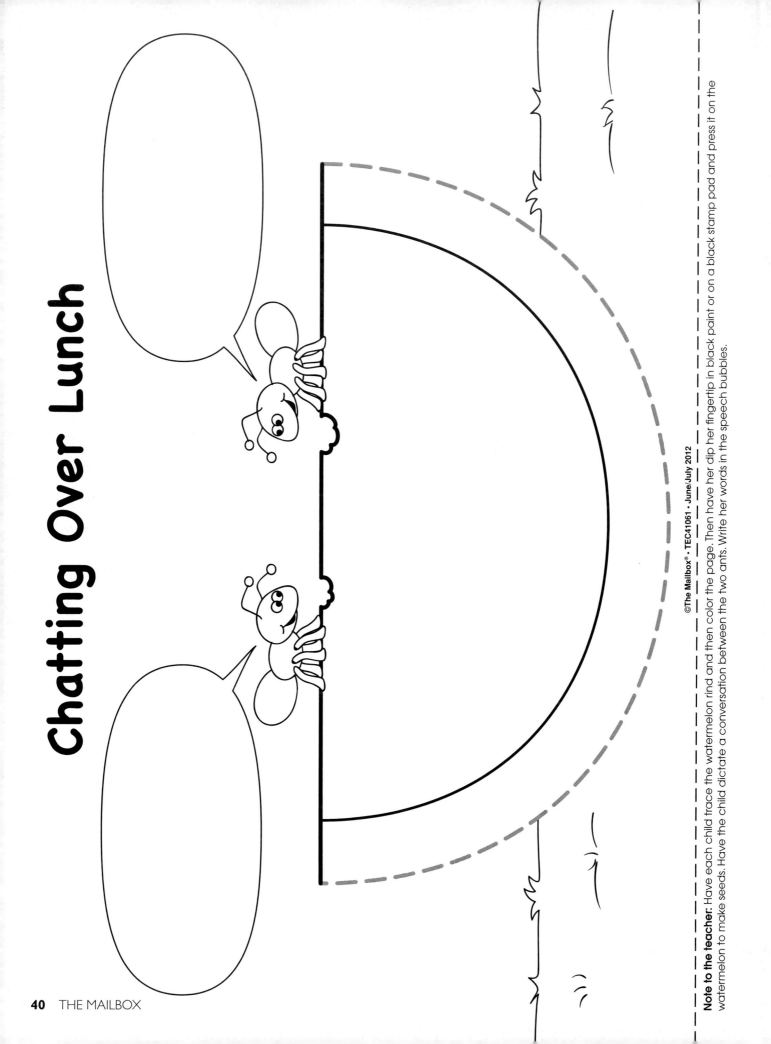

©The Mailbox® • TEC41061 • June/July 2012

Note to the teacher: Have each child trace the watermelon rind and then color the page. Then have her dip her fingertip in black paint or on a black stamp pad and press it on the watermelon to make seeds. Have the child dictate a conversation between the two ants. Write her words in the speech bubbles.

CIRCLE TIME

Who's Knocking?

Obtain a photo of each child. Enlarge the schoolhouse pattern on page 58 and make a copy. Then cut out the schoolhouse, making sure to trim around the door so it opens. To play, place the schoolhouse on the floor and secretly hide a youngster's photo behind the door. Knock several times on a surface. Then lead students in chanting, "One, two, three, four—who's that knocking at the door?" At the end of the chant, open the door to reveal the photo. Encourage students to identify their classmate; then replace the photo and repeat the process.

adapted from an idea by Candy Grzadziel
Elgin, IL

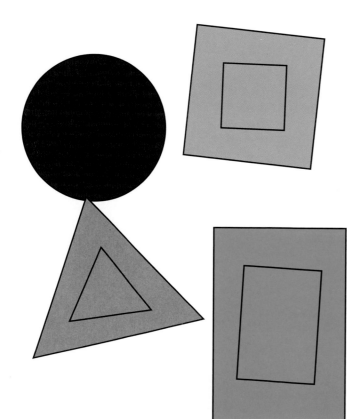

Shape Search

Youngsters practice shape matching with this fun game! Scatter a class supply of shapes around the room. For each shape, place a larger matching shape in the center of the circle-time area. Review the shapes with youngsters. Then encourage each child to find one shape, bring it back to the circle, and place it atop the corresponding shape. After verifying that the shapes are matched correctly, lead youngsters in singing the song shown, ending with a round of applause.

(sung to the tune of "The Muffin Man")

We found all the matching shapes,
The matching shapes, the matching shapes.
We found all the matching shapes.
Let's give ourselves a hand!

Trisha Orend
Orend Family Child Care
Port St. John, FL

Get Up and Go!

Little ones will have a blast playing this movement game! Arrange a class supply of chairs, facing inward, in a horseshoe shape and have each child sit in a chair. Instruct a student from one end of the horseshoe to gallop around the outside of the chairs toward the other end. As he gallops, direct the child sitting next to the vacated chair to quickly sit in it; the remaining youngsters shift over one seat as well. When the galloping child reaches the other end of the horseshoe, he sits in that vacant chair. Continue in the same way until everyone has had a turn to gallop.

Karla David
Options State Preschool—Cedargrove
Covina, CA

Apple Picking

Mount a poster board tree on a wall and place a basket nearby. To begin, instruct little ones to close their eyes while you use Sticky-Tac adhesive or tape to attach several personalized apples to the tree. Then have youngsters open their eyes. Sing the song shown, prompting each child to pick an apple from the tree if she sees one labeled with her name. After checking for accuracy, have the students put their apples in the basket. Have youngsters close their eyes again and repeat the process until each child has had a turn to go apple picking.

(sung to the tune of "If You're Happy and You Know It")

If your name is on an apple, pick it, please.
If your name is on an apple, pick it, please.
If your name is on an apple,
If your name is on an apple,
If your name is on an apple, pick it, please!

Becky Crutsinger
Weatherford Christian School
Weatherford, TX

Kevin.

Roll, Say, and Switch

Give one child a ball. Ask her to name a classmate and then roll the ball to that child. After she rolls the ball, lead her in reciting the chant shown, inserting the selected child's name and the appropriate pronoun. Have the remaining youngsters pat their legs as she speaks. At the end of the chant, prompt the two youngsters to switch places. Then direct the child who has the ball to name a classmate who has not had a turn. Continue in the same manner, inviting the last child who takes a turn to name a classmate of her choice.

I know a [boy] named [Kevin].
Yes, [Kevin] is [his] name.
Switch places with me, [Kevin].
That's how we play the game!

adapted from an idea by Michele Sterner
Future Faces
Endwell, NY

Red or Yellow

Scatter enough red and yellow items around the room for each child to find one. Place a red apple cutout and a yellow school bus cutout in the middle of the circle. Then instruct each child to find one object that matches either color and bring it back to his seat. After all the youngsters are settled in, invite a student to show his object, tell what it is, and then name the color. When he's finished, have him place the item atop the matching-color cutout. Prompt the remaining youngsters to say "Crunch!" when an item is placed on the apple and "Beep, beep!" when one is placed on the bus. Continue until everyone has had a turn.

April Pace
Scope Educational Services
Levittown, NY

Listen, Listen

Store in a sack a collection of items associated with familiar words representing sounds. For example, a stuffed toy cat (*meow*), a rubber duck (*quack*), a toy train (*choo, choo*), a clock (*tick-tock*), and a plastic frog (*ribbit, ribbit*). Invite a volunteer to take an item from the sack. Then lead the group in reciting the chant shown, inserting the name of the item. Next, encourage youngsters to make the item's sound. Set the item aside and continue until the sack is empty.

Listen, listen,
What do you hear?
I hear a [item's name]
With my listening ears!

Roxanne LaBell Dearman
NC Early Intervention Program for Children Who Are Deaf
    or Hard of Hearing
Charlotte, NC

Planting a Rainbow by Lois Ehlert

Where's the Mouse?

Youngsters will need the keen eyes of a wise old owl to play this observation game! To prepare, cut out a gray construction paper copy of the mouse pattern on page 47 and attach a roll of tape to the back. To play, have youngsters pretend to be owls. Explain that owls eat mice. Instruct your little owls to close their eyes. While their eyes are closed, attach the mouse somewhere in the classroom. Have the owls open their eyes and fly about the room looking for lunch. When an owl spots the mouse, he says, "Whoooo! Whoooo!" and then reveals its location. Remove the mouse and play several more rounds of this fun game.

adapted from an idea by Karen Smith
Little Tid-Bits
Fresno, CA

Five Yummy Doughnuts

Display five felt doughnuts on your flannelboard. Place a container near the board and give each of five children a piece of play money. To begin, guide youngsters in counting the doughnuts aloud. Then lead the group in saying the rhyme, inserting a child's name. Prompt that child to drop her coin in the container, take a doughnut, and return to her seat. Guide students in counting the remaining doughnuts; then repeat the activity, inserting the appropriate number and a different child's name until all the doughnuts are gone.

Down around the corner at the bakery shop,
There are [five] yummy doughnuts with frosting on top.
Along came [child's name] with money to pay,
So [she] bought one doughnut and walked away.

Allison Annand
Hollis Primary School
Hollis, NH

Real or Make-Believe?

Display a two-column chart like the one shown. Next, say, "Some people think monsters are real and others think they are make-believe. Let's find out what our class thinks!" Recite the chant shown, inserting a youngster's name where indicated. Then help the child place a personalized sticky note on the chart to reflect how he feels. Continue in the same way with each child. Guide little ones in counting and comparing the notes in each column. Then conclude the activity with a discussion, leading youngsters to understand that monsters are make-believe.

Monsters, monsters,
Are they real?
[Child's name], show us
How you feel!

Amy Jandebeur
Frogs to Fairy Dust Childcare and Preschool
Yukon, OK

Preschool Pilgrimage

Make an oversize yarn or masking tape boat outline on the floor for youngsters to sit in. Briefly share about the Pilgrims' voyage aboard the *Mayflower*. Explain how the ocean water could sometimes be calm or rough during their journey. Then have youngsters pretend they are Pilgrims sailing aboard the *Mayflower*. Announce words that begin with /k/ like *calm* or /r/ like *rough*. When a word begins with the /k/ sound, prompt your pint-size Pilgrims to sit still as if sailing on calm ocean water. When a word begins with /r/, have youngsters rock back and forth pretending to sail on rough ocean waves. After several rounds, hold your hand above your brow, look off in the distance, and then call out, "Land ho!" to conclude the activity.

Donna Olp
St. Gregory the Great Preschool
South Euclid, OH

Mouse Pattern
Use with "Where's the Mouse?" on page 45.

TEC41057

Tapping Bells

Youngsters learn to track print from left to right with this musical activity! Write the words to the chorus of "Jingle Bells" on chart paper. To make a musical pointer, securely attach jingle bells to one end of a craft stick. Lead little ones in singing the song, gently tapping the pointer as you track the print. When you sing the word "Hey!" (and again at the end of the chorus), add some musical flair by giving the pointer a few lively shakes.

 tip For a fun and festive syllable activity, make a few jingle bell pointers and give one to each child. Name a holiday-related word. Then have students say the word, shaking their bells for each syllable.

Jingle bells

Jingle bells, jingle bells,

Jingle all the way.

Oh what fun it is to ride

In a one-horse open sleigh. Hey!

Jingle bells, jingle bells,

Jingle all the way.

Oh what fun it is to ride

In a one-horse open sleigh.

Rebecca.

Cold Snowball

Try this chilly twist on the familiar game Hot Potato! Play some lively music and have youngsters pass a faux snowball—such as a white foam ball or a large white pom-pom—around the circle as if it were very cold! Stop the music, signaling students to stop. Prompt the child holding the snowball to call out a classmate's name and then toss the snowball to that child. Restart the music and continue the activity, reminding students who hold the snowball to toss it to someone who hasn't had a turn.

Carol Link
Browning Pearce Elementary
San Mateo, FL

The Name Game

Make a duplicate set of student name cards. Arrange a class supply of chairs in a circle facing outward. Place each card from one set under a different chair. Play a recording of music and have children walk around the chairs. Stop the music and have each child sit in the nearest chair, take the card from beneath his seat, and hold it in front of his chest. Draw a card from the remaining set. Then encourage that child to walk slowly around the circle of chairs and locate his name card. After the child has found his card, direct youngsters to put the cards back under the chairs. Then restart the music.

Mary Robles
Portland, OR

Stocking Surprise

Youngsters practice letter identification with this sweet idea! Obtain a class supply of individually wrapped candy canes, plus a few extra. Tape the extra candy canes to the back of separate alphabet cards. Put the class candy canes in the bottom of a holiday stocking with the alphabet cards on top. To begin, pretend to discover the stocking and say, "Someone left a stocking surprise! I wonder what's inside." Slowly remove a card so the candy cane is facing the group; then say the chant shown. At the end of the chant, turn the card around, prompting youngsters to name the letter. Continue with the other cards; then surprise each child with a candy cane treat to take home.

A letter is stuck to this candy cane!
When I turn it around, please tell me its name.

Tejaswini Duggaraju
Sunrise Co-Op Preschool
Renton, WA

Read and Rhyme

To prepare, cut out a copy of the cards on page 59. Program a sentence strip, leaving spaces in which to insert the cards. Put the strip in a pocket chart and place the object cards as shown. Place the animal cards nearby. To begin, insert an animal card in the first space. Pause at the end, helping youngsters decide which card will finish the rhyming sentence. Have a child insert the card. Then lead youngsters in reading the sentence aloud. Remove the cards. Then repeat the activity with the remaining cards.

Carole Watkins
Crown Point, IN

Little 🐱 , are you in the big 🎩 ?

Where Is Waddles?

Teach and reinforce positional words with a little help from Waddles the penguin! Gather a stuffed toy penguin (or a penguin cutout) and a white pillow (iceberg). Introduce Waddles, telling youngsters how this energetic penguin is always on the go! Then lead students in singing the song shown as you make the penguin "waddle" around the iceberg. At the end of the song, position the penguin *on*, *behind*, *in front of*, *beside*, *over*, or *under* the iceberg. Then ask, "Where is Waddles?" prompting youngsters to describe the penguin's position in relation to the iceberg.

(sung to the tune of "Pawpaw Patch")

Where, oh where could Waddles be going?
Where, oh where could Waddles be going?
Where, oh where could Waddles be going?
Where, oh where is he waddling to?

Cari Charron,
Quesnel CCRR,
Quesnel, British Columbia, Canada

Shake It Up!

Place candy conversation hearts in a clear plastic bottle and secure the cap in place. Then have a volunteer sit in the center of the circle with her eyes covered. Play music and have students pass the bottle around the circle. Stop the music and prompt the child with the bottle to hold it behind his back and his classmates to hold their hands behind them as well. Next, have the child shake the bottle. Then prompt the volunteer to open her eyes and guess who has it. If she guesses correctly, have the child reveal the bottle. If not, have her close her eyes and the child shake the bottle again. After a second guess, reveal who has the bottle. Repeat with a different volunteer.

Barb Stefaniuk, Kerrobert Tiny Tots Playschool, Kerrobert, Saskatchewan, Canada
Melissa Weimer, Stepanski Early Childhood Center, Waterford, MI

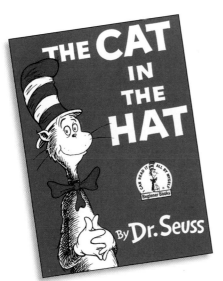

Thing 1 and Thing 2

After a read-aloud of Dr. Seuss's *The Cat in the Hat*, lead youngsters in this class-patterning activity. In advance, make a class supply of white circle cutouts and label half of them "Thing 1" and the remaining half "Thing 2." Attach rolled tape to the back of each circle. To begin, hand circles to a few youngsters and have them attach the circles to their shirts. Help them stand in a row to make a pattern. Next, review the pattern with the group, prompting students to tell what comes next. Then hand another child an appropriate label. Lead the class in saying the pattern again. Repeat the process until each child is involved in the pattern.

Christine Brock, Davila Day School, Chula Vista, CA

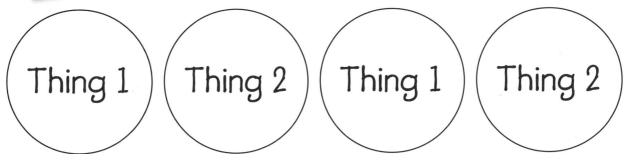

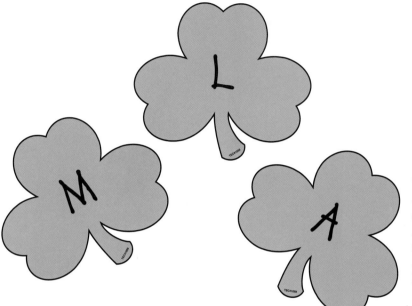

Shamrock Patch

Students will be eager to play this letter-recognition game! Label a class supply of shamrock cutouts (pattern on page 60) with a few different letters. Arrange the shamrocks in a large circle on the floor (shamrock patch). Play some music and have your little leprechauns stroll around the patch. Stop the music, signaling each leprechaun to stop and "pick" the shamrock closest to him. Announce a letter, prompting youngsters with the corresponding shamrocks to hold them in the air. After confirming they are correct, invite those students to do a little leprechaun jig! Then direct all the leprechauns to place the shamrocks back on the floor and repeat the activity.

adapted from an idea by Sharon Berkley
Son Shine Christian Preschool
Pasadena, TX

Pop! Pop! Pop!

Youngsters practice color recognition and gross-motor skills with this fun idea! Make a class supply of colorful popcorn cutouts (pattern on page 60). Give each child a cutout and have youngsters stand in a group. Ask little ones to pretend they are popcorn kernels in a cooking pot. Then direct youngsters to subtly bob up and down as you recite the chant shown. At the end of the chant, prompt students with the designated kernel color to hold it in the air and jump up and down enthusiastically. Repeat the activity, replacing the underlined word with a different color word until all the popcorn kernels have "popped."

Popcorn kernels in the pot,
See the [red] ones pop, pop, pop!

adapted from an idea by MacGregor Nursery School
MacGregor, CA

 For extra fun, secure popcorn kernels in a clear, lidded container and shake the container each time youngsters jump up and down!

Muddy Muck

Place a large sheet of brown bulletin board paper (mud puddle) or a brown blanket on the floor. Gather several number cards and have little ones stand around the mud. Lead youngsters in saying the chant shown. At the appropriate time, hold a card in the air, prompting students to say the number. At the end of the chant, have little ones count to the designated number and then jump in the mud and stamp their feet. After a few moments, say, "Oooey, gooey, muddy muck! Get your little feet unstuck!" signaling youngsters to step out of the mud and return to their spaces. Repeat the activity several times using other number cards. How fun!

Standing round a mud puddle with a big grin,
We'll count to number [number name] and then jump right in!

adapted from an idea by Tricia Kylene Brown
Bowling Green, KY

Great Gardening!

Cut out a class supply minus one of the flower shapes in several different colors. (Go to page 249 for a flower card.) Attach each flower to a craft stick. Invite a volunteer to be the gardener and then hand her a toy watering can. Give a flower to each remaining child; then have those youngsters kneel in rows of matching flowers. Next, recite the rhyme shown, encouraging the gardener to "water" the appropriate row of flowers when the rhyme ends. Prompt each child in that row to slowly rise to a standing position. Have the gardener switch places with a classmate; repeat the process until all the flowers have grown big and tall.

[Child's name, child's name], with flowers so small,
Water the [color name] ones so they'll grow tall!

Sue Fleischmann
Milwaukee, WI

Pond Sights

Cut out a copy of the cards on page 61. Have students pretend they're standing near a pond; then lead them in singing the song shown. At the appropriate time in the first verse, display the duck card. Then encourage youngsters to mimic the duck when appropriate. Repeat the activity with each remaining card, using the following suggestions: *frog, ribbit; fish, swish; turtle, snap; dragonfly, buzz; beaver, slap.*

(sung to the tune of "Old MacDonald Had a Farm")

We took a walk down to the pond
To see what we could see,
And in the pond there was a [duck]
As happy as could be!
With a [quack, quack] here, and a [quack, quack] there,
Here a [quack], there a [quack], everywhere a [quack, quack].
We took a walk down to the pond
To see what we could see.

Kimberli Usselman
Victor, NY

Recycling Fun

For this fun activity, you will need several clean, empty tin cans and a "recycling bin." (Inspect the cans for sharp edges or cover the edges with masking tape.) To play, have youngsters close their eyes while you partially hide one of the cans in the area. Next, say, "Recyclers, recyclers, where's the tin? It needs to go in the recycling bin!" Then prompt youngsters to open their eyes and visually look for the can. The first child to spot the tin can calls out, "I found the tin for the recycling bin!" Then he retrieves the can and puts it in the bin. Repeat the activity with each remaining can.

Jennifer Nichols
Project Excel
Monticello, NY

...8, 9, 10, Pop!

How high can youngsters count before a bubble pops? They'll find out with this activity! Dip a wand into bubble solution and gently blow on it to make a large bubble. As the bubble floats through the air, prompt youngsters to count aloud, stopping only when the bubble pops. Write on chart paper the last number counted; then repeat the activity several more times. When the bubble blowing is done, help students compare the numbers, identifying the highest number they counted to and the lowest.

Elizabeth Allen
Chesterbrook Academy
Naperville, IL

Shark!

Little ones get a real gross-motor workout with this island-themed idea! Place an oversize island-shaped cutout on the floor. Gather students on the island and say, "Swim, if you please, in the tropical breeze!" prompting little ones to jump into the ocean and "swim" around the island. After a few moments, call out "Shark!" signaling youngsters to quickly exit the water and return to the island. Check that the water is "safe" and repeat this fun activity!

adapted from and idea by Bonne Fuller
Dotlen Academy
Pottstown, PA

Friendly Fireflies

Copy and cut out a supply of firefly cards from page 62. Get a clear plastic jar and a large die. Spread the fireflies on the floor and place the jar nearby. To play, have students take turns rolling the die, counting aloud the dots, and "catching" that many fireflies to put in the jar. After all the fireflies are caught, lead youngsters in singing the song shown. Then "release" the fireflies and play another round!

(sung to the tune of "Shoo Fly")

Fireflies are fun to see.
Fireflies are fun to see.
Fireflies are fun to see,
But now it's time to set them free!

Jennie Jensen
Clarence, IA

Rock Miners

Label each of a class supply of rock cutouts with either a letter or number; then scatter the rocks around the classroom. To begin, ask little ones to pretend they are rock miners. Instruct each child to find one rock and bring it back to your circle-time area. When all the miners have returned, have each one display his rock and tell whether it's labeled with a letter or number. Ask him to identify the symbol and then place the rock, according to its symbol, into a pile with letters or numbers. Continue until all the rocks are sorted into the appropriate piles.

Mary Robles
Portland, OR

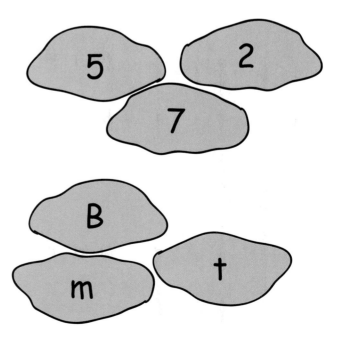

Stolen Treasure

Place in the middle of the circle a toy treasure chest (or other container) filled with gold plastic coins (or yellow pom-poms). Stack number cards nearby. Recite the rhyme shown, inserting a student's name where indicated and displaying a number card during the last line for the group to identify. Next, have the designated "pirate" remove that many gold coins from the treasure chest as the group counts each one aloud; then have him take the gold to his seat. Repeat the process with other youngsters until there is no gold left.

Arrrr! Arrrr! Look what we found:
A treasure chest buried in the ground!
Pirate [child's name] came along one day.
[She] took [number] gold coins and ran away!

Cari Charron
Red Bluff Strong Start
Quesnel, British Columbia, Canada

Ant Invasion!

For this letter-sound association activity, gather a picnic basket and real or plastic picnic-related food, each item with a different beginning sound. For each food, label a cutout copy of an ant card from page 62 with the first letter of the food's name. Put the food in the basket, helping students identify each type of food. Then spread the ant cards nearby and say, "Uh-oh, we have some uninvited picnic guests!" Then choose an ant card and ask students to identify the letter and its sound. Next, invite a volunteer to remove a food that begins with that letter sound. After confirming a correct choice, have her place the food and the ant card aside. Repeat the process until the basket is empty.

Marcie Case
First United Methodist Preschool
Stuart, FL

Schoolhouse Pattern
Use with "Who's Knocking?" on page 42.

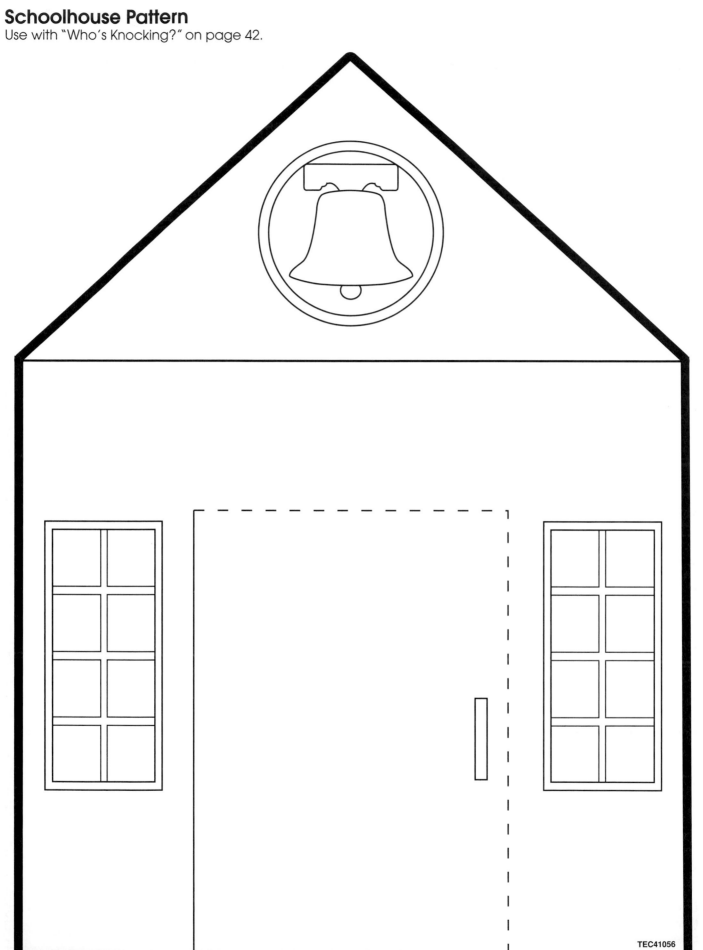

TEC41056

TEC41058

TEC41058

TEC41058

TEC41058

TEC41058

TEC41058

TEC41058

TEC41058

Shamrock Pattern
Use with "Shamrock Patch" on page 52.

Popcorn Pattern
Use with "Pop! Pop! Pop!" on page 52.

TEC41060

TEC41060

TEC41060

TEC41060

TEC41060

TEC41060

Firefly Cards
Use with "Friendly Fireflies" on page 56.

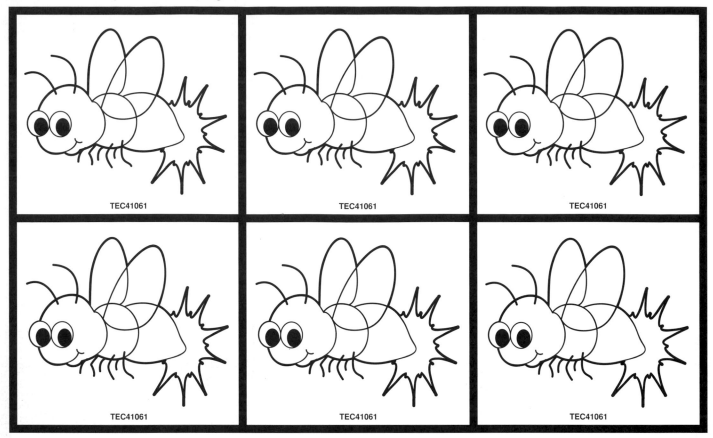

Ant Cards
Use with "Ant Invasion!" on page 57 and "Bug Boppers" on page 209.

Classroom Displays

CLASSROOM DISPLAYS

Every Piece Is Important!

Tillian — Dean — Sarah — Aiden — Hunter — Julie — Danny — Pia — Bianca — Rajan — Christy — Jerry

Puzzle-cut a white foam board sheet (or poster board) so there's one puzzle piece for each child. Encourage each student to draw a self-portrait on her piece and then help her label it with her name. Assemble the puzzle pieces on a board or wall and add the title shown.

Stephanie Greene, The Ivy League School, Smithtown, NY

Welcome
to
Preschool!

For this cute display, have each child glue a head shot photo of himself to a green circle cutout. Have him attach other green circles and paper strips (antennae) to make a worm. Then display each child's worm near an over-size apple cutout as shown.

Jessica Guy
Toddle Inn Daycare
LaCrosse, WI

A Birthday Bouquet

No room for a birthday bulletin board? No problem! Get an oversize plastic vase and place a variety of colorful plastic flowers in the vase. Write each child's name and birthdate on a card, secure it to a floral pick, and insert the pick in the bouquet. If desired, display the vase near a wall with the title shown. For added fun, switch out the flowers to match colors associated with each season!

Sara Peterson
The Goddard School
Suwanee, GA

We're Learning "Egg-citing" Things This Year!

Here's a fun way to display important preschool information! Have each child make a simple Humpty Dumpty craft. Then display the projects on a brick wall background. Add your classroom goals and standards to the display.

Donna Olp, St. Gregory the Great Preschool, South Euclid, OH

Jumping Into Autumn!

To make this cute display, help each child cut out a photo of himself jumping. Then have him paint his hand with fall colors and press it onto a green construction paper leaf, adding more paint to his hand as needed to give the leaf an autumn look. Display the projects and the photos so it appears youngsters are jumping in a big pile of leaves.

Jodi Zeis
Richland School District Two
Columbia, SC

We're All Wrapped Up in Halloween!

To make a mummy, invite each child to glue torn white crepe paper strips to a white tagboard body cutout (pattern on page 74). Trim the edges of the cutout. Then have her glue black paper circles (eyes) to the head. Mount the mummies on a board or wall with the title shown.

For this hygienic display, attach the poem shown to a piece of bulletin board paper. Have each child make a colorful handprint on the paper. Then encourage him to sprinkle sand and oatmeal on his print before the paint dries. Add soap bubble cutouts to the paper. Then display it on your wall.

adapted from an idea by Cynthia Jackson
E. A. Palmer Head Start
Prichard, AL

Little fingers like to play
In mud and paint and sand all day.
To get those fingers squeaky clean,
Wash the fronts and backs
And in between!

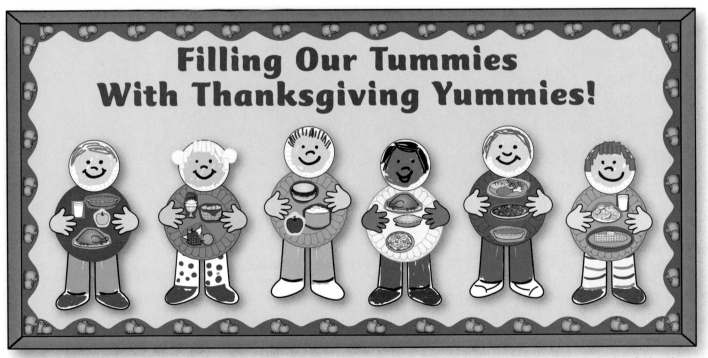

Give each child a small paper plate (head) attached to a large paper plate (tummy). Have him add details to the head; then have him cut out magazine pictures of his favorite Thanksgiving foods and glue them to the tummy. Help him attach hand cutouts to the plate so it appears he's holding the tummy; then invite him to add construction paper legs and feet.

James Butler
Laburnum Elementary-Federal Programs Preschool
Richmond, VA

CLASSROOM DISPLAYS

Taste

Touch

Hear

Smell

See

Our "Sense-ational" Holiday Tree!

For this multisensory display, attach an oversize tree cutout and cards to your wall. Then have students create and add the following ornament options!

 **See:** Decorate lightbulb cutouts with colorful glitter.

Hear: Attach pipe cleaner hangers to jumbo jingle bells.

Taste: Attach wrapped candy canes.

 Smell: Spread glue on colorful jumbo craft sticks and then sprinkle cinnamon on the glue. Glue yarn hangers to the sticks.

 Touch: Glue soft and fuzzy pom-poms to small tagboard circles.

Jaime Jamieson, Waiting to Grow Preschool, South Portland, ME

For this frosty display, have each child cut and glue winter wear from paper or fabric and attach it to a bear cutout (pattern on page 75). Mount the bears on a board with cotton batting snow and the title shown. Then invite youngsters to attach self-adhesive craft foam snowflakes to the sky.

Rebecca Flores and Cassondra Powell
Mason Square Head Start
Springfield, MA

To create this serene holiday display, draw windows on a length of bulletin board paper and attach a door cutout. Attach the paper to a larger length of dark paper and then mount the display on a wall. Help each child make a simple menorah craft like the one shown. Then tape a menorah to each window. Add stars, a moon, and the title shown.

Margie Goldberg, Washington Hebrew Congregation Early Childhood Center, Potomac, MD

CLASSROOM DISPLAYS

Great Thinkers!

Show youngsters a picture of Rodin's famous sculpture *The Thinker*. (An Internet image search will turn up plenty of options!) Ask students what they believe he is thinking about. Next, have each student pose for a photo in which he's imitating the sculpture. Then, in a thought bubble, encourage him to draw a picture of what he might be thinking about. Display the photos and bubbles as shown.

Beth Halpin, Just Children, Trevose, PA

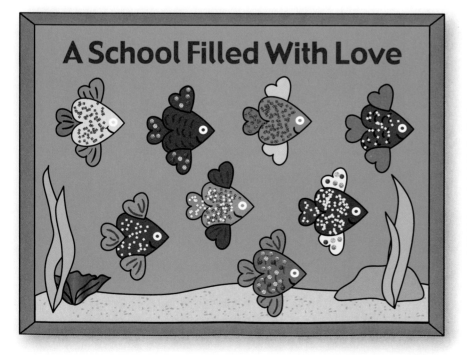

A School Filled With Love

To make this adorable display, invite each child to glue together four assorted heart cutouts to make a fish. Encourage her to add a hole reinforcer eye and body details using items such as markers, sequins, and glitter. Display the projects with the details and title shown.

Mandy Brown and Erin Pool
Bright Horizons
Lisle, IL

Preschool Shoppers

This display is sure to create an appetite! Have each child cut or tear pictures of food from store circulars. Then have her make a grocery list by gluing the pictures to a sheet of decorative paper, programmed as shown, and dictating or writing the names of each food beside its picture. Mount each list around a large paper grocery bag and add the title shown.

Nancy Foss, Wee Care Preschool, Galion, OH

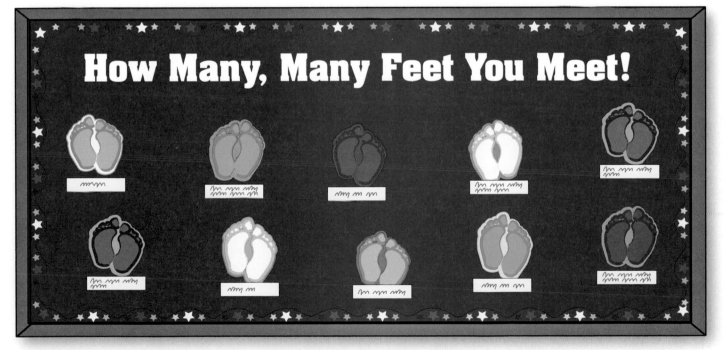

After a read-aloud of Dr. Seuss's *The Foot Book*, paint the bottoms of each child's feet and have him press them onto a sheet of paper to make footprints. Then have him tell something he does with his feet for you to record on a paper strip. Trim around each set of footprints and mount them with the strips and title shown.

Ada Goren, Winston-Salem, NC

April Showers Bring May Flowers

For this personalized display, trim a photo of each child holding her arms out as shown. Invite her to decorate a flower cutout and an umbrella cutout (patterns on page 76); then help her attach a pipe cleaner stem to the flower and a pipe cleaner handle to the umbrella. Display the cutouts and photos as shown.

Tamara Johnson, Hart County EHS/HS/PreK, Hartwell, GA

Radical Rainbow!

Invite students to colorize a large rainbow cutout using bingo daubers or paint. Then give each youngster a child cutout (pattern on page 76) in his favorite rainbow color. Have him draw facial details on the cutout and tell why that color is his favorite. Record his words on the cutout and display it with a length of yarn leading to the corresponding color on the rainbow.

Donna Olp
St. Gregory the Great Preschool
South Euclid, OH

CLASSROOM DISPLAYS

This Class Is "Berry" Special!

For this sweet display, have each child use a foam paint roller to roll light yellow paint onto a piece of bubble wrap. Have her press a red strawberry cutout on the painted surface and then remove the cutout. Encourage her to glue a green star cutout (leaves) to the top of the strawberry. Have her write her name on the leaves. Then display the strawberries as shown.

Margaret Cromwell
Grace Episcopal Preschool
Georgetown, TX

To make this summertime footwear, invite each child to decorate a tagboard flip-flop with summer-related stickers. Then punch three holes in the flip-flop and help him attach pipe cleaners. (See enlarged flip-flop for details.) Mount the projects on a board or wall with beach-related details and the title shown.

Julie Shupe, Shupe Daycare, Raytown, MO

Body Pattern
Use with "We're All Wrapped Up in Halloween!" on page 66.

TEC41057

TEC41058

Umbrella and Flower Patterns

Use with "April Showers Bring May Flowers" on page 72.

Child Pattern

Use with "Radical Rainbow!" on page 72.

TEC41060

TEC41060

TEC41060

INSTANT SEASONAL ACTIVITIES

Instant Seasonal Activities

Fantastic Formation!

After a read-aloud of *Swimmy* by Leo Lionni, discuss with little ones how the fish stayed safe by swimming together as a unit. Then help youngsters line up to take a walk. Explain that by walking together in a line, they too will stay safe just like Swimmy and his friends! *Carla Impalli, Valley View Elementary, Califon, NJ*

Classroom Tour

Have youngsters pretend to board a school bus. Then tour the room, stopping the bus at each area of interest and giving a brief overview of each area. For added fun, pretend to have a flat tire you need to quickly fix or encourage youngsters to wave at imaginary pedestrians!

The Name Song

Display a student's name card and help youngsters identify the name. Then lead the group in singing the song shown, inserting the appropriate name and letter. *Lisa White, Emmanuel United Methodist Kindergarten, Memphis, TN*

(sung to the tune of "Old MacDonald Had a Farm")

[Ella, Ella, *E, E, E*]—
[*E*] starts [Ella's] name!
[Ella, Ella, *E, E, E*]—
[*E*] starts [Ella's] name!

Ella

Guess Who?

Invite a child to stand facing away from the group. Prompt one of his classmates to ask, "Can you guess my name?" Then have the child guess the classmate. If he guesses correctly, lead the group in a round of applause. If he does not, prompt the classmate to repeat the question. After three guesses, have the classmate reveal her identity to the guesser. *Connie Meyer, Hurstbourne Baptist Day School, Louisville, KY*

Joshua!

School Tools

Conceal in a backpack several school-related items, such as a crayon, a stapler, scissors, tape, and a glue bottle. Provide clues, guiding youngsters to guess what an item is. When the item is guessed, remove it from the backpack and reveal it to the group. Continue until the backpack is empty.

Instant Seasonal Activities

Gather and Count

Scatter brown pom-poms (acorns) in your circle-time area. Invite two students (squirrels) to gather acorns in separate baskets. After all the acorns are gathered, enlist the help of the group to count the acorns in each basket and compare the amounts. Play until each child has had a turn to be a squirrel. *Roxanne LaBell Dearman, Western NC Early Intervention Program for Children Who Are Deaf or Hard of Hearing, Charlotte, NC*

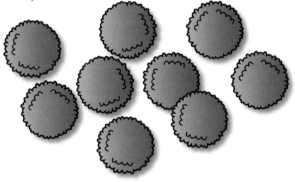

Fabulous Faces!

Tell students that jack-o'-lanterns can have many different faces. Have little ones pretend to be jack-o'-lanterns and demonstrate faces that are sad, happy, excited, scared, scary, mad, silly, and worried. Use great dramatic flair when responding to youngsters' faces!

Turkey Troubles

Have little ones pretend to be turkeys, strutting around the classroom and gobbling. After several moments, say, "It's Thanksgiving Day!" and prompt the little turkeys to quickly hide. Say, "I wonder where those turkeys went?" Then play another round.

Alike and Different

In advance, gather several fall leaves and place them in a small paper bag. During circle time display two leaves from the bag. Invite little ones to name likenesses and differences between the leaves. Repeat the activity with other pairs of leaves. *Roxanne LaBell Dearman*

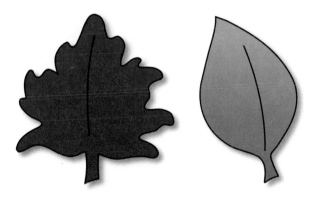

Fall Colors

In the center of your circle-time area place sheets of construction paper in the following colors: red, yellow, orange, and brown. Then give each child a craft stick (or other manipulative) and have him put his stick on the paper that represents the fall color he likes best. To conclude the activity, lead students in counting each group of sticks to determine which fall color most students prefer. *Roxanne LaBell Dearman*

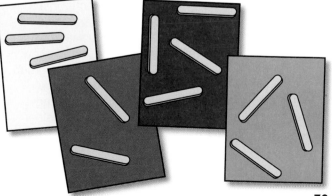

Instant Seasonal Activities

Lovebug Hug

Play some soothing music and encourage your little lovebugs to flutter their wings and move to the tempo. Then stop the music and call out, "Lovebug hug!" prompting each child to give the classmate nearest to her a hug. Or have the students hug themselves, if desired. **Ada Goren, Winston-Salem, NC**

Lion, Lamb, or Leprechaun

Place number cards from 1 to 10 in a bag. Invite a child to pull a card from the bag and identify the number. Then have her announce "lion," "lamb," or "leprechaun." If she says "lion," the group says "roar" that many times. If she says "lamb," youngsters say "baa" that many times. If she says "leprechaun," students leap like a leprechaun that many times! **Karen Guess, St. Richard's School, Indianapolis, IN**

L-O-V-E

Have youngsters stand in a circle. Lead the group in saying "L-O-V-E" as you walk around the circle and tap a different student each time you say a letter. When you say the letter *E*, prompt the child who gets tapped to sit down. Continue in the same way until one child is left standing. Then play another round. **Ada Goren**

L-O-V-E.

Breezy or Windy

Gently fan children with a sheet of tagboard and prompt them to sway like they're in a gentle breeze. Then vigorously fan youngsters, prompting them to pretend they're being blown by a big gust of wind! Repeat for several rounds. **Karen Guess**

Can You Spell *Lamb?*

Display a sentence strip labeled "lamb" in a pocket chart. Gather letter cards that spell the word and place them facedown along with a few distracters. Invite a child to take a card and show it to the group. If the letter is in the word, the group says "baa" and the child places the card in the chart below the appropriate letter. If not, youngsters roar like a lion and she sets the card aside. Continue until the word is complete.

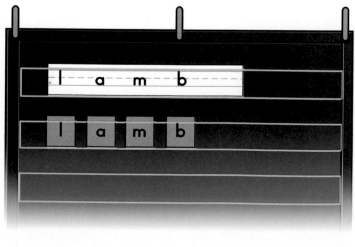

Instant Seasonal Activities

At the Pond

Have youngsters stand in a circle and pretend they're fishing in a pond. After a few moments, hold a number card in the air and have youngsters identify the number. Then prompt your little fishermen to "reel in" their fish, leading them in counting aloud as they turn their imaginary reels the corresponding number of times. *Tricia Kylene Brown, Bowling Green, KY*

Twitchy Tadpoles

Have each child curl up on the floor and pretend to be a tadpole asleep in its egg. Then call out, "Twitchy tadpoles!" and prompt youngsters to pretend to hatch from their eggs and swim around. After a few moments, encourage your tiny tadpoles to hop around like frogs! *Tricia Kylene Brown*

Springtime Charades

Invite a volunteer to stand and face the group. Whisper to her a spring-related action, such as stamping in a puddle, flying a kite, or planting a seed. Encourage her to perform the action, and then have youngsters guess what she's doing. After the action is guessed, select a different volunteer and repeat the activity. *Tricia Kylene Brown*

She's planting a seed!

Bee Behavior

Tell youngsters that bees are more active during the day and less active at night. Then turn down the lights (nighttime) and have your little bees huddle, pretending to rest in their hive. Next, turn up the lights (daytime) and prompt the bees to "fly" around the room, buzzing as they go. Turn the lights down again, signaling the bees to return to the hive.

I Spy Rainbow Colors

Display a picture of a rainbow. Point to one of the arcs and ask youngsters to identify the color. Then have students visually scan the room to find items that are that color. When a child spots an item, he says, "I spy rainbow [red]!" and then identifies the item. After several youngsters each take a turn, repeat the process with a different color.

Ice-Cold Ice Cube

Ask, "What would happen to an ice cube if you held it in your hand?" After a brief discussion, have students pass an ice cube around the circle as you lead them in saying the rhyme shown. When the ice can no longer be passed, ask little ones to name other things that melt and to explain why.

Pass the ice cube round and round.
Try not to drop it on the ground.
Ice-cold ice cube going round,
Slowly melts without a sound.

Terrific Tentacles!

Draw an octopus head on the board. Then ask students eight questions, such as summer-related or skill-review questions. As each question is answered, draw a tentacle on the octopus. After all the questions have been answered, lead little ones in counting the tentacles aloud.

Picnic Packing

Set out an empty container (picnic basket). Ask each child, "What would you bring on a picnic?" After she responds, have her place the imaginary item in the basket. After everyone has added to the basket, engage little ones in a pretend picnic!

Ocean Critters

Divide the class into two groups. Assign each group an ocean animal, such as a crab and a seal. Then have students stand in a designated area (ocean) while you stand a distance from them (shoreline). Call out, "Ocean critters swim ashore!" signaling youngsters to travel toward you, mimicking their assigned animals as they move. After a few moments, call out, "Ocean critters float and rest!" prompting them to stop. Repeat the process until all the critters reach the shoreline. *Mandi Ellis, Patchogue, NY*

Scoop and Lick

Little ones will love making these imaginary frozen treats! Simply display a number card for students to identify; then have them "scoop" that many ice cream scoops atop an imaginary cone, counting aloud as they scoop. When the scooping is done, invite youngsters to "lick" their treats!

KIDS IN THE KITCHEN

Kids in the Kitchen

Little ones develop fine-motor skills while making this yummy snack!

Supersimple Jelly Roll

Ingredients for one:
slice of bread
light whipped cream cheese
jelly or jam

Utensils and supplies:
rolling pin
plastic knife for each child
large paper plate for each child

Teacher preparation:
Arrange the ingredients and supplies near a colored copy of the step-by-step recipe cards (see page 85).

Janet Boyce, Cokato, MN

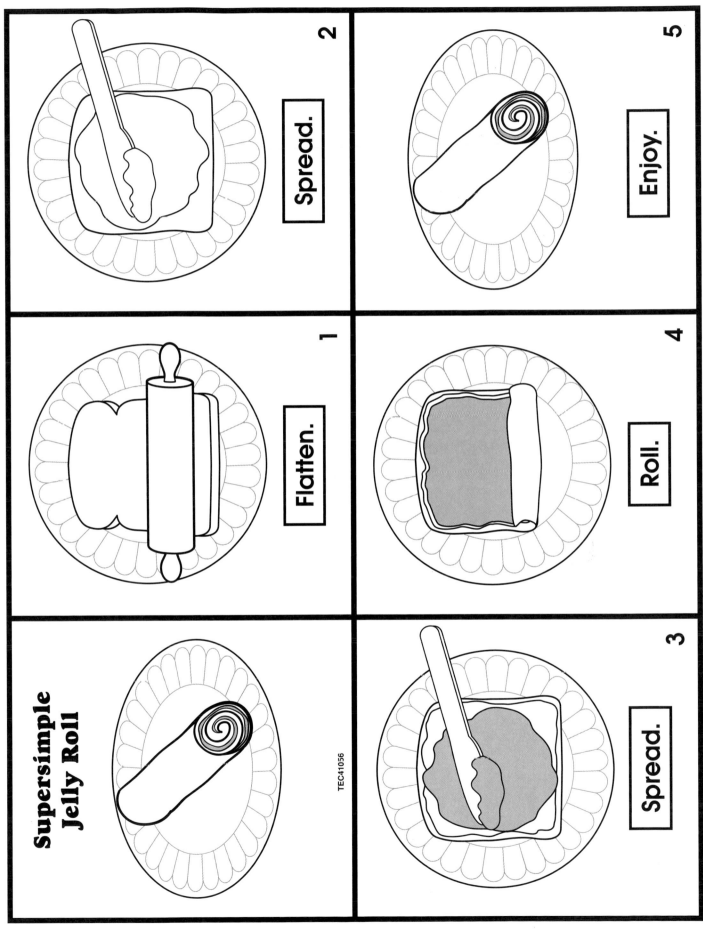

Supersimple Jelly Roll

1 — Flatten.

2 — Spread.

3 — Spread.

4 — Roll.

5 — Enjoy.

TEC41056

Kids in the Kitchen

These yummy cookies are the perfect treat for any fall celebration.

Candy Corn Cookies

Ingredients for one:
soft sugar cookie
white frosting
orange sugar crystals
yellow sugar crystals

Utensils and supplies:
plastic knife for each child
paper plate for each child

Teacher preparation:
Arrange the ingredients and supplies near a colored copy of the step-by-step recipe cards (see page 87).

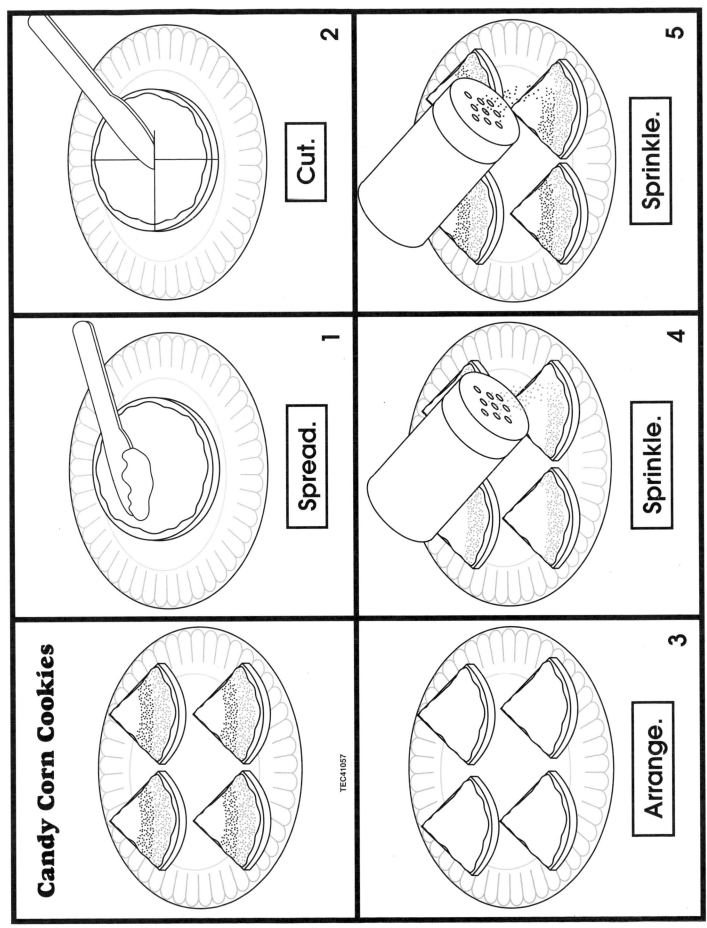

Candy Corn Cookies

1 — Spread.

2 — Cut.

3 — Arrange.

4 — Sprinkle.

5 — Sprinkle.

TEC41057

Kids in the Kitchen

On a chilly winter day, these edible snowballs go perfectly with a cup of cocoa!

Snowballs

Ingredients for one:
3 vanilla wafer cookies
cream cheese spread
flaked coconut

Cindy Kern
ChildSavers
Richmond, VA

Utensils and supplies:
disposable plate
plastic knife
plastic bowl for coconut

Teacher preparation:
Arrange the ingredients and supplies near a colored copy of the step-by-step recipe cards (see page 89).

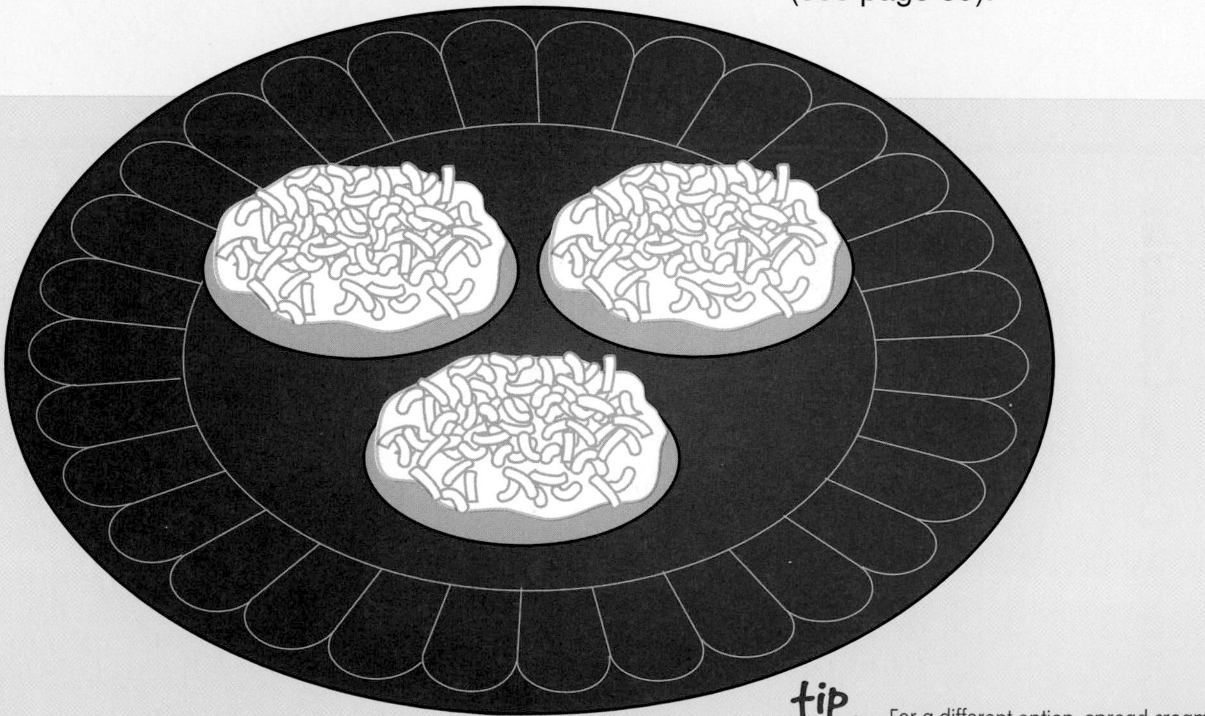

tip → For a different option, spread cream cheese on a cracker and sprinkle chopped cauliflower on top!

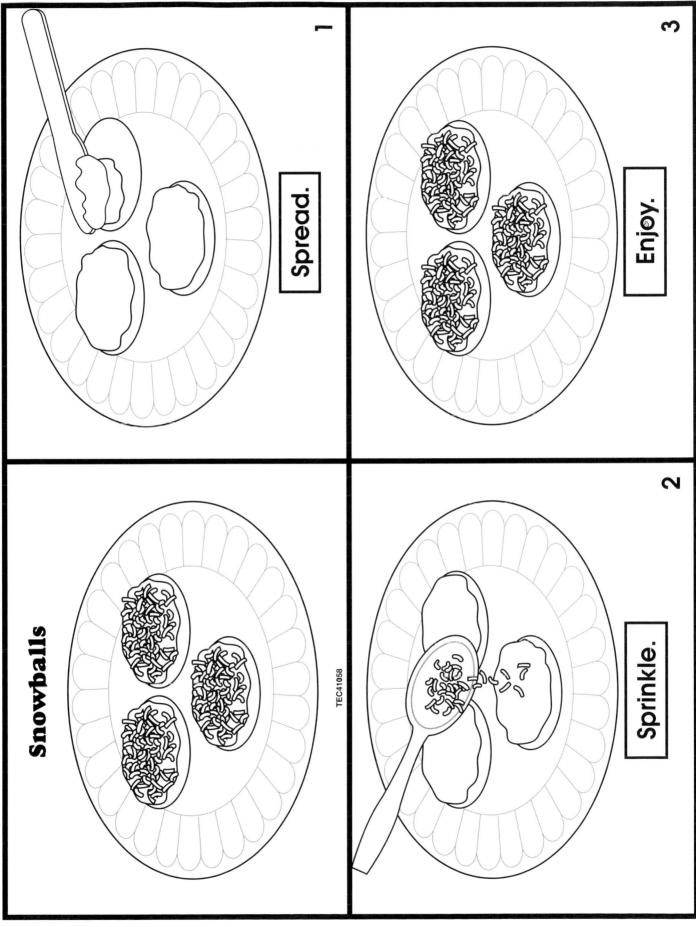

1

Spread.

3

Enjoy.

Snowballs

TEC41058

2

Sprinkle.

Kids in the Kitchen

Youngsters pilot yummy planes into the fluffy clouds with this fun snacktime activity.

Airplanes in the Clouds

Ingredients for one:
whipped topping
vanilla frosting
six graham cracker sticks

Betty Jean Roper
Tutor Time
Stevenson Ranch, CA

Utensils and supplies:
paper plate
large spoon
plastic knife

Teacher preparation:
Arrange the ingredients and supplies near a colored copy of the step-by-step recipe cards (see page 91).

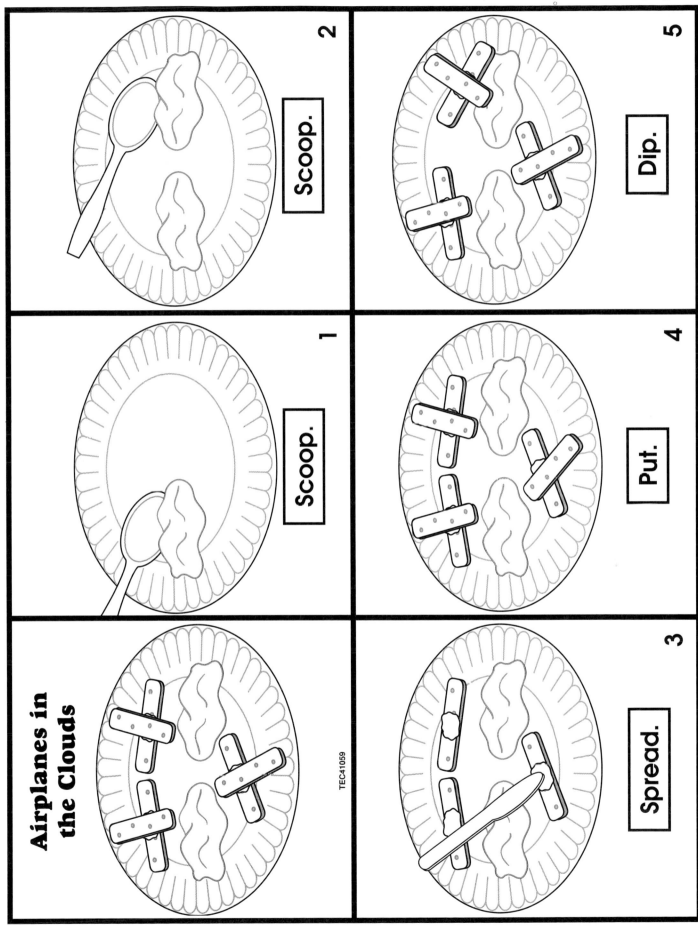

5

Dip.

2

Scoop.

1

Scoop.

4

Put.

Airplanes in the Clouds

TEC41059

3

Spread.

Kids in the Kitchen

Celebrate spring being in full bloom with this yummy snack.

Cherry Blossoms

Ingredients for one:
6 pretzel sticks
strawberry cream cheese

Utensils and supplies:
disposable plate

Teacher Preparation:
Arrange the ingredients and supplies near a colored copy of the step-by-step recipe cards (see page 93).

Janet Boyce
Cokato, MN

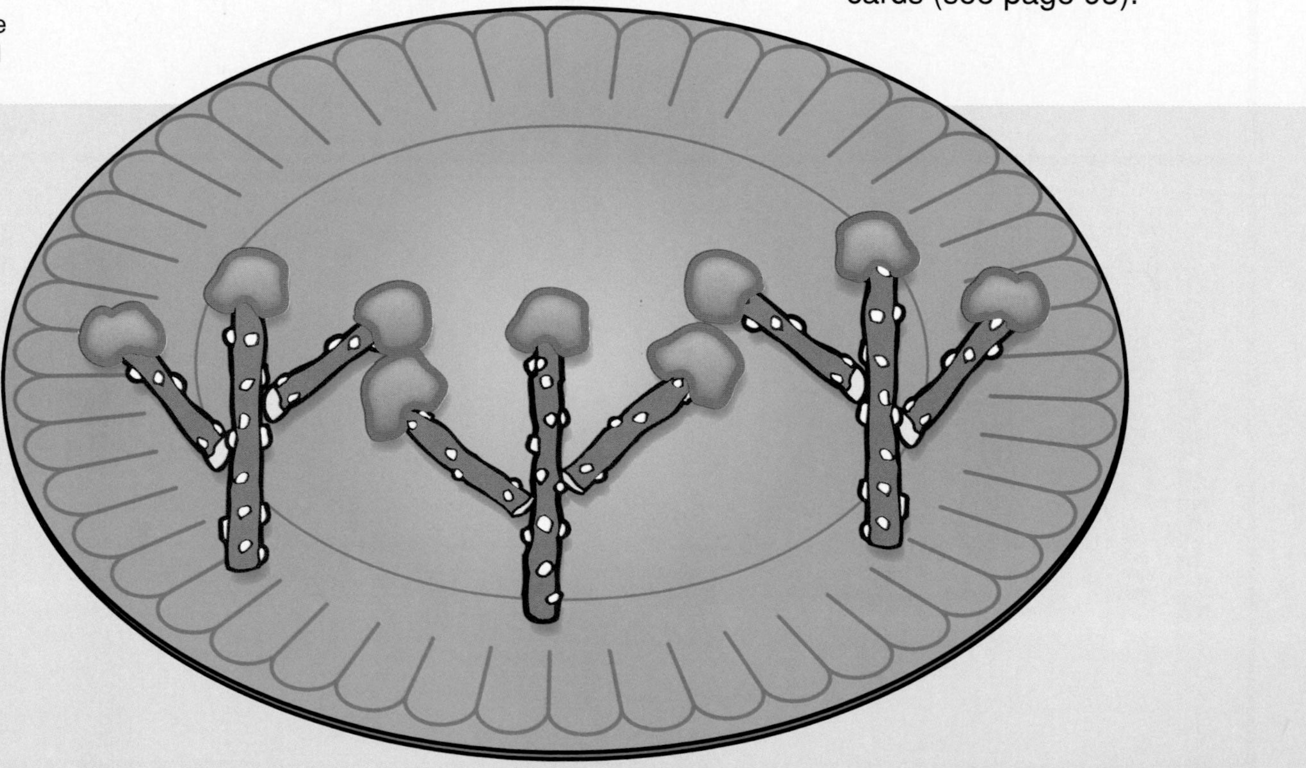

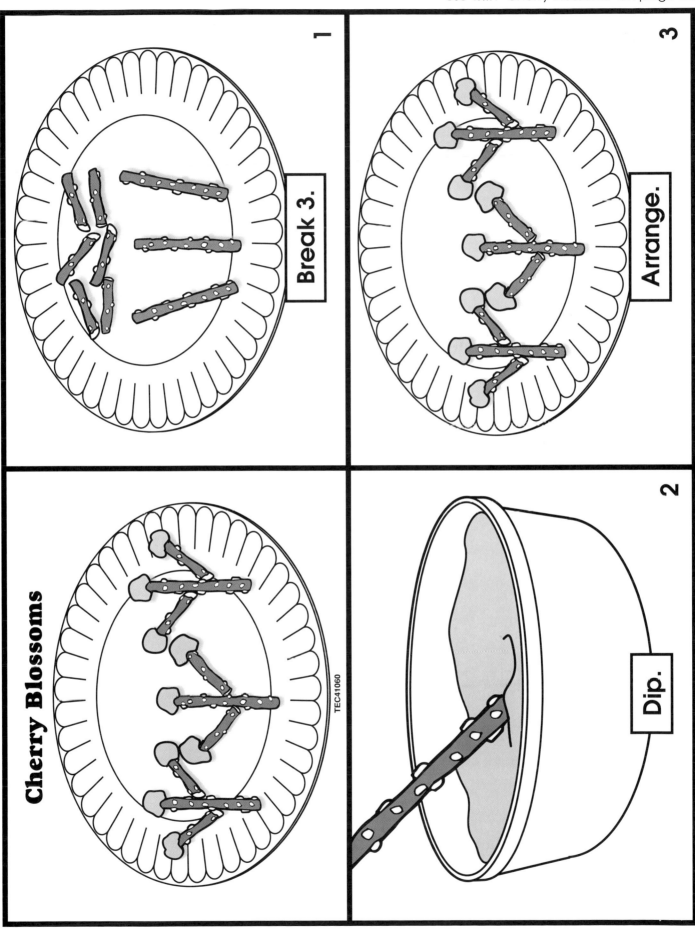

1

Break 3.

3

Arrange.

Cherry Blossoms

TEC41060

2

Dip.

Kids in the Kitchen

Snack on this healthy alternative to a traditional s'more during a camping unit.

Fruit S'mores

Ingredients for one:
2 graham crackers
whipped cream cheese
thinly sliced strawberries and bananas

Kady Sator
Love and Learning Home Child Care
Greeley, CO

Utensils and supplies:
paper plate
plastic knife

Teacher preparation:
Arrange the ingredients and supplies near a colored copy of the step-by-step recipe cards (see page 95).

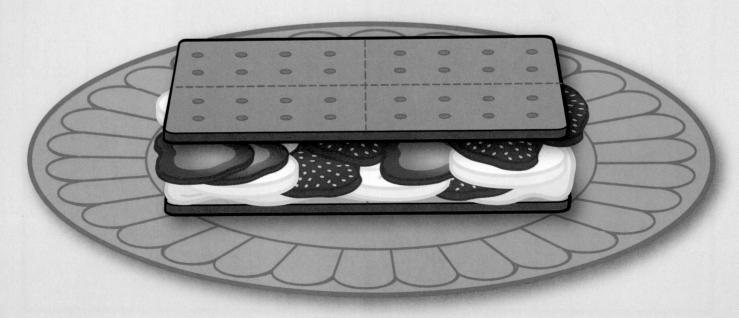

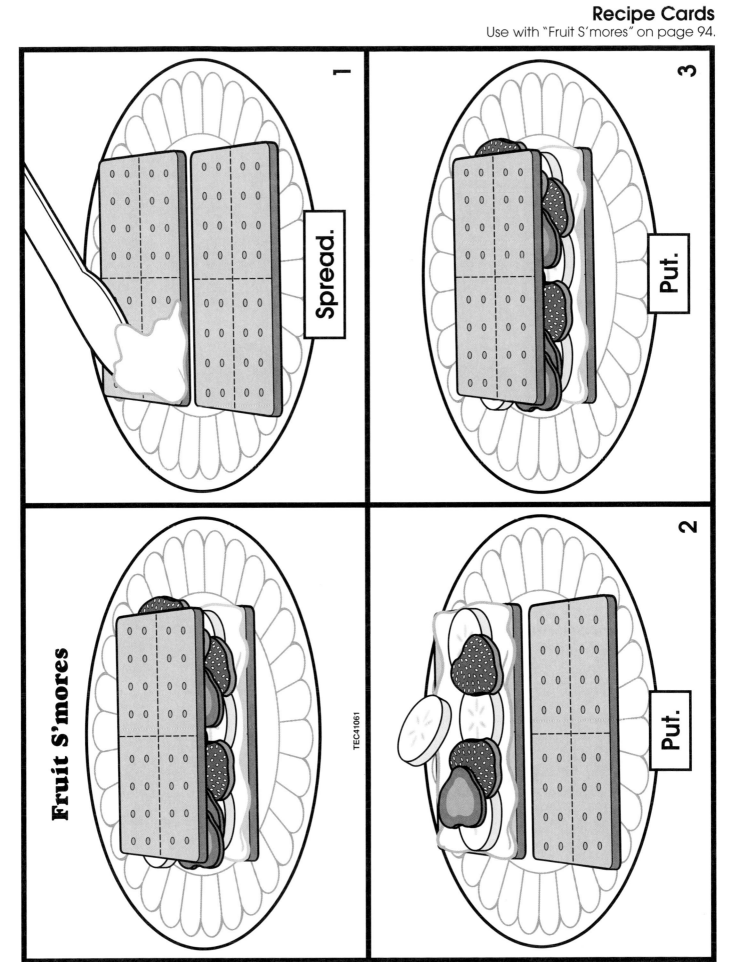

TEC41061

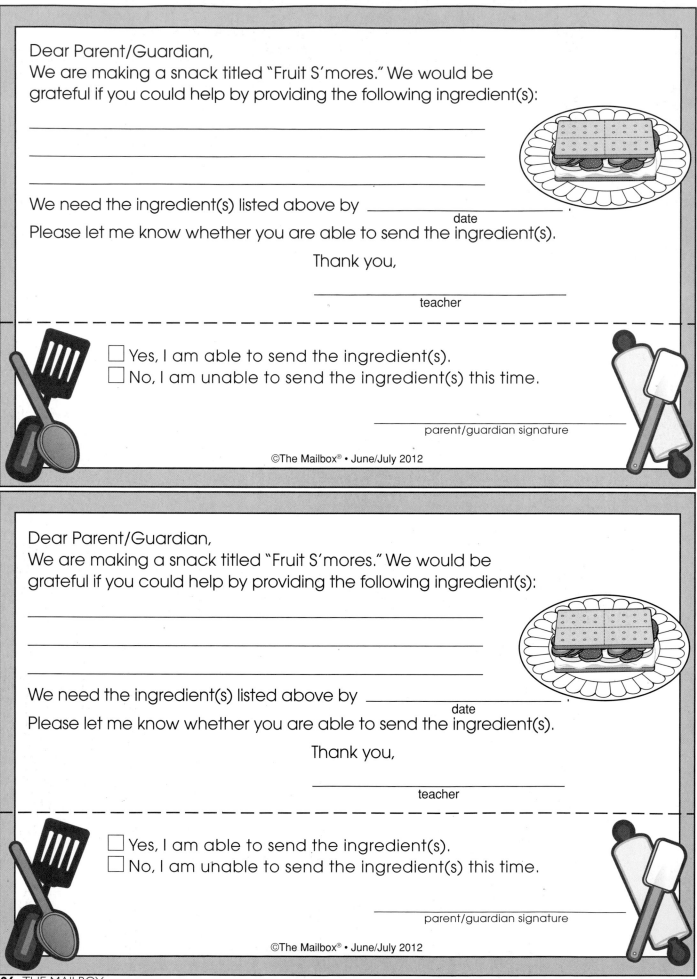

Dear Parent/Guardian,
We are making a snack titled "Fruit S'mores." We would be grateful if you could help by providing the following ingredient(s):

_____

_____

_____

We need the ingredient(s) listed above by _____.
date
Please let me know whether you are able to send the ingredient(s).

Thank you,

_____
teacher

☐ Yes, I am able to send the ingredient(s).
☐ No, I am unable to send the ingredient(s) this time.

_____
parent/guardian signature

©The Mailbox® • June/July 2012

Dear Parent/Guardian,
We are making a snack titled "Fruit S'mores." We would be grateful if you could help by providing the following ingredient(s):

_____

_____

_____

We need the ingredient(s) listed above by _____.
date
Please let me know whether you are able to send the ingredient(s).

Thank you,

_____
teacher

☐ Yes, I am able to send the ingredient(s).
☐ No, I am unable to send the ingredient(s) this time.

_____
parent/guardian signature

©The Mailbox® • June/July 2012

LEARNING CENTERS

Learning Centers

Simply Irresistible
Art Center

Provide squeeze bottles of glue and white paper. A child gently squeezes glue onto a sheet of paper to create a personal design. When the glue is dry, she paints over the design with watercolors. The glue resists the paint, revealing her lovely design.

Dee Hamlin
Jovita Christian Preschool
Edgewood, WA

Pinch and Pull
Play Dough Center

Youngsters develop their pincer grasps with this fun idea! Set out play dough with several items—such as a small teddy counter, a pattern block, and a jumbo paper clip—hidden inside. A youngster pinches off small chunks of play dough, searching for the hidden items. When he finds one, he pulls it out of the dough and sets it aside. He continues until he finds all the items.

Tracy Henderson
Brook Hollow Preschool
Nashville, TN

Crayon Color Match
Math Center

Place at a table an oversize poster board crayon along with assorted paper scraps that include the crayon color. Each student visits the table and finds scraps that match the color of the crayon. Then she cuts or tears the scraps and glues them to the crayon. If desired, periodically repeat the activity using different-color crayon cutouts.

adapted from an idea by Becky Ford
Growing Tree Preschool
Chambersburg, PA

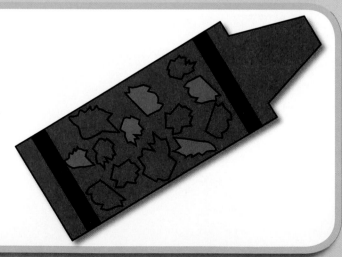

Letter Search
Literacy Center

Label craft foam circles (or milk caps) with letters and hide them in a container of uncooked rice. Provide a slotted spoon and a programmed sorting container for each letter. A child uses the spoon to dig through the rice and find a chip. He places the chip in the appropriate container. Then he repeats the process.

Amber Dingman
Play 'n' Learn Family Child Care and Preschool
Sterling, MI

Magnify It!
Discovery Center

Provide large and small magnifying glasses as well as magnifying sheets. Place them at a table with a variety of items from the classroom. Youngsters investigate the items—and each other—with the magnifiers!

Linda Heavrin
Benton, IL

You're Invited!
Dramatic-Play Area

Stock your dramatic play area with party goods and decorations. Also provide paper for party invitations, crayons, and a class list. A youngster writes out several party invitations (referring to the class list as needed) and delivers them to the intended guests. Then she returns to the area to put the finishing touches on the party before the guests arrive.

Karen Eiben
The Learning House Preschool
LaSalle, IL

Learning Centers

Feed the Squirrel
Fine-Motor Area

Cut out a copy of the squirrel pattern on page 108 and then cut out the mouth. Attach the squirrel to a box with a precut hole that aligns with the squirrel's mouth. Provide a bowl of brown pom-poms (acorns) and tweezers. A youngster uses the tweezers to pick up an acorn and "feed" it to the squirrel. She continues until the squirrel has "eaten" all the acorns.

Lisa Kerns
Trinity Preschool of Berwyn
Berwyn, PA

Perfect Pizza
Sensory Center

Place prepared bread dough, a rolling pin, counters (toppings), empty spice bottles, and a pizza pan in your sensory center. If desired, also provide a box to use as a makeshift oven. A child kneads the dough and then flattens it with a rolling pin. He adds toppings and pretends to shake on spices, pausing to sniff the spicy aroma. After "baking" the pizza, he slices it with the pizza cutter. (Refrigerate the dough between center times.)

Anne Hanlon
Early Learning Center
Sheboygan, WI

Autumn Leaves
Literacy Center

Program a paper strip as shown. Set out construction paper leaves, the letter stamps needed to spell *autumn*, and stamp pads in a variety of fall colors. Using the programmed strip as a guide, a student stamps the word *autumn* onto a leaf. If desired, mount the finished leaves on a tree cutout and title the display "Autumn Is Amazing!"

Barb Stefaniuk
Kerrobert Tiny Tots Playschool
Kerrobert, Saskatchewan, Canada

Toothy Critters!
Math Center

This counting activity has a not-so-scary monster! Make a simple monster cutout with a large mouth. Provide a die and several white triangle cutouts (teeth). A child rolls the die and counts the numbers. Then she places the same number of teeth on the monster. She continues until the monster's mouth is full of teeth!

Camelia Kline
Kids-R-Special
Fairmont, WV

Berry Squish
Art Center

Partially fill resealable plastic bags with whole cranberries. Seal each bag, making sure to squeeze the air out before sealing it. Provide a rolling pin, disposable cups, white construction paper, and small paintbrushes. A child rolls the rolling pin over the bag until the berries are completely squished. Then she opens the bag, drains the contents into a cup, and paints with the berry juice.

Stacey Pellicano
DeSales Catholic School
Lockport, NY

Pumpkin Stand
Dramatic-Play Area

Ask parents for donations of pumpkins and gourds to put in your dramatic-play area. Provide items such as bushel baskets, empty boxes, a scale, shopping bags, a toy cash register, and play money. Also provide nonfiction books about pumpkins and gourds. Students visit the center and role-play workers and customers at a pumpkin stand.

Debbie Paquin
Smiling Faces Family Child Care
Chester, MD

Learning Centers

Penguin Prints
Art Center

Provide large iceberg-shaped cutouts along with a shallow container of pink paint and a sponge trimmed so it resembles a penguin's foot. A child dips the sponge in the paint and stamps it on an iceberg. He continues in the same way to create a trail of penguin footprints.

Angela Dunham
All Aboard Preschool
Cincinnati, OH

Whirling Snowfall
Fine-Motor Area

Fill a plastic tub with water and add items such as craft foam snowflakes, snowflake confetti, and small white pom-poms. Provide clear plastic jars with lids, plastic tweezers, and a soup ladle. A youngster uses the tweezers to pick up and drop items into a jar. Then she uses the ladle to fill the jar with water. She tightens the lid onto the jar, with help as needed, and then shakes the jar to create a whirling snowfall!

Kristi Webler
The Goddard School
Venetia, PA

Gingerbread People
Play Dough Center

Follow the recipe shown to make gingerbread play dough. Provide person-shaped cookie cutters, a rolling pin, and craft items such as mini pom-poms, sequins, craft foam bows, and pieces of rickrack and yarn. A youngster uses the items to make and decorate pretend gingerbread people!

Gingerbread Play Dough

2 c. flour	1 tbsp. ground cinnamon
1 c. salt	1 tbsp. ground ginger
2 tbsp. vegetable oil	1 c. water

additional vegetable oil as needed to improve consistency

Mix the ingredients together. Knead until the dough is smooth.

Mary Ann Craven
Fallbrook United Methodist School
Fallbrook, CA

Learning Centers

Cat and Mouse
Discovery Center

Attach cat and mouse cutouts (patterns on page 109) to metal lids from frozen juice concentrate cans. Place the lids at a table along with a magnet wand for each one. Attach a mouse-hole cutout to one end of the table. Partners choose either a cat or a mouse. Then they each use a magnet wand to drag the lids along the surface of the table, pretending the cat is chasing the mouse! After a few moments, the mouse scurries to the mouse hole. Then the partners switch lids and begin again.

Jan Boyce
Cokato, MN

Rollin' Along
Block Center

Place one or two rolls of thick toilet paper in your block center. Students use blocks to build a neighborhood. Then they roll out strips of toilet paper to make the roads, taping the ends of each road to the floor to secure them in place. When the neighborhood and roads are complete, youngsters engage in pretend play, driving toy vehicles along the roadways.

Mindy Wisecup
Illiopolis Elementary
Illiopolis, IL

Spill and Grab
Fine-Motor Area

Youngsters develop and strengthen their pincer grasp at this center! Provide a pair of tweezers and a disposable cup filled with jumbo paper clips. A child spills the paper clips onto a surface. Then she uses the tweezers to pick up each paper clip and place it back in the cup. Each day, provide a different item to spill and grab, such as pom-poms, drinking straw halves, pipe cleaner pieces, round-end toothpicks, crumpled tissue paper, and small craft foam shapes.

Shelley Hoster
Jack & Jill Early Learning Center
Norcross, GA

Learning Centers

Pots of Gold
Math Center

Set out ten black pot cutouts (pattern on page 109), each labeled with a number from 1 to 10. Provide ten disposable cups, each containing from one to ten yellow tagboard circles (gold coins). A youngster chooses a cup, spills the contents, and counts the coins. Then he finds the pot labeled with the corresponding number and places the coins above the pot. He continues with each remaining cup.

Barbara Zuber
Hammonton Early Childhood Education Center
Hammonton, NJ

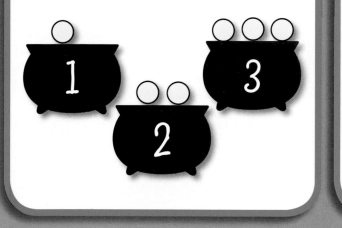

Fancy Floss Designs
Art Center

Place folded white tooth cutouts and shallow containers of paint at a table. For each container of paint, provide a strand of dental floss tied to a craft stick. A child unfolds a cutout. Then she drags a strand of floss through paint and lays it on one side of the tooth. She folds the tooth back over and lightly presses her hand on it as she uses the stick to drag the floss out of the folded paper. She repeats the process with other strands of floss and colors of paint until she is satisfied with her work.

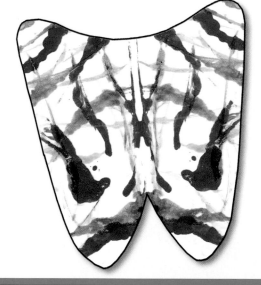

Letter Shopping
Literacy Center

Label a paper grocery bag with a letter. Then provide clean food boxes and containers that have that letter on the label and others that do not. (Encourage youngsters to focus on the big letters on the packaging.) If a label has the letter, a child pretends to scan the item and then places it in the bag. If the item does not, he sets it aside. **For an extra challenge,** use two grocery bags with different letters and have the child sort the packaging into the appropriate bags.

Susan Norton
Busy Bee Preschool
Thatcher, AZ

Colorful Egg Basket
Art Center

Cut a basket shape from plastic canvas and attach it to a tabletop. Provide shallow containers of paint and a potato half for each color. A child places a sheet of paper atop the basket and rubs the side of an unwrapped crayon across the paper. She continues in the same way with other crayons. When the rubbing is finished, she removes the paper, dips the cut side of a potato in paint, and presses it above the basket to make an egg shape. She repeats the process several times. When the paint is dry, she decorates the eggs with markers.

Mary Ann Craven
Fallbrook United Methodist School
Fallbrook, CA

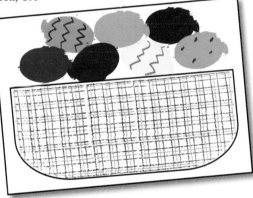

Unique Butterfly
Block Center

Place in your block center a poster-size butterfly cutout. Provide assorted wood and plastic blocks along with items to create butterfly details, such as milk caps, pom-poms, and pattern blocks. A student places blocks along the edge of the butterfly. When he's finished, he uses the remaining items to add butterfly details. How unique!

Roxanne LaBell Dearman
NC Early Intervention Program for Children Who Are Deaf
    or Hard of Hearing
Charlotte, NC

Sound Sort
Literacy Center

Set out three containers: two labeled with different letters and one unmarked. Provide a collection of items (or pictures) that begin with each letter sound and several that do not. A youngster chooses an item and says its name and beginning sound. Then she places the item in the container labeled with the corresponding letter. If the item doesn't begin with either letter sound, she places it in the unmarked container. She repeats the process with each remaining item.

Marie E. Cecchini
West Dundee, IL

Learning Centers

Busy Bee
Gross–Motor Area

Obtain several plastic flowerpots (or pails) and decorate each one so it resembles a different-colored flower. Provide a supply of pom-poms (pollen) that correspond to the color of each flower. Explain that bees spread pollen from flower to flower. A child takes a handful of pollen and pretends to be a bee buzzing around the flowers. As he buzzes around, he pauses to drop or toss a piece of pollen into the pot with the corresponding flower. He continues in the same way until all the pollen is dispersed into the appropriate pots.

Tricia Kylene Brown
Bowling Green, KY

Lunch Log
Math Center

Label each of 12 frog cutouts (pattern on page 207) with a number from 1 to 12. Attach the frogs to a paper log as shown. Cut out a copy of the fly cards on page 110 and stack them facedown near the log. A youngster flips the top card and counts the flies aloud. Then he places the card above the frog with the corresponding number. He continues in the same way with each remaining card.

adapted from an idea by Tara Green
Lincoln Heights Elementary
Fuquay-Varina, NC

A Bevy of Bulbs
Sensory Center

Fill your sensory table or a large plastic tub with soil. Provide assorted flower bulbs, plastic gardening tools, gardening gloves, and a magnifying glass. A student uses the magnifying glass to examine the flower bulbs, commenting on and comparing the details as he studies them. Then he uses the tools and accessories to plant the bulbs in the soil.

Christine Manning
Charlotte, NC

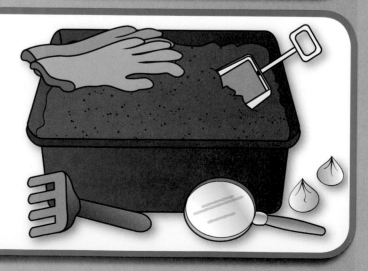

Sparkling Waves!
Art Center

A child visits this center and fingerpaints a tray with blue and green paint; then he places a sheet of construction paper atop the paint and rubs his hands across it. He removes the paper, squeezes wavy lines of glue across the painted page, and then sprinkles glitter on the glue. The resulting artwork looks like whitecaps on the ocean.

Ada Goren, Winston-Salem, NC

tip → For extra pizzazz, have each child attach craft foam or confetti ocean critters to the artwork!

Boat Float
Water Table Center

To make a mini sailboat, press a small lump of play dough or clay into a plastic soda bottle lid. Attach a construction paper triangle to a toothpick; then insert the toothpick into the play dough. Float a fleet of mini sailboats in your water table. A student waves a sheet of cardboard or blows on the sailboats to maneuver them around in the water.

Connie Massingill, Dawn 'til Dusk Daycare, Zionsville, IN

Ocean Park
Dramatic-Play Area

Place a blue blanket or bedsheet (water) on the floor in your dramatic-play area. Stock the area with toy dolphins and whales and plastic pails containing craft foam fish (for feeding the sea animals). Also provide items such as sunglasses, towels, empty sunscreen bottles, a toy cash register, play money, and admission tickets. Youngsters pretend to be sea animal trainers putting on a show for visitors at an ocean-themed park.

Jennifer Gemar, Tripp-Delmont School District, Tripp, SD

Cut out

TEC41057

Cat and Mouse Patterns

Use with "Cat and Mouse" on page 103.

TEC41059

TEC41059

Pot Pattern

Use with "Pots of Gold" on page 104 and "Leprechaun's Gold" on page 16.

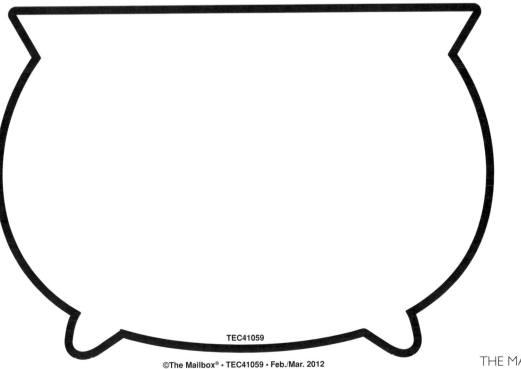

TEC41059

Fly Cards
Use with "Lunch Log" on page 106.

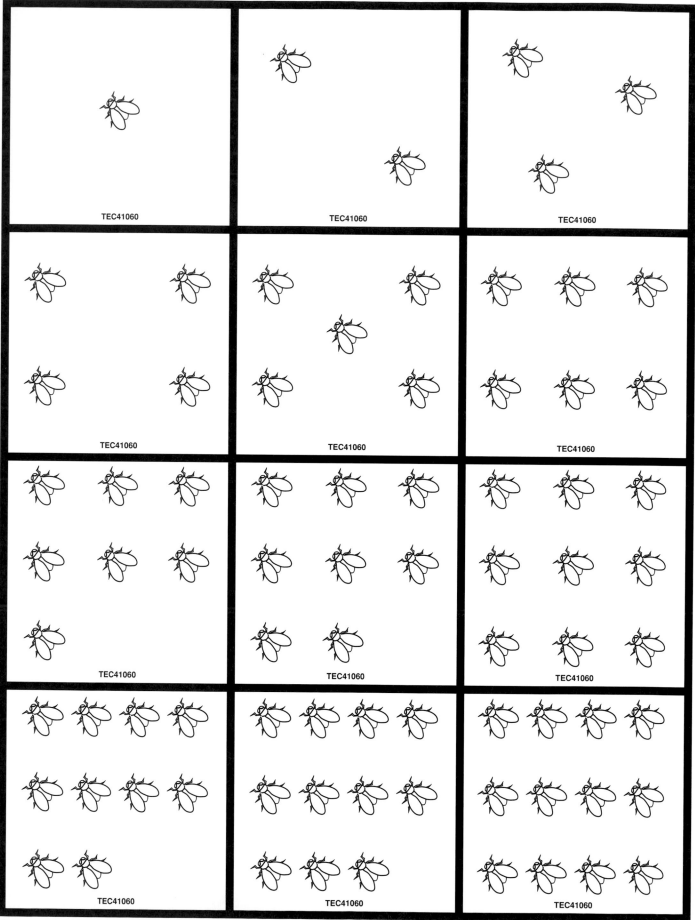

TEC41060

TEC41060

TEC41060

TEC41060

TEC41060

TEC41060

TEC41060

TEC41060

TEC41060

TEC41060

TEC41060

TEC41060

OUR READERS WRITE

Magic Play Dough

Add a little color to the school year with magic play dough. I prepare a batch of white play dough. Then, for each child, I form a ball of dough with a couple of drops of food coloring and a sprinkle of glitter in the center. On the first day of school, I give each child a ball of play dough and invite him to work the dough in his hands. I tell him that if it changes color, he will have a great school year. It is hard for youngsters to contain their excitement as the play dough begins to change color. **Kerri Barnes, Neal Child Development Center, Bryan, TX**

f **"I LOVE your magazine. I have been using it in my classroom since 1990."—Cajsa Howland Sheen via Facebook**

f **"Great teaching ideas! My students love them all!"—Jennifer Marcinkus Chumbley via Facebook**

Morning Greeting

Students like to receive morning greetings in different ways, so I design a greeting sign. On the sign, I post the following pictures: a character smiling, a character waving, two characters high-fiving, and two characters hugging. When the child arrives, she points to the greeting she needs to get her day off to a good start! *Karen Vino, Hazleton Area School District, Hazleton, PA*

THE BIRTHDAY THRONE

Invite each little one to be king or queen for his or her birthday. I use craft items to decorate an inexpensive chair. Then I attach a large birthday cake cutout near the top of the chair and make number and candle cutouts that youngsters can attach to the cake. When it is a child's birthday, I have him display the appropriate number and set of candles. Then I invite him to sit in the throne during circle time and storytime. *Heather Taube, Saint Mary of the Assumption School, Avilla, IN*

The MAILBOX BLOG

🔲 **"Thank you for the wonderful ideas that you provide every month! I look forward to my new edition like it's Christmas morning!"—Rolanda Staley, Aiken, SC, via The Mailbox® Blog**

We had a special person visit our class. Ask your child what our visitor brought with her.

TALK ABOUT IT

To help parents jump-start conversations about their children's day, I display a small dry-erase board near the classroom door. Prior to dismissal, I write on the board a conversation starter related to something we did in class. Parents use the conversation starter to talk with their children about the school day.

Camille Ruggirello, Trinity Preschool, Walden, NY

Bathroom Clock

Owen
Brandi
Katie
Jack
Pete
Eliza
Knox
Amy

Use this unique clock to remind little ones that it is bathroom time. I label a simple construction paper clock with youngsters' names. Then I display the clock. When it is time to begin bathroom time, I say, "Tick tock, bathroom clock; it's your turn, [child's name]." The child moves the hand on the clock so it points to her name. I continue in this manner until each child has visited the bathroom. **Brooke O'Dell, Minds in Motion, Nashville, TN**

Multisensory Months

I teach youngsters the months of the year using a multisensory approach. For each month, I break its name into syllables and add a motion for little ones to repeat as they say the syllables. For example, youngsters pretend to pick an apple as they say each syllable in *September*. This method has been particularly successful for my special-needs students!

Maryanne Kadish, The Tobin Montessori School, Cambridge, MA

This is me and my teacher.

SPECIAL BUDDIES

Each day, I choose a child to be my special buddy. About thirty minutes before the end of rest time, I wake my buddy so we can do a special activity together, such as playing a game, putting together a new puzzle, or doing an art activity. My little ones can't wait until it is their turn to be my special buddy.

Janice Hicks, The Nurturey Preschool and Daycare, Gaithersburg MD

Pleasing Pumpkin

This papier-mâché art project is perfect to use during a fall harvest unit or near Halloween. I blow up a large punching balloon. Then, right before beginning the project, I mix warm water and flour to make a soupy liquid. I help small groups of students dip newspaper strips in the flour mixture, remove excess liquid, and place the strips on the balloon. We apply several layers and allow several days for them to dry. Then I have youngsters use diluted glue to attach orange and black tissue paper so the project resembles a jack-o'-lantern! *Jeanette Anderson, Jeanette's Tots, Otsego, MN*

Fire Drill Time Filler

During our wait to return to the building after a fire drill, I ask my students questions about fire drills, such as "What is that loud noise?" or "What do we need to do when we hear the fire alarm?" If time permits, I also ask questions about firefighters and police officers and their jobs. Not only does this activity keep students busy, but it also reinforces the purpose of the drill. *Erin McGinness, The Learning Patch, Newark, DE*

FALL BANNER

After the leaves begin to fall, I take my students on a walk and invite them to collect leaves. When we return, I give each child a length of Glad Press 'n Seal wrap. I help him place the wrap sticky-side up and then put the leaves on one half of the wrap. Next, I help him fold the wrap in half and press on it to seal it. Finally, I staple a folded strip of paper to the top of the banner and add a yarn hanger. *Mileen McGee, George O. Barr Elementary, Silvis, IL*

PHOTO PARADE

My little ones and classroom visitors love this adorable display. I take a photo of each child wearing his Halloween costume. I also have him wave in the photo so it looks like he is waving at the parade watchers. I post the photos in a line on the wall outside our classroom so that people who pass by the wall can enjoy our Halloween parade. *Amy Hart, Saint Sylvester School, Pittsburgh, PA*

Simple Stained Glass

Want a creative use for leftover laminating film? Try this! I give a leftover piece of laminating film to each child and invite her to use permanent markers to draw designs or a picture on the film. Then I attach the finished projects to the classroom windows. For added fun, die-cut the laminating film to make seasonal shapes. *Donna Ream, Ms. Donna's Daycare, Plainfield, IL*

Feed the Turkey!

For Thanksgiving Day, my class participates in a food drive for the local food pantry. This adorable turkey box is perfect for collecting the food! I cut a hole in the box so food can be put in it. I have students fringe-cut feather cutouts. Then I attach the feathers and a turkey body to the box. When a child brings in food, I help him "feed" the turkey! *Sally Sypen, Redeemer Christian Nursery School, Ramsey, NJ*

Word of the Day

When my class returns from breakfast each morning, we stop at the door and I ask each child, "What is your magic word for the day?" He names the word; I repeat it and give him a hug. (Youngsters can choose a real word or a silly, made-up word.) It is a fun way to greet my little ones each morning. *Lori Gelbke, Community Child Care Center, Kimberly, WI*

Puzzle Wreaths

This simple craft idea can be a magnet or an ornament. Throughout the year I save pieces from incomplete puzzles. In addition, I buy a couple of cheap puzzles at a thrift store or a garage sale. I spray-paint the pieces green. Then each child glues several pieces to a painted cardboard ring to make a wreath. When the glue is dry, he adds small red pom-pom berries and a bow. Then I help him add a magnet to the back or a loop for hanging. **Ruth Zabelin, Riviera, TX, via The Mailbox Blog**

f *"The Mailbox* **is an excellent resource for my teaching plans. Thank you for helping me find great ideas to implement in my lessons each and every week."—** *Cathy Jo McCall via Facebook*

Scents of the Season

Tickle little ones' noses with this sense-of-smell activity. I punch holes in the lids of opaque containers. In each container, I place something with a distinctive smell that is related to the season, such as crushed candy canes, a clipping from an evergreen tree, or a cinnamon candle. I place the jars at a center and encourage youngsters to sniff and try to identify the different scents. *Danielle Lockwood, Colchester, CT*

PRINTED ART

Encourage youngsters to use an out-of-the-ordinary object to create one of a kind art projects! I ask parents to donate the bottom portions of trunk that they cut from their live Christmas trees. I put these tree pieces in my art center along with shallow containers of paint. A child dips the pieces in paint and makes prints on a sheet of paper. **Susan Perry, Avon Nursery School, Avon, MA**

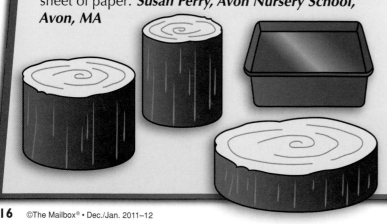

The **MAILBOX** BLOG

R **"I totally love** *The Mailbox* **website and magazines!"—***Karen Lesmerises, Allenstown, NH, via The Mailbox Blog*

FIVE LITTLE SNOWMEN

Parents love these adorable keepsake ornaments. I paint each child's hand white. Then I place an empty ball ornament (found at craft stores) on her palm and bring her fingers around the ball to make a print. After the paint dries, I help her fill the ball with icicle decorations and confetti. Then I add faces to each finger and thumbprint to make snowmen. *Michelle Weiler, Morrison, IL*

The MAILBOX BLOG

I have made many games and activities from ideas in *The Mailbox.* I love this magazine!"—*Cindy MacDonald, Raynham, MA, via The Mailbox Blog*

SNOW PAINTING

Let the snow be your canvas for this fun outdoor activity. I fill spray bottles with tinted water. Then I head outside with my students. I invite each child to spray the colored water onto the snow to make a unique work of art. I take a photo of each masterpiece for the student to share with his family. *Danielle Lockwood, Colchester, CT*

Toy Trade

Instead of having parents purchase a new gift for a holiday gift swap—try this! A couple of weeks prior to our gift swap, I send a note to parents asking them to wrap a gently used toy and send it to school on a designated day. I always keep a couple of extra toys on hand in case a child does not bring a toy. Parents like this idea because they do not have to go to the store, plus it helps make room for new toys! *Coya Clayton, Kids Inc., Marion, IA*

f *"The Mailbox* magazine is a great resource for fun skill- and theme-based activities for preschool children."—*Janette Eicken Janssen via Facebook*

Seasonal Stories

My students love to share these simple booklets with their families. Make a supply of small stapled booklets with seasonal gift wrap covers and place them in your writing center. Then tell little ones to draw and write about their holiday memories. *Rebecca Juneau, Highland Elementary, Lake Stevens, WA*

A Sweet Collage

When youngsters are making a collage, I use sweetened condensed milk as an alternative to glue. I have my little ones paint a thin layer of the milk on their papers. Then they press tissue paper squares over the milk. Sweetened condensed milk doesn't dry as fast as glue. Plus it's perfect for younger preschoolers who frequently put their fingers in their mouths. Before the collages are sent home, I cover each one with a piece of clear Con-Tact paper. *Kelly Nielsen, JCDC Little Tree House, Janesville, WI*

The **MAILBOX** BLOG

"I really love reading all the tips and ideas from my fellow teachers. *The Mailbox* magazines are great!"—*Linda Stoffan, Rio Rancho, NM, via The Mailbox Blog*

Buggy Observations

A couple of weeks prior to beginning a bug unit, I head outside to collect a variety of dead bugs. I place the bugs in plastic tubes. Then I add a generous amount of clear hand-sanitizing gel to each tube. I use tape to secure the cap on each tube. The gel suspends the bugs so they are easy for youngsters to observe. It also preserves them for a long time! *Karla Broad, Our Savior Preschool, Naples, FL*

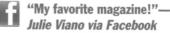

"My favorite magazine!"— *Julie Viano via Facebook*

RECYCLABLE ROBOT

At the beginning of my unit on recycling, I send home a note asking each family to send in clean recyclable materials. When we receive the materials, we use tape and glue to attach the products to make a robot. When it is finished, we name our robot and put it on display! My youngsters and their parents always enjoy this activity! *Peggy Lawrence, Sandpiper Preschool, Portage, IN*

Marigolds for Mom

My heart you touch.
My hand you hold.
Please accept this marigold.
I planted it with a finger or two
Because it's Mother's Day.
And I love you!

Two weeks prior to Mother's Day, I have each youngster decorate a small flower pot with colorful sticky dots. Then I help her plant marigold seeds in the pot. We care for our seeds until the last school day before Mother's Day. On this day I tie the poem shown to each child's pot. Then I have him take it home and give it to his mother or another special woman. *Cindy Peno, A Bizzy Bunch Preschool, Gonzales, LA*

Spring Planting

A funnel is a helpful tool to use during seed-planting projects. After a student has created a hole in the dirt for her seeds, I place the small end of the funnel in the hole. Then I give her a few seeds and have her drop them in the funnel. I direct her to remove the funnel and fill the hole with dirt. This simple idea ensures that seeds are planted perfectly every time. *Teresa Gallentine, Jordan Creek Elementary, West Des Moines, IA*

The MAILBOX BLOG

BUBBLES!

Review the /b/ sound with this entertaining activity. I add dishwashing liquid to our water table and provide an old-fashioned egg beater. When a child visits the area, he practices the /b/ sound as he beats the water to make bubbles. *Margaret Cromwell, Grace Episcopal Preschool, Georgetown, TX*

Fun Flannelboards

Here's an easy way to create professional-looking flannel-board pieces for a fraction of the price. I print clip art pictures on iron-on transfer paper. Then I iron the pictures on white felt. Not only are the pieces nice-looking and durable, but I can create pieces for any story or unit. *Jennifer Schear, Wright Elementary, Cedar Rapids, IA*

Our Readers WRITE...
(and EMAIL and BLOG and TWEET and POST)

Personalized Postcards

At the end of the year, I have each child draw a picture on a blank postcard. Then I label the postcards and store them for safekeeping. During summer break, I use the postcards to write thank-you notes for end-of-the-year gifts or just to send notes of encouragement. My youngsters are thrilled to receive notes from their teacher on the postcards they created. *Jennifer Silvetti, Camp Hill Presbyterian School, Camp Hill, PA*

Dear Amber,
Thank you for the candle. It smells wonderful. I hope you are enjoying your summer.

Love,
Ms. Silvetti

Amber Jones
123 Elm Street
Camp Hill, PA

SOCKS AND SNEAKERS

Looking for a way to encourage parents to dress their children in proper footwear for outdoor play? I send a copy of this adorable poem home to each family. It is a fun way to remind families that sneakers and socks are the best footwear for outdoor play. *Donna Britt and Sherry Britt, Persimmon Ridge Head Start, Jonesborough, TN*

Those flip-flops are adorable.
Your sandals are so cute.
And you look very stylish
In your clogs and cowboy boots.

But when you're on the playground,
Where there's dirt and mulch and rocks,
The safest things for you to wear
Are sneakers and some socks!

The mulch can scratch your ankles.
The rocks can stub your toes.
You might take a tumble
And bop your little nose!

Your teachers want to keep you safe.
We think you're very sweet.
So please wear socks and sneakers
To protect your little feet!

A Clean Shave

I love to spray non-mentholated shaving cream on my classroom tables and then have youngsters use their fingers to explore and write. To make the cleanup quick and easy, I cut a disposable plastic plate in half and use a plate half to scoop the shaving cream off the table. Then I wipe the table with a damp sponge! *Melissa Herman, Wee Folk School, Frederick, MD*

The MAILBOX BLOG

PROBLEM SOLVED!

Problem Solved!

Your Solutions to Classroom Challenges

I gather **old die-cuts** laminated with Con-Tact covering and store them in a container. If a youngster is wiggly or has sensory needs, I give him the box. He can sit and use his fingers to pick the lamination from the die-cut. This tip really helps my youngsters stay focused!

Alison Davis, St. Catherine Academy Pre-K, New Haven, KY

Experts say a normal attention span is three to five minutes per year of a child's age.

I use a simple phrase to get my little ones to sit quietly on their chairs. Whenever we go to our chairs for snacktime or a center activity, I say, **"Sit square on your chair."** My students know this means to sit ready to listen with their legs beneath the table.

Debbie Abbatte, Start Smart Academy, Flemington, NJ

How do you calm *wiggly youngsters?*

My class finds the scent of lavender very calming. So on particularly wiggly days, I pull out my **lavender hand lotion.** I encourage students to sit quietly, and then I squirt a small amount of lotion on each child's hands. They quietly sit and rub it in, smelling the light scent of the lotion. It never fails to calm my little ones!

Lynn Hanney, A Childs Haven Valrico, FL

I have youngsters **sing this song** with me before circle time to calm those wiggly hands! At the end of the first, second, and fourth lines, have students gently tap their legs.

Denise Brown, Childserve Child Care Center, Johnston, IA
Amanda Shinn, Kinder Cassel, Champaign, IL

(sung to the tune of "If You're Happy and You Know It")

Put your hands in your lap, in your lap.
Put your hands in your lap, in your lap.
Put your hands in your lap and leave them just like that.
Put your hands in your lap, in your lap.

It's your turn! We're always looking for your tips, ideas, and suggestions. **Go to themailbox.com/mailboxideas.**

Problem Solved!

Your Solutions to Classroom Challenges

When it is time to clean up, I tell my youngsters we are going to play the magic toy game. I secretly choose a toy that is out of place. Each child quickly cleans the room in hopes that he will put away the magic toy. After the room is clean, I reveal the magic toy and award the child who put it away a small sticker and a round of applause.

Lynn Harbuzinski, Always Home, Westfield, NJ

Messy classroom?
What is your most effective cleanup tip?

One tool I always keep handy for cleaning up is a squeegee. I can use it to clean up crumbs, glitter, and other messes with just a few quick swipes. My little ones enjoy using this wonderful cleanup tool as well!

John Simas, East Rochester Elementary, East Rochester, NH

I set a timer during center time to help my group keep track of time as well as to alert them when it is cleanup time. When my little ones hear the timer ring, they stop working and recite the following rhyme: "When our classroom timer rings, it's time to clean up all our things!" This reminds my youngsters what is expected of them.

Molly Drake, Blackheath Pre-kindergarten Center, Long Beach, NY

I choose a snappy fast-paced song to be my cleanup song. Then I record it on a cassette, inserting a few silent pauses during the song. At cleanup time, I play the recording. When youngsters hear the music stop, they freeze and look around the room to see what still needs to be cleaned up. When the music starts again, cleanup resumes.

Susan Pufall, Red Cliff Early Head Start, Bayfield, WI

"Cleaning up with children around is like shoveling during a blizzard."
Author Unknown

It's your turn! We're always looking for your tips, ideas, and suggestions. **Go to themailbox.com/mailboxideas.**

Problem Solved!

Your Solutions to Classroom Challenges

After setting up the naptime mats, I have my class line up near the naptime area. In turn, I whisper something special into each child's ear and then invite her to quietly tiptoe to her mat and lay down. This simple idea really helps to set the tone for naptime.

Kathy Hagenbuch, Growing Tree Child Care Center, Whitehall, PA

A day without a nap is like a cupcake without frosting.
—Terri Guillemets

To begin naptime, I turn on my magic candle (flameless candle). At the end of naptime, I invite a child to "blow out" the candle. The magic candle is perfect for naptime because it gives off a lovely, soothing glow.

Maria Carrubba, St. Gabriel School, Philadelphia, PA

How do you help youngsters have a successful naptime?

I gather several small lidded boxes, such as baby wipe containers, and decorate them. In each box, I put objects students can use quietly, such as puzzles, a pencil and a small notepad, plastic linking blocks, or plastic toy animals. If it is obvious that a child is unable to sleep, I invite him to choose a box, bring it back to his naptime area, and play with the materials in the box. Ten minutes before the end of naptime, I have youngsters return their boxes.

Cindy Kern, Childsavers, Richmond, VA

Do you have some little ones who are afraid of the dark? Here's a solution! In a safe location, I display a strand of white lights. At the beginning of naptime, I turn on the "night-night" lights. My youngsters think they are cool, plus it calms those who are afraid of the dark. For added fun, I substitute the strands to match holidays: orange for Halloween, red for Christmas, and green for St. Patrick's Day!

Kyleen Cook, In the Zone, Ocean Springs, MS

It's your turn! We're always looking for your tips, ideas, and suggestions. **Go to themailbox.com/mailboxideas.**

Problem Solved!

Your Solutions to Classroom Challenges

When my **glue sticks** start drying out, I rehydrate them instead of throwing them away! I seal each glue stick and a damp paper towel in a resealable plastic bag. (Hint: Snack-size bags work great.) Then I set each bag aside for a couple of days, and the glue sticks are as good as new!

Monica Stapleton
Warner Christian Academy
South Daytona, FL

Did you know?
Around 1750, the first glue patent was issued in Britain. The glue was made from fish!

Here's a great way to reuse **milk jug lids** and conserve glue. I squeeze a small amount of glue into separate lids for individual youngsters to use. The lids are easy to refill and can be cleaned without water. I simply let the lids air-dry and then peel the glue residue out of the lid.

Penny Brown
Little Red Schoolhouse
Salem, OR

Glue can be aggravating! *How do you tame your troubles with glue?*

For projects that need glue in just the right places, I highlight the area with a yellow highlighter. When youngsters see highlighted areas, they know exactly where to put the glue. This works especially well for little ones who are new to using glue.

Vickii Nesbit
Little Lambs Preschool
Williston, VT

To help youngsters learn to use squeeze bottles of glue, I give each student a sheet of black paper and have her attach hole reinforcers to it. Then I provide squeeze bottles of tinted glue. I encourage her to put a drop of glue in the center of each reinforcer, reminding her to gently squeeze the bottle to control the amount of glue that comes out.

Jodi Reiner
St. Catherine of Siena Preschool
Carrollton, TX

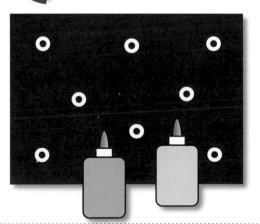

It's your turn! We're always looking for your tips, ideas, and suggestions. **Go to themailbox.com/mailboxideas.**

Q & A Problem Solved!

Your Solutions to Classroom Challenges

Our class loves to play this fun variation of **Red Light, Green Light**. I announce "yellow" to move in slow motion, "purple" to move in reverse, "orange" to move left, and "blue" to move right. This game always results in lots of giggles because not everyone (including me) remembers the colorful directions!

Rebecca Luckmann, Fairlawn Preschool, Columbus, IN

I fill time and fine-tune **observation skills** with this game! I invite a child to be the change artist and stand in front of the group. After youngsters observe the child, I have him leave the area with an adult helper and change his appearance in some way. For example, he might remove a shoe, roll up a pant leg, or put a sticky dot on his forehead. Then he returns to the area, and youngsters guess what's different.

Ashley Foster, Tendercare Learning Center—Jefferson, Clairton, PA

You have unexpected time between activities! *What do you like to do with your little ones?*

I give one domino to each child. I place an extra domino on the floor, count the dots on either end, and ask if anyone has a domino with the same dot set. A child who has the same dot set matches it to the domino on the floor. He **counts the dots** on the unmatched end of his domino, and then we repeat the process. When no other matches can be made, we continue with the unmatched end of the starter domino.

Michelle Gwinn, Wood County Schools, Parkersburg, WV

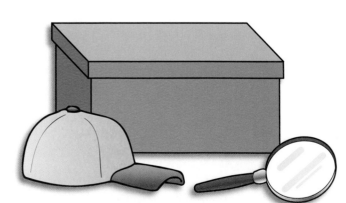

I fill a story box with assorted items, such as a hat, a key, an apron, a magnifying glass, a bell, and a shopping list. To use the box, I remove an item, such as the hat, and say, "One day, the blustery wind blew my hat away!" I invite my students to **add to the story**; then I remove other items, in turn, to add new story elements.

Litsa Jackson, Covington Integrated Arts Academy, Covington, TN

It's your turn! We're always looking for your tips, ideas, and suggestions. **Go to themailbox.com/mailboxideas.**

Science Explorations

Solid and Liquid

Little ones explore what happens when a variety of items are placed in water!

Materials:
salt
dry sponge
wood block
3 clear containers of water
spoon

STEP 1

Show students the salt, the sponge, and the block. Have youngsters handle each item. Explain that each one is a solid, which means it has a shape that will not change on its own. Then have students scan the room. Ask, "What other solids do you see?" Have youngsters share their thoughts.

STEP 2

Say, "Let's see what happens when we mix a solid with a liquid, such as water." Have youngsters help you put salt in a container of water. Encourage each child to stir the contents, observe what happens, and share his observations. Explain that the salt dissolves and becomes part of the liquid.

STEP 3

Hold up the sponge and ask students to predict what they think will happen when you place it in water. After students share, place the sponge in the second container. Encourage youngsters to feel the sponge, leading them to understand that the sponge absorbs the water. The sponge keeps its shape but becomes soft and flexible.

STEP 4

Have youngsters repeat the process with the block and the third container, leading them to realize that the block does not dissolve in or absorb water.

This Is Why

Whether a solid dissolves, is malleable, or is unchanged depends on its solubility and density (the amount of matter in a given volume or space). The density depends on how tightly packed the matter is.

Curious Cotton Ball Behavior!

Little ones will be intrigued with this unique sink and float exploration!

idea contributed by Cassie Campbell
Bourbon County Preschool Head Start, Paris, KY

Materials:

clear disposable cup	vegetable oil
clear container	water
2 cotton balls	spoon

STEP 1

Show the oil and ask, "What do you know about vegetable oil?" After youngsters share their thoughts, have them rub a small amount of oil between their fingertips and describe how it feels. Have them clean their fingers and repeat the process with water. Ask, "How are oil and water the same? How are they different?"

STEP 2

Pour a small amount of oil into the cup and then place a cotton ball in the oil. Have youngsters help you stir the cotton ball to saturate it with oil. Encourage each child to observe the cotton ball and share his observations.

STEP 3

Fill the container with water. Have youngsters handle a plain cotton ball. Then ask, "If the oil-soaked cotton ball and a plain cotton ball are dropped in the water, which one will sink and which one will float?" Have students share their thoughts and explain their reasoning.

STEP 4

Put the oil-coated cotton ball and a plain cotton ball in the container. When the plain cotton ball becomes saturated with water, youngsters will see it sink to the bottom of the container, while the oil-soaked cotton ball stays afloat!

This Is Why

Water and oil are both liquids; however, oil does not dissolve in water, so the two liquids separate. Because oil is less dense (lighter) than water, it floats on the water's surface, which is why the oil-soaked cotton ball stayed afloat.

Science Explorations

Fizz and Foam

What happens when vinegar and baking soda mix? Youngsters find out with this sizzling investigation!

idea contributed by Melissa Talley, Early Learning, Champaign, IL

Materials:
clear 12-ounce plastic bottle
vinegar
baking soda
measuring cup
funnel
plastic tub or deep tray

STEP 1

Display the vinegar and baking soda. Ask youngsters what they know about each item. Prompt them to notice that the vinegar is a liquid and the baking soda is a solid. Then invite each child to rub the baking soda between her fingertips, smell it, and then taste it. Have her describe the baking soda. Then encourage her to repeat the process with the vinegar.

STEP 2

Place the bottle in the plastic tub and put the funnel in the bottle. Pour about one-half cup of vinegar into the bottle. Ask, "What do you think will happen if we put baking soda in the vinegar?" Encourage students to share their thoughts and explain their reasoning.

STEP 3

Put about one-quarter cup of baking soda into the bottle and then quickly remove the funnel. Have youngsters observe what happens and describe what they see. Then have students sniff the ingredients to see if the vinegar's odor has changed. Encourage each child to share her observations.

This Is Why

When baking soda and vinegar mix, it causes a chemical reaction. This reaction creates a gas, which causes the ingredients to bubble and foam.

For added fun, repeat the experiment with a clean bottle. This time, pour a mixture of baking soda and unsweetened Kool-Aid powder into the vinegar!

Science Explorations

Rainy Day Dress!

Little ones explore and compare the materials used for rainy day clothing to those used for everyday wear. What a fun way to investigate absorption!

Materials:
raincoat
T-shirt
eyedropper
container of water

STEP 1

Show youngsters the raincoat and the T-shirt and encourage them to touch the materials and discuss their observations. Ask, "When would you wear a coat like this?" and "When would you wear a T-shirt?" Allow several youngsters to share their thoughts.

STEP 2

Ask students what they think would happen if they dripped water onto the coat. Then have a child use an eyedropper to drip water on the coat. Encourage youngsters to discuss what happened. Why do they think this happened? Repeat the process with the T-shirt. Explain that the coat repels the water and the T-shirt absorbs the water. Prompt students to name other items they believe would repel or absorb water.

STEP 3

Ask students whether it is smarter to wear the coat or the T-shirt on a rainy day. Encourage youngsters to explain their thoughts, leading them to draw conclusions about the purpose of raingear.

What Next?

Place water, the eyedropper, and several different materials at a center. You may consider providing fabric, cardboard, vinyl, Bubble Wrap cushioning material, and paper. Encourage youngsters to drip water on the various items and discuss whether the items repel or absorb water.

Gelatin Germination

Gelatin isn't just for dessert anymore! Surprise your youngsters with this unique planting experience.

idea contributed by Jennifer Avegno
Carousel Preschool, Cypress, CA

Materials:
unflavored gelatin
    mix (such as Knox
    Unflavored Gelatin)
water
mixing bowl and spoon

clear plastic cup
plastic wrap
vegetable seeds
potting soil

STEP 1

Show the box of gelatin and ask, "Has anyone ever helped make gelatin?" After youngsters respond, ask, "Do you like to eat gelatin?" Then invite youngsters who say "no" to explain why and children who say "yes" to tell their favorite gelatin flavor.

STEP 2

Encourage students to tell what they know about planting seeds. Then ask, "Do you think seeds will grow if we plant them in gelatin?" After students share their thoughts, invite them to help make the gelatin. Then partially fill a cup with the mixture and let it set.

STEP 3

Invite youngsters to lightly press a few seeds just under the gelatin's surface. Cover the cup with plastic wrap, place it in sunlight, and then have youngsters observe it daily for growth. Since unflavored gelatin is clear, youngsters will be able to study the growth quite easily!

STEP 4

After the seedlings sprout to about an inch or two, remove the gelatin along with the seedlings and transplant them into soil.

What Next?

Have a snack of flavored gelatin! Consider having students use plastic knives to cut fruit into small pieces and add it to prepared gelatin. It's a terrific and healthy snack!

Songs & Such

Songs & Such

Apple Seeds

This adorable action rhyme is sure to be perfect for the beginning of the school year!

Eat an apple to the core.
Find one seed; find several more.
Plant them in a little cup.
Wait until a sprout pops up.
When the sprout has several leaves,
Plant it in your garden, please.
Then one day you'll look and see
Your sprout is an apple tree!

Make a fist (apple).
Hold up one finger and then all five.
Cup hands.
Press hands together and move them overhead.
Push hands apart and wiggle fingers.
Pat the floor.
Place hand above eyes.
Point.

Marie E. Cecchini
West Dundee, IL

What's Your Name?

Here's a sweet song that helps youngsters learn each others' names! Sing the first line of the song, substituting your name. Then gesture to a child as you sing the second line of the song. After he says his name, lead students in singing the remaining lines. Continue with each youngster.

(sung to the tune of "Are You Sleeping?")

I'm [Ms. Erin]. I'm [Ms. Erin].
What's your name? What's your name?
Oh, [his] name is [John]. Oh, [his] name is [John].
Super name! Super name!

Erin McGinness
Great New Beginnings Early Learning Center
Newark, DE

Raise Your Hand

Encourage little ones to raise their hands in the classroom with this catchy song!

(sung to the tune of "The Farmer in the Dell")

Please, keep your answers in.
Please, keep your answers in.
Raise your hand in the air.
Please, keep your answers in.

Doria Owen, William Paca Old Post Road Elementary
Abingdon, MD

Quiet Preschool Voices

Remind youngsters to use inside voices by leading them in this soothing song.

(sung to the tune of "Clementine")

Inside voices, inside voices,
We talk softly in our room.
Inside voices, inside voices,
We talk softly in our room.

adapted from an idea by Kathryn Wilson
New Hope Elementary
Henderson, NC

Songs & Such

Leaves on the Move

Youngsters use real leaves as props for this fun action song! Give each child a colorful fall leaf. Then lead the class in singing the song and moving their leaves appropriately.

(sung to the tune of "The Wheels on the Bus")

The leaves in the air [go up and down],
[Up and down, up and down].
The leaves in the air [go up and down]
All around the town.

Continue with the following: *twirl round and round, go whooshing by, fall gently down*

Teena Ingram
Highlands Christian Preschool
Calistoga, CA

Beep, Beep, Beep

Familiarize youngsters with the sound of a smoke alarm with this little song!

(sung to the tune of "Mary Had a Little Lamb")

Smoke alarms say "beep, beep, beep,
"Beep, beep, beep, beep, beep, beep."
Smoke alarms say "beep, beep, beep"
When there's smoke in the room.

If there's smoke, get down and crawl,
Down and crawl, down and crawl.
If there's smoke, get down and crawl.
There's fresh air near the floor.

LeeAnn Collins
Sunshine House Preschool
Lansing, MI

Green Acorn, Brown Acorn

Show youngsters an acorn and explain that the acorn is green in the summertime. When fall arrives, acorns usually turn brown and fall from the tree. Guide little ones in reciting this catchy chant. See page 148 for an adorable two-sided acorn puppet to use as a prop during this chant!

I'm a little acorn—look at me!
I live high in an old oak tree.
My face is green but will soon be brown
When leaves start to flutter to the ground.

Sarah Booth
Hughesville, PA

Very Scary!

Here's a song that's just perfect for the Halloween season! Cut out a copy of the patterns on page 149 and attach them to a wall. Lead students in singing the song, removing the named cutout when indicated and making it "run away" during the final line.

(sung to the tune of "Where Is Thumbkin?")

Where is [Pumpkin],
Where is [Pumpkin]?
Here I am!
Here I am!
How are you this evening?
Very scary, thank you!
Run away. Run away!

Continue with the following: *Spider, Black Bat, Skeleton, Monster*

Laura Swanson
College of Lake County Lakeshore Child Care
Waukegan, IL

 tip You can also give each child her own set of cutouts and encourage her to manipulate them as described!

Songs & Such

Hello, Mittens!

Youngsters say hello to warm winter clothing with this catchy song! Lead students in singing the song as they wiggle their hands in the air. Repeat the song several times with the suggestions shown, prompting students to accompany each verse with appropriate movements.

(sung to the tune of "Good Night, Ladies")

Hello, [mittens]!
Hello, [mittens]!
Hello, [mittens]!
You keep my [hands] so warm!

Continue with the following: *boots/feet, hat/head, scarf/neck, sweater/body*

Linda Howes
Branchville, NJ

Lots of Pairs!

This engaging chant helps youngsters develop new vocabulary! After performing the chant, have students name and locate other body part pairs, such as knees, elbows, ankles, and shoulders.

Two things, two things make a pair,	*Hold up two fingers.*
And on me, I'll show you where!	*Point to self.*
A pair of eyes, a pair of feet,	*Touch eyes and then feet.*
A pair of ears to hear—that's neat!	*Touch your ears.*
A pair of hands to clap, clap, clap	*Clap three times.*
And fold up nicely in my lap.	*Fold hands in lap.*

adapted from an idea by Jennifer Schear
Wright Elementary
Cedar Rapids, IA

Happy Holidays!

Celebrate common winter holidays with this easy-to-learn song!

(sung to the tune of "Clementine")

Happy Kwanzaa!
Happy Christmas!
Happy Hanukkah to you!
Happy Kwanzaa!
Happy Christmas!
Happy Hanukkah to you!

May your days be very merry!
May your nights be merry too!
Happy Kwanzaa!
Happy Christmas!
Happy Hanukkah to you!

adapted from an idea by Cynthia Dennis
Omega Day Care Center
South Ozone Park, NY

 tip Do you have little ones perform for their families before the holidays? This song would be an adorable conclusion to the program!

Napping Critters

Here's an informative sing-along that focuses on cold-blooded hibernators!

(sung to the tune of "Are You Sleeping?")

[Frog] is sleeping.	*Fold hands against cheek.*
[Frog] is sleeping	
In the ground,	*Pat the floor.*
In the ground.	
Wonder when he'll come out.	*Throw hands out to sides.*
Wonder when he'll come out.	
In the spring,	*Clap to the beat.*
In the spring.	

Continue with the following: *turtle, snake, toad*

Christine Lennon and Melanie Fitzgerald
Alternatives for Children
Southampton, NY

Songs & Such

Hooray for Phil!

Groundhog Day is February 2! Celebrate this quirky day with a splendid little song!

(sung to the tune of "This Old Man")

Groundhog Day, Groundhog Day,
Cheer for Phil. Hip hip hooray!
Will he run and hide or
Promise early spring?
What prediction will Phil bring?

Jacqueline Schiff, Moline, IL

Did You Get One?

Here's a sweet and simple valentine song! Write each child's name on a separate heart cutout (patterns on page 150) and stack the hearts. Read the name on the first heart and then lead students in helping you sing the first verse of the song. Reveal the heart with great enthusiasm and give it to the child. Then lead students in singing the final verse. Continue with each remaining heart.

(sung to the tune of "The Muffin Man")

Oh, did you get a valentine,
A valentine, a valentine?
Oh, did you get a valentine,
A valentine from me?

Oh, yes, you got a valentine,
A valentine, a valentine.
Oh, yes, you got a valentine,
A valentine from me!

It's a Rainbow!

Give each child a strip of construction paper to match one of the colors in the song. As you lead students in singing, have them raise their strips when they hear their colors. Then, during the final line, have students wiggle their strips in the air!

(sung to the tune of "Hush, Little Baby")

Rainbow violet,
Rainbow blue,
Rainbow green,
And yellow too.
Rainbow orange,
Rainbow red,
Rainbow shining overhead!

Laurie Rhoads
YWCA Children's Alley
Boulder, CO

Chug, Chug, Chug

Line students up and lead them in chugging around the classroom as you sing the song. Repeat the song slowly, prompting students to chug slowly. Then sing a quick version of the song as little ones change their movements appropriately.

(sung to the tune of the chorus of "Jingle Bells")

Chug, chug, chug, chug, chug, chug,
Chugging down the track.
See our little choo-choo train—
It's chugging down and back!
We are cars all lined up,
Chugging just like so.
Hear our whistle toot, toot, toot
As down the track we go!

Lindsey Bachman
YWCA Early Learning Center
Duluth, MN

Songs & Such

Silly String!

When youngsters get wiggly, give each child a small length of string (or yarn) and have them perform this silly chant, encouraging them to make appropriate movements with their silly string for each line.

Silly string wiggles from side to side.
Then my silly string likes to hide!
Silly string makes circles big and small.
Silly string bounces just like a ball.
Shake the string up and shake the string down.
Shake that silly string all around.
Move it really fast and move it really slow.
Silly string moves wherever you go!

Linda Salinas
Mt. Ararat Baptist Church Preschool
Stafford, VA

Sit Next to Me!

This interactive birdie-themed song is sure to be a favorite with your little ones! Recite the first verse five times, increasing the number appropriately for each verse. Then recite the second verse five times, reducing the number appropriately and ending the final verse with "No little birdies to wave goodbye." This rhyme can be acted out, performed as a fingerplay, or demonstrated with props on a flannelboard!

[One] little [birdie] sitting in a nest
Doing what little birdies do best!
Along came another birdie, nice as can be.
"Birdie, birdie, sit next to me!"

[Five] little [birdies] sitting in a nest
Doing what little birdies do best.
One birdie says, "I want to fly!"
So all the other birdies waved goodbye!

Tabitha Bahr
Beech Tree House Center for Child Development
Indianapolis, IN

We Recycle!

Here's a song just perfect for your Earth Day celebration. Don't forget, Earth Day is April 22!

(sung to the tune of "Are You Sleeping?")

We recycle; we recycle.
Yes, we do! Yes, we do!
We care for our planet; we care for our planet.
You should too; you should too.

Sandra Swink, Miss Millie's Child Care Center, Maiden, NC

Five Little Tortillas

Spotlight Cinco de Mayo with this engaging chant! If desired, attach circles of light brown felt (tortillas) to your flannelboard and then have a youngster remove a tortilla for each couplet.

Five tortillas, cooking in a pan.
One jumped out and ran, ran, ran!
Four tortillas, brown on each side.
One fell out and ran to hide.
Three tortillas, flat and round.
One ran away without a sound.
Two tortillas, not a lot.
One ran away—it was too hot!
One tortilla, looking pretty neat,
Until it heard the words "Let's eat!"

Jo Ellen Brown, Hawthorne Child Development Center Preschool, Albuquerque, NM

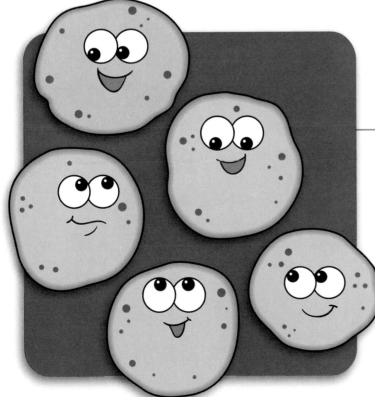

Songs & Such

Active Animals

Prompt little ones to practice animal moves with this action song!

(sung to the tune of "Are You Sleeping?")

Frogs go hopping,
Hop, hop, hopping!
Kangaroos—they hop too!
Horses gallop proudly.
Monkeys leap so loudly.
Pigeons fly
Way up high.

Jacqueline Schiff, Moline, IL

Pirate Play

Youngsters are sure to enjoy this simple pirate-themed chant! Lead students in reciting the first stanza four times, having students hold up fingers to represent pirates and say "Arrrr!" once for each pirate playing. Then prompt students to recite the final verse.

[One] little pirate(s) went out to play
On a pirate ship one day.
He had such enormous fun,
He called on another pirate friend to come.
[Arrrr! Arrrr!]

Five little pirates went out to play
On a pirate ship one day.
They had such enormous fun,
They played and played till the day was done!

Jeanne McLaughlin
Saint Andrew's Preschool
San Bruno, CA

Our Flag

Familiarize youngsters with the parts of the American flag with this jaunty little song!

(sung to the tune of "The Farmer in the Dell")

Our country's flag has stripes.
Our country's flag has stripes.
Thirteen red and white in all!
Our country's flag has stripes.

Our country's flag has stars.
Our country's flag has stars.
Fifty white stars in all!
Our country's flag has stars.

Donna Ream
Ms. Donna's Daycare
Plainfield, IL

Wiggle Time!

Are your little ones feeling wiggly? Try this cute chant to banish those wiggles!

Put your hands on your [head]
And wiggle to the floor!
Put your hands on your [head]
And wiggle to the floor!
Then shake your hips
And shake them some more!
Put your hands on your [head]
And wiggle to the floor!

Songs & Such

Off to Kindergarten!

Have your little ones sing this engaging and simple song at a preschool graduation ceremony!

(sung to the tune of "The Itsy-Bitsy Spider")

My itsy-bitsy preschool
Seems so far away.
I am getting big now.
I'm growing every day.
Now I'm off to kindergarten—
Time to learn and play!
Yes, I am off to kindergarten.
Let's all shout, "Hooray!"

Robert Whitney, St. Elizabeth's School, Philadelphia, PA

Silly Fishies!

This twist on a traditional rhyme has super engaging actions! Lead students in performing the first verse five times, reducing the number appropriately and changing "fishies" to "fishy" in the final verse.

[Five] silly fishies swimming in the sea,
Teasing Mr. Crab—"No, you can't catch me!"
Along comes Mr. Crab as quiet as can be
And snaps one fishy right out of the sea.

Make a wiggling fish motion with all five fingers.
Put hands on hips and shake hips side to side.
Tiptoe in place.
Make a snapping motion with hands.

Lisa Anderson, Hildebrandt Learning Centers, Carlisle, PA

Little Clowns

Your little ones will love this action rhyme!

(sung to the tune of "London Bridge")

Little clowns, [jump up and down],
[Up and down, up and down].
Little clowns, [jump up and down]
And then sit down.

Continue with the following: *sway side to side; lean back and forth; use marching feet; nod yes, yes, yes; walk quietly; crawl on the floor*

Ann Bruehler
Immanuel Lutheran Early Childhood Center
Charleston, IL

Squeaky Clean!

Encourage little ones to sing this song twice as they are washing their hands. No doubt those hands will be squeaky clean!

(sung to the tune of "Row, Row, Row Your Boat")

Wash, wash, wash your hands.
Wash your hands so clean!
Wash on top and underneath
And even in between!

Lori Lide
Tritt Elementary
Marietta, GA

Note to the teacher: To make a two-sided puppet, color one acorn green and the other acorn brown. Cut out a copy of the pattern and fold it on the dotted line. Glue the acorns together with a craft stick sandwiched between them.

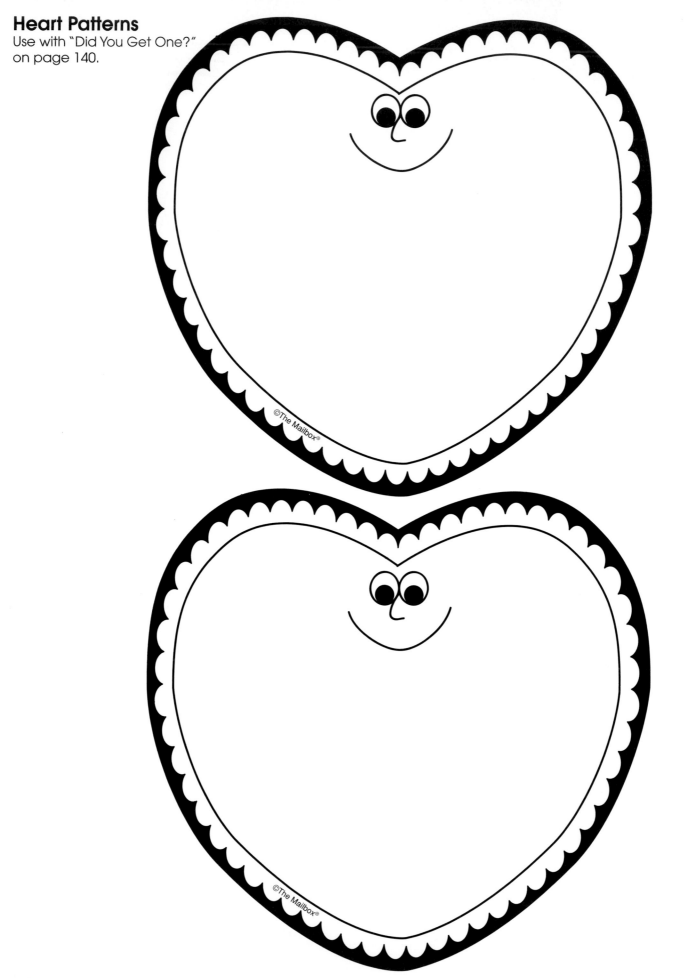

©The Mailbox®

©The Mailbox®

STORYTIME

Storytime

The Pigeon Finds a Hot Dog!
Written and illustrated by Mo Willems

The pigeon stumbles across a delicious-looking hot dog and is just about to take a bite when an inquisitive duckling appears and puts a damper on the joyous moment!

ideas contributed by Roxanne LaBell Dearman
Early Intervention for Children Who Are Deaf or Hard of Hearing
Charlotte, NC

> The duckling wants to eat the hot dog!

Before You Read
Display the cover of the book and read its title aloud. Draw youngsters' attention to the pigeon and have them describe what they see. Then point out the duckling and ask, "What might the duckling be thinking?" After youngsters share their thoughts, read aloud this entertaining tale about a pigeon, a hot dog, and a very clever duckling.

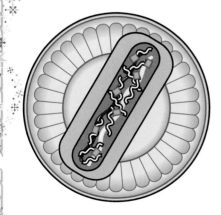

After You Read
The duckling wants mustard on the hot dog. With this cute project, your youngsters can load up on a slew of tasty condiments! Give each child a paper plate, a construction paper hot dog bun, and a hot dog cutout. Provide squeeze bottles of red and yellow paint (ketchup and mustard), white crinkle shreds (sauerkraut), and green paper confetti (pickles). Have him glue the bun to the plate and then the hot dog to the bun. Then encourage him to add desired condiments to the hot dog. If desired, have each child hold up his hot dog and then share his favorite part of the story.

Bunny Cakes

Written and illustrated by Rosemary Wells

While Ruby makes her surprise cake for Grandma's birthday, Max innocently creates a bit of kitchen chaos. After several trips to the store and unsuccessful attempts to get the ingredient he wants, Max finally thinks of a perfect way to solve the problem!

ideas contributed by Roxanne LaBell Dearman
Early Intervention for Children Who Are Deaf or Hard of Hearing
Charlotte, NC

> Yuck! I don't want a cake with a worm in it!

Before You Read

Conceal cake ingredients and utensils inside a grocery bag. (Consider using items such as flour, milk, an egg, a measuring cup, a cake pan, a mixing bowl, and a spoon.) Also tuck a rubber worm in the bag. Remove each item (except for the worm), guiding students to realize that all the items are used when making a cake. Next, peek in the bag and say, "Oops! There's one more thing." Then pull out the worm, which is sure to elicit plenty of comments! Finally, read the story aloud, enlightening youngsters as to why a worm was included in the cake-making accessories.

After You Read

Give each child a copy of page 163 and invite her to make a shopping list of items she would need to make a surprise cake of her own. Encourage her to "write" the names of the items on the page and draw a picture of each one. When they're finished, invite little ones to use their lists in the dramatic-play area to pretend to shop for the items and make their surprise cakes.

Storytime

Literacy Ideas for Teachers®

Time to Sleep
Written and illustrated by Denise Fleming

Bear sniffs once and then twice, captivated by the aroma of winter air. Before settling in for her winter nap, she heads off to tell Snail, who tells Skunk, who tells Turtle, and so on, until Ladybug rushes off to tell Bear, who is already fast asleep in her cave.

ideas contributed by Ada Goren, Winston-Salem, NC

Before You Read
Display the cover of the book and read its title aloud. Tell youngsters that today's story is about forest animals discovering that it's time for their winter naps. Then invite little ones to tell how they know when it's time for them to go to sleep. After each child has had the opportunity to share, read the book aloud so students can see whether the animals in the story use the same clues they do to know when it's time to sleep.

It's time to sleep when mommy says so!

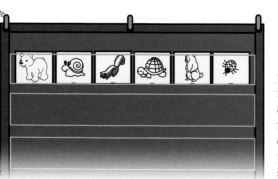

After You Read
Scatter a cutout copy of the cards on page 164 near a pocket chart. Ask, "Which animal is the first to smell winter in the air?" After youngsters determine that it is Bear, invite a child to place the bear card in the pocket chart. Then reread the book, pausing to let students name each new critter and to place its card in the chart. Then, if desired, place the book and cards at a center for independent sequencing practice!

'Twas the Night Before Thanksgiving

Written and illustrated by Dav Pilkey

In this tall turkey tale, Farmer Mack Nugget reveals to a group of visiting students the grim demise in store for his turkeys. But the youngsters turn the tables on Mack Nugget, hiding the turkeys beneath their jackets and taking them home to be treated as Thanksgiving guests!

I would hide a turkey under my bed!

Before You Read

Show youngsters the cover of the book and have them describe what they see. Next, tell students the story is about eight tiny turkeys that get hidden away to keep them from becoming Thanksgiving dinner! Then ask, "If you wanted to hide a turkey, where would you hide it?" After each child has had a chance to share his thoughts, have little ones settle in for this tall tale with a surprise ending!

After You Read

Youngsters are sure to enjoy looking and feeling just like the schoolchildren with their hidden turkeys! In advance, hot-glue craft feathers to a pillow. Invite a child to put on an oversize jacket. Then help her stuff the pillow under the jacket so that some of the feathers stick out. Remind her that the schoolchildren have a difficult time walking around with their concealed turkeys. Invite her to walk around and discuss whether it is difficult. Next, take her photo. Then display the photos with the title "Save the Turkeys!"

Sarah Karns, Christian Community Child Center, Oshkosh, WI

Storytime

The Gingerbread Man
Retold by Jim Aylesworth

A freshly baked gingerbread man tauntingly outruns a host of hungry pursuers, until he meets a tricky fox!

My grandma bakes cookies on a tray like that!

Before You Read

Conceal items—such as a rolling pin, a baking tray, a container of ground ginger, and a gingerbread man cookie cutter—in a bag. Tell little ones you are going to give clues to help them guess today's story. Remove the bowl, the rolling pin, and the tray and have youngsters offer guesses to identify the story. Next, reveal the ground ginger and then the cookie cutter, guiding youngsters to guess that the story is *The Gingerbread Man*. Finally, have little ones settle in for this entertaining retelling of a favorite children's classic.

After You Read

Engage little ones in a story alternative that has the Gingerbread Man leading them to a hidden snack! Cut out a copy of the gingerbread man pattern on page 165. Hide a class supply of gingerbread man cookies somewhere in the room. In follow-the-leader fashion, hold up the gingerbread man and chant, "[Hop, hop] as fast as you can! Follow me. I'm the gingerbread man!" Periodically prompt the group to stop, and then insert a new gross-motor movement in the chant. Finally, lead youngsters to discover the hidden snack!

adapted from an idea by Michelle Freed, Peru State College, Peru, NE

Snow Music

Written and Illustrated by Lynne Rae Perkins

A young boy opens the door to admire the beauty of fresh-fallen snow when suddenly, his dog bolts out the door! While searching for his dog, the boy and a companion experience a myriad of interesting snowy sights and sounds.

> I like to catch snow-flakes on my tongue!

Before You Read

Display the cover of the book, drawing students' attention to the snow globe. Hand a child a real snow globe. Encourage her to shake the globe. Then have her share something she likes about a snowy day. After each child has the opportunity to share her thoughts, tell youngsters that today's story is about a young boy who experiences lots of snowy sights and sounds while searching for his lost dog.

After You Read

Set out "snow paint" (white tempera paint thickened with flour), plastic figures and vehicles similar to the ones in the story, and iridescent glitter. Revisit the page spreads that depict tracks in the snow. Then have each child spread a thick layer of snow paint on a sheet of tagboard, encouraging him to say "peth, peth, peth" to imitate the sound of snowfall in the book. Invite him to make tracks in the snow using desired props and then sprinkle glitter onto the snowy scene.

Storytime

Literacy Ideas for Teachers®

Animals Should Definitely <u>Not</u> Wear Clothing.

Written by Judi Barrett
Illustrated by Ron Barrett

Should a porcupine wear a sweater? Is it convenient for a hen to wear pants? Does a kangaroo really need a coat with a pocket? The simple text and humorous pictures in this cleverly written book answer these questions, and more!

ideas contributed by Ada Goren, Winston-Salem, NC

> I saw a little dog at the park wearing a red sweater!

Before You Read

Display a stuffed toy dog wearing an article of clothing, such as a sweater. Ask, "Have you ever seen a real dog wearing a sweater?" After youngsters respond, explain that pet stores sell doggy clothing—such as shirts, sweaters, raincoats and boots—and specialty items like Halloween costumes. Then display the cover of the book and ask, "Do you think a porcupine should wear a sweater?" After each child has had the opportunity to share, have little ones settle in for this entertaining read-aloud that shows why most animals should definitely not wear clothing!

After You Read

The animals in this story are clearly experiencing wardrobe malfunctions. Try this mix-and-match game to find out what youngsters think about other animals and their clothing options. Cut out and laminate a copy of the cards on page 166. Place the animal cards and clothing cards facedown in separate piles. Invite a volunteer to turn over a card from each pile and identify the animal and the clothing item. Then encourage youngsters to tell why they think the animal should or should not wear that clothing. After students share their thoughts, set the cards aside and continue. This activity can be repeated again and again with different possibilities each time!

158 ©The Mailbox® • Feb./Mar. 2012

Storytime

My Friend Rabbit

Written and illustrated by Eric Rohmann

Mouse knows that no matter what his best friend, Rabbit, does, trouble is sure to follow. But he lets Rabbit play with his new toy airplane anyway. No sooner does Rabbit get his paws on the plane, the trouble begins. Watch out! Rabbit has an idea that leads to even bigger problems!

ideas contributed by Ada Goren, Winston-Salem, NC

Rabbit tries to ride on the plane, and he breaks it!

Before You Read

Display the cover of the book and read its title aloud. Then ask youngsters to study the picture and describe what they see. Next, tell students today's story is about two best friends who run into a big problem. Then have little ones predict what they think the problem is. After students share their thoughts, have them settle in for this entertaining read-aloud with out-of-the-box problem solving!

Dear Rabbit,
   To get the airplane out of the tree....have the elephant shake the tree with its trunk!

Love,
Robin

After You Read

Rabbit's plan to rescue the toy airplane creates utter chaos, although it gets the job done. Then at the end of the story, Rabbit and Mouse are faced with the same dilemma! Invite your youngsters to dictate a letter to Rabbit giving airplane-rescue advice. Then have her illustrate her advice. If desired, bind the pages together to make a class book titled "Preschool Problem Solvers!"

Hedgie's Surprise

Written and illustrated by Jan Brett

Henny longs to hatch a brood of peeping chicks, but how can she when the Tomten keeps stealing her eggs? With the help of her clever friend Hedgie, the Tomten's thievery ends and Henny's dream comes true!

egg	✕✕✕✕✕ |||
oatmeal	||||

Before You Read

Draw a two-row chart on your board with illustrations of an egg and a bowl of oatmeal. Then, in turn, ask each child, "Would you prefer eggs or oatmeal for breakfast?" After she responds, draw a tally mark in the appropriate row on the graph. If she doesn't like either food, move on to the next child. When the graphing is complete, help youngsters count the tally marks to determine whether more children like eggs or oatmeal for breakfast. Then explain that the boy in the story prefers eggs for breakfast, but the hen that lays them wishes he didn't!

After You Read

Youngsters review the items Hedgie places in Henny's nest with this fun game! Cut out a copy of the cards on page 167. Set out a large nest cutout and scatter the cards facedown nearby. Invite a volunteer to flip two cards. If the pictures match, have him place the cards on the nest. If they do not match, have him turn the cards facedown again. If he flips a hedgehog card, prompt the group to say, "Puffa-puffa. Stick-stick!" Then have him turn the card back over. Continue until all the food and acorn cards are on the nest. To conclude the activity, flip the remaining pair of hedgehog cards to prompt a final "Puffa-puffa. Stick-stick!" chant. How fun!

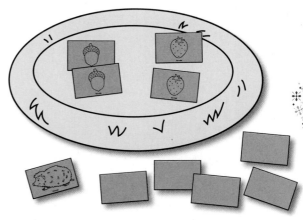

Bonus activity! Give each youngster a single set of the cards from page 167 and have her attach them to a strip of paper in story order.

Storytime

If You Give a Pig a Party
Written by Laura Numeroff
Illustrated by Felicia Bond

"If you give a pig a party, she's going to ask for some balloons." But this story doesn't stop there, because the pig will also want to put on her favorite dress, try to find her friends, ride some bumper cars, get some ice cream, and many other things—all leading her right back to the party.

I would have a big cake, and we would play freeze dance!

Before You Read

Display the cover of the book and read its title aloud. Tell little ones that today's story is about a pig that eagerly contributes ideas to a party plan. Then invite youngsters to tell how they would plan a party, the foods they would serve, and the activities they would do. After each child has the opportunity to share, read the book aloud so students can see whether the pig's party turns out like one they would plan.

If you give a preschooler a party, __Micah__ will ask for

ice cream!

After You Read

Invite students to create their own story sequel called "If You Give a Preschooler a Party." Give each child a copy of page 168. Also provide markers or crayons and party-related stickers or stamps. Help each child write his name in the space provided. Encourage him to dictate or write words to complete the sentence; then have him illustrate his words. Bind the pages together to make a class book.

Marsupial Sue

Written by John Lithgow
Illustrated by Jack E. Davis

A young kangaroo named Marsupial Sue doesn't feel happy doing what kangaroos do. So she tries hanging out with other Australian animals and doing what they do. After enduring some unexpected mishaps, she realizes that being a kangaroo isn't so bad after all!

Hopping makes my legs tired!

Before You Read

Students are sure to be sympathetic to Marsupial Sue's dilemma with this prereading activity! Show little ones the cover of the book and ask them to identify the animal. Then set a timer and invite youngsters to hop like kangaroos. When the timer goes off, ask students if they would like to be a kangaroo that hopped all day. After each child has a chance to respond, read aloud this thought-provoking tale with the reassuring message that we can be happy with who we are.

I'm happy to be me because I am funny and can run fast!

After You Read

Label a class supply of speech bubbles with the prompt "I'm happy to be me because…" Give each child a paper plate and encourage her to draw a self-portrait with a happy face. Then invite her to use yarn and construction paper scraps to add desired details. When the self-portrait is finished, encourage her to complete the prompt by dictating or writing words on a speech bubble. Attach the speech bubbles to the plates and mount them on a board titled "Happy to Be Me!"

Surprise Cake Ingredients

Critter Cards

Use with "After You Read" on page 154.

TEC41057

TEC41057

TEC41057

TEC41057

TEC41057

TEC41057

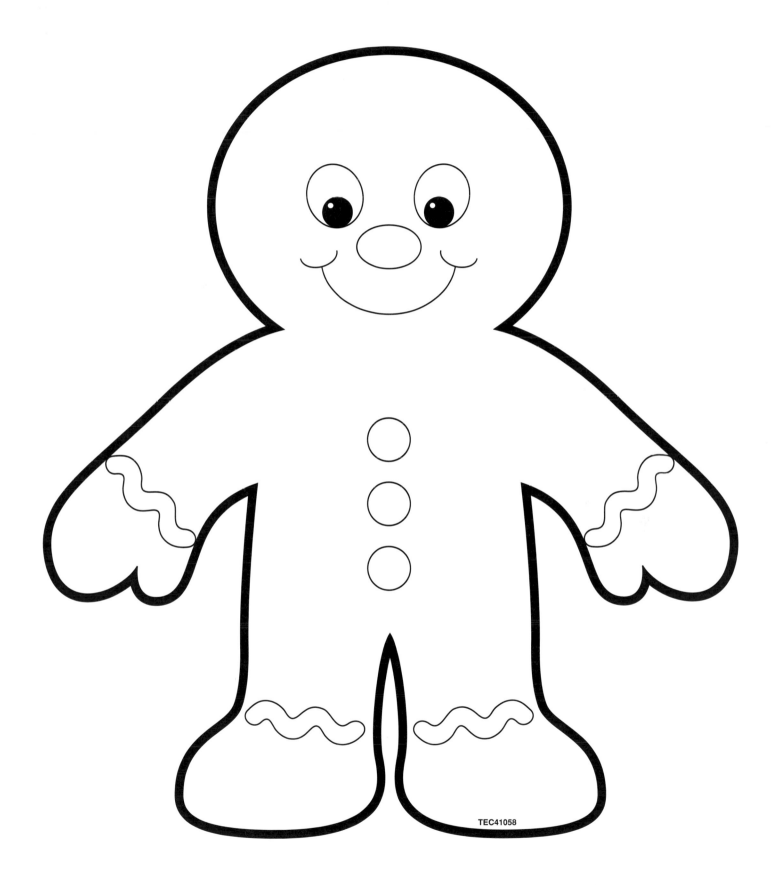

TEC41058

Picture Cards

Use with "After You Read" on page 158.

TEC41059

TEC41059

TEC41059

TEC41059

TEC41059

TEC41059

TEC41059

TEC41059

TEC41059

TEC41059

TEC41059

TEC41059

TEC41060

TEC41060

TEC41060

TEC41060

TEC41060

TEC41060

TEC41060

TEC41060

TEC41060

TEC41060

If you give a preschooler a party,

_____ will ask for

Note to the teacher: Use with "After You Read" on page 161.

BOOK UNITS

Transportation Trio

This "wheel-y" fun selection of transportation-related books is sure to delight your little ones!

Little Blue Truck
Written by Alice Schertle
Illustrated by Jim McElmurry

Little Blue Truck is very friendly. He is so kind that he tries to help a rude dump truck that is stuck in the muck. When Little Blue Truck's friends help out, the dump truck learns the value of kindness.

Friendly Trucks
Getting acquainted with classmates

Little Blue Truck beeps at all of his friends. Your little ones can beep at their friends too! Give each child a paper-plate steering wheel and signal students to "drive" around the room. After several seconds of driving, give another signal for youngsters to stop. Encourage each child to look at the driver nearest to him; say, "Beep, beep, beep!"; and wave. Then signal students to resume driving. Continue for several rounds.

Muddy Masterpiece
Responding to a story through art

By the end of the story, Little Blue Truck is covered with mud! Have each child color a copy of the truck on page 173 blue. Then help her cut it out and glue it to a sheet of paper. Have her load a paintbrush with brown paint and tap it against the pointer finger of her opposite hand, spritzing the paper with flecks of brown paint. This little blue truck sure is a mess!

"Teep, Teep, Teep!"
Manipulating phonemes

Write "Little Blue Truck says, 'Beep!'" on a sentence strip and place the strip in your pocket chart. Gather several consonant cards. Read the sentence aloud as you move your finger beneath the words. Say, "I wonder, if I change one of the letters, will 'beep' sound different?" Have a child choose a consonant card and place it over *B* in *Beep*. Then read the sentence aloud. After the giggles die down, say, "Well, that's not right. A truck says 'beep,' not [new word]." Continue with other consonant cards.

Little Blue Truck says, "Teep!"

Red Light, Green Light

Written by Anastasia Suen
Illustrated by Ken Wilson-Max

A little boy creates streets, tunnels, and tollbooths for his toy cars and trucks in this engaging rhyming story.

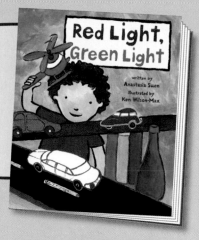

●○●○ Pretend Play ○●○●

Responding to a story through play

Your youngsters can make a creative world just like the little boy in the book! Gather books, toy people and animals, plastic containers, unsharpened pencils, and other unique items. Then place the items in your block center along with a variety of car and truck toys. A youngster uses the items to make roads, intersections, tunnels, and buildings. Then he "drives" the automobiles around his pretend world!

●○●○ Bright Lights ○●○●

Sorting by color

Provide a variety of red, yellow, and green collage items. Gather a small group of students and have each child glue three white circles to a sheet of black paper as shown so it resembles a stoplight. Tell them that a stoplight is red on top and green on the bottom. Emphasize that there is also a yellow light in the middle. Then prompt a child to choose a red item and glue it to the top light. Then have her glue a green item to the bottom light and a yellow item to the middle light. Now that she has the lights labeled with the appropriate colors, have her continue to glue desired items to the lights, sorting them appropriately.

●○●○ Modern Art ○●○●

Responding to a story through art

The black roads and bright colors in this artwork are reminiscent of the illustrations in the story! Have each youngster attach strips of black electrical tape to a sheet of bright paper as desired. Then encourage her to glue car die-cuts to the page.

The Goodnight Train

Written by June Sobel
Illustrated by Laura Huliska-Beith

The goodnight train takes off, carrying children and animals through a whimsical, dreamlike landscape. By the end of the journey, nighttime has arrived. The train chugs into its station, and the passengers drift off to sleep.

☽☆☾ All Aboard! ☽☆☾

Gross-motor skills, participating in a group activity

Give each child a copy of a train ticket from page 174. Then pretend to be the conductor as you call each child to "board" an imaginary train, collect youngsters' tickets, and line them up. When all the students have boarded, get into place as the engine. Lead youngsters around the room, encouraging them to make train noises. Prompt them to stand on tiptoes as they travel over mountains and crouch near the floor as they go through valleys and tunnels. Finally, slow the train and return to the circle-time area, encouraging students to lie down and pretend to sleep.

☽☆☾ Bedtime Traditions ☽☆☾

Dictating information

Little ones make a goodnight-train display with this fun idea! After a read-aloud of the story, ask each child what she does before she goes to bed. Write her words on a rectangular cutout. Have her glue wheel cutouts to the rectangle so it resembles a train car. Attach all the train cars to a wall. Then attach an engine cutout (enlarge a copy of the train engine pattern on page 174) in front of the cars. During group time, read each youngster's dictation aloud.

☽☆☾ Clack, Clack, Clack ☽☆☾

Rhyming

Point out to students that the goodnight train sways and bounces as it rolls along. Prompt students to sway side to side as you lead them in saying "clickety-clack, clickety-clack, clickety-clack." Next, help students come up with a nonsense word that rhymes with *clack*. Repeat the process, prompting students to sway and repeat the phrase "clickety-[rhyming word], clickety-[rhyming word], clickety-[rhyming word]." Continue for several rounds.

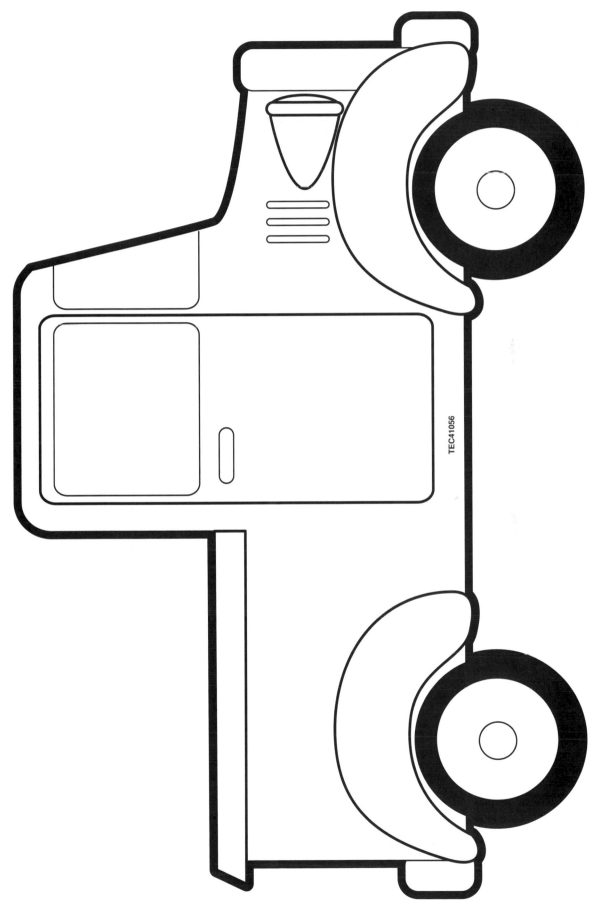

TEC41056

Train Ticket Patterns
Use with "All Aboard!" on page 172.

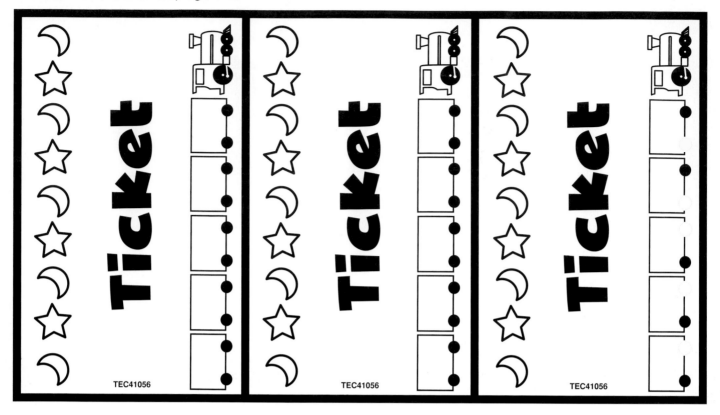

TEC41056   TEC41056   TEC41056

Train Engine Pattern
Use with "Bedtime Traditions" on page 172.

TEC41056

Pumpkin Jack

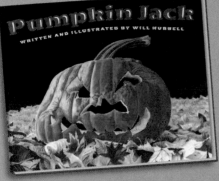

by Will Hubbell

Tim carves a jack-o'-lantern and names it "Jack." When Jack begins to rot, Tim puts him in the garden. After a while, he's covered with snow. Spring arrives, and a plant sprouts where Jack had been sitting. Soon it's time to carve a new Jack!

From Pumpkin to Mush
Sequencing

Youngsters put the story in order with this activity! For each child, fold a 6" x 18" piece of paper to make four panels. Have each child color a copy of the cards on page 177. Next, help her cut them out. Scramble the cards. Then have her place them on the paper to show Jack's progression from Halloween decoration to sprouting pumpkin plant. Have her point to and describe each picture.

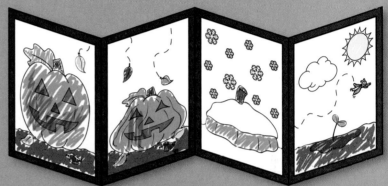

Frosty Jack
Responding to a story through art

Encourage little ones to make this art project that resembles Jack in the snowy garden. Give each child an orange paper plate. Then have her draw a face on her plate and attach a stem cutout. Next, have her paint the top of the resulting jack-o'-lantern with a mixture of white paint and flour. While the paint is wet, encourage her to sprinkle white or iridescent glitter on the project. Display the projects with the title "Goodbye, Fall; Hello, Winter."

Jack in the Box
Investigating living things, observation, prediction

This pumpkin will end up looking just like Jack! After carving a class pumpkin and putting it on display, place it in a clear container and then secure the lid on the container. Ask little ones to predict what will happen to the pumpkin. Then encourage youngsters to observe the pumpkin each day, noticing that it begins to decay just as Jack did! Prompt them to compare their pumpkin to the pictures of Jack in the book.

Roxanne LaBell Dearman, NC Early Intervention Program for Children Who Are Deaf or Hard of Hearing, Charlotte, NC; Tara Travis, Cherokee Elementary, Alexandria, LA

 tip → Don't have a big container? Put a piece of pumpkin in a small, clear container for youngsters to observe.

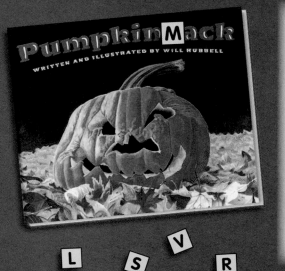

What's That Name?
Manipulating phonemes

Tim decides that a jack-o'-lantern as good as the one he created needs a great name. So he names it "Jack." Your little ones can help you come up with some equally good names for this jack-o'-lantern! Gather several small consonant cards and place them facedown. Hold up the cover of the book and run your finger beneath the title as you read it aloud. Tell students that you have thought about giving Tim's pumpkin a new name. Have a child choose a card. Say the letter's sound. Then lightly tape the card over the *J* in *Jack*. Read the new name and ask students if they think this is a better name. After they share their thoughts, remove the card. Repeat the activity with the remaining cards.

TEC41057

TEC41057

TEC41057

TEC41057

Goodnight Moon

Written by Margaret Wise Brown
Illustrated by Clement Hurd

"Goodnight clocks and goodnight socks..." The little bunny in this classic bedtime story bids the items in his room "goodnight" as he settles down for sleep.

*ideas contributed by Ada Goren
Winston-Salem, NC*

That's interesting!

Clement Hurd, *Goodnight Moon*'s illustrator, originally wanted the main characters in the story to be human. Margaret Wise Brown and her editor eventually decided that Clement was a better painter of rabbits than people!

A Case Full of Clues
Connecting to prior knowledge

Pique students' interest in a read-aloud of this classic story! Gather bedtime-related items, such as a toothbrush, a stuffed animal, a book, a pair of child's pajamas, and a nightlight. Place the items in a pillowcase. Invite students to remove the items; then guide little ones to identify what the items have in common. When students conclude that the items relate to bedtime, explain that the story you're about to read is about a bunny at bedtime. Then have students settle in for a soothing read-aloud of the story.

Marvelous Mush!
Manipulating phonemes

Focus on the mush in the story with this phonological awareness activity! Gather a plastic bowl and say, "A comb and a brush and a bowl full of sush!" Youngsters will no doubt immediately inform you that you have used the wrong word. Give the bowl to a child and have her say the line using the correct word. Then say, "Oh, I understand! Let me try again." Take the bowl and repeat the line, once again tacking a different initial sound on the word *mush*. Continue in the same way until you say the line correctly with great dramatic flair!

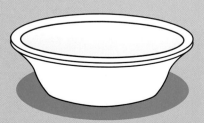

Bug, Rug!
Rhyming

This activity combines observation skills with rhyming practice! Gather a small group of youngsters. Then open the book to a random spread of the colored pages. Silently determine a word, such as *bug*, that rhymes with an object on the page. Ask, "What rhymes with *bug*?" Then help students name items on the page, encouraging them to discover that there is a rug on the page and *rug* rhymes with *bug*. Continue with other words.

I hope those cats go away, because they probably want to eat me!

The Mouse's Story
Expanding a story

Turn to the first color page spread in the book and have little ones notice the mouse. Encourage students to tell you what the mouse might say. Then write their words on a sticky note and attach it to the page. Continue with other pages and then reread the story, adding the mouse's commentary!

My Own Room
Dictating information

After looking closely at the great green room in the story, have students create their own special rooms! Prompt each student to cut out magazine pictures of furniture and toys and attach the pictures to a sheet of green paper programmed with the starter shown. Then have the child dictate information to finish the sentence.

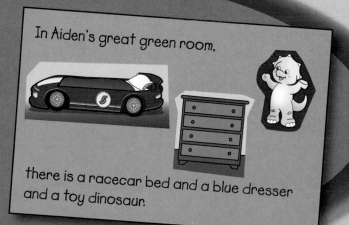

In Aiden's great green room, there is a racecar bed and a blue dresser and a toy dinosaur.

Note to the teacher: Help each child cut out a copy of the cards and sort them into rhyming pairs on a sheet of green paper (the great green room). Once they are paired, have her glue them in place.

My Many Colored Days

Written by Dr. Seuss
Paintings by Steve Johnson and Lou Fancher

Throughout this book of whimsical rhymes, the reader experiences a kaleidoscope of colors, a myriad of moods, and a menagerie of animals.

ideas contributed by Margaret Aumen
Emory United Methodist Nursery School
New Oxford, PA

What Am I Today?
Color recognition, dramatizing a story

During a rereading of the book, youngsters reinforce color recognition and act out the animals in the story! Prepare a class supply of paper squares in red, blue, brown, yellow, gray, orange, green, purple, pink, and black and give one to each youngster. Begin to reread the book, pausing after the page spread that shows the horse. Then ask youngsters who have a red square to hold it in the air. After confirming each square is red, prompt those youngsters to mimic a horse. Repeat the process for each consecutive page spread, pausing after the "Mixed-Up Day" to have all the children in the group act out their designated animal!

I Feel...
Making text-to-self connections

Dr. Seuss expresses feelings and moods through a variety of color connections, but how do your little ones connect color to the way they feel? Give each child a copy of page 183. Encourage her to think of a personal experience and tell how it made her feel. For example, was she happy, sad, angry, excited, or scared? Next, find out what color she thinks best represents that feeling. Write the color word in the space provided and have her dictate words to complete the sentence. Then have her color the person that color and add desired details to the page. Bind the pages together along with a cover to make a class book titled "Our Many Colorful Feelings."

Mixed-Up Puzzle Pile
Color words

Youngsters develop literacy skills with these easy-to-make color-word puzzles. Get craft foam rectangles in each color represented in the book. Use a permanent marker to label each rectangle with its color word; then puzzle-cut each rectangle into several pieces. Store each puzzle in a separate envelope labeled with the color word written in that color. To begin, mix all the pieces from all the puzzles together on the floor. According to your class size, give each child or pair of children a different envelope. Help them "read" the color word, making sure to point out the color of the word. Then have youngsters find all the puzzle pieces in that color and assemble the puzzle. If desired, have youngsters mix the puzzle pieces again, switch envelopes, and repeat the activity.

My Many Colorful Days
Responding to the story through art

Budding young artists show how emotions are communicated through color. Provide black construction paper, a supply of colorful tissue paper squares, and glue. Invite each child to glue assorted tissue paper squares to a sheet of paper. As he works, encourage him to tell a feeling or mood that each color best represents. To complete his work, have him glue a trimmed photo of himself to the page along with a strip titled "My Many Colorful Days."

My Many Colorful Days

Read and Rhyme
Identifying rhyming words

With this activity, students identify and supply rhyming words. Reread the book aloud, emphasizing the rhyming words on each page and then pausing to have youngsters identify the rhyming word pair. (For younger children, you may wish to read only the rhyming text.) After each rhyming pair is identified, encourage students to supply additional real or nonsense rhyming words.

Blue, too, shoe!

I feel _____

when

by _____

Chickens Aren't the Only Ones

Written and illustrated by Ruth Heller

Colorful illustrations and rhyming text take the reader through a delightful discovery of unique egg-laying insects and animals.

ideas contributed by Ada Goren, Winston-Salem, NC

Handle With Care
Participating in a group activity

After reading the book aloud, engage little ones in this interactive guessing game! Tuck an animal picture card (see page 185) into each of several plastic eggs. Arrange students so they're seated in a circle and hand a child one of the eggs. Then have youngsters pass the egg around the circle as you lead them in singing the song shown. At the end of the song, invite students to guess what animal is inside the egg. Then have the youngster holding the egg remove the card and name the animal. Set the egg aside and repeat the activity with a different egg.

(sung to the tune of "Row, Row, Row Your Boat")

Pass, pass, pass the egg.
Round and round, it goes.
Inside there's an animal.
What is it? Do you know?

Hidden Hatchlings
Contributing to a class book

Give each child a paper programmed with the prompt shown. Encourage her to draw an animal that hatches from an egg (other than a chicken) on an egg cutout. Have her glue the egg to the page; then help her attach a blank egg cutout atop the first one to make a flap. Encourage her to dictate or write the name of the animal to complete the prompt. Then bind the pages together along with a cover to make a book titled "Hidden Hatchlings."

If chickens aren't the only ones, then what's inside this egg?
It's a <u>turtle</u>!

So Many Critters!
Building vocabulary

After a couple readings of the book, give a child an unsharpened pencil with an egg cutout attached (pointer) and encourage her to point to an animal on the page and then name it. Continue with other youngsters, challenging them to remember animals such as the duckbill platypus, the salamander, and the seahorse.

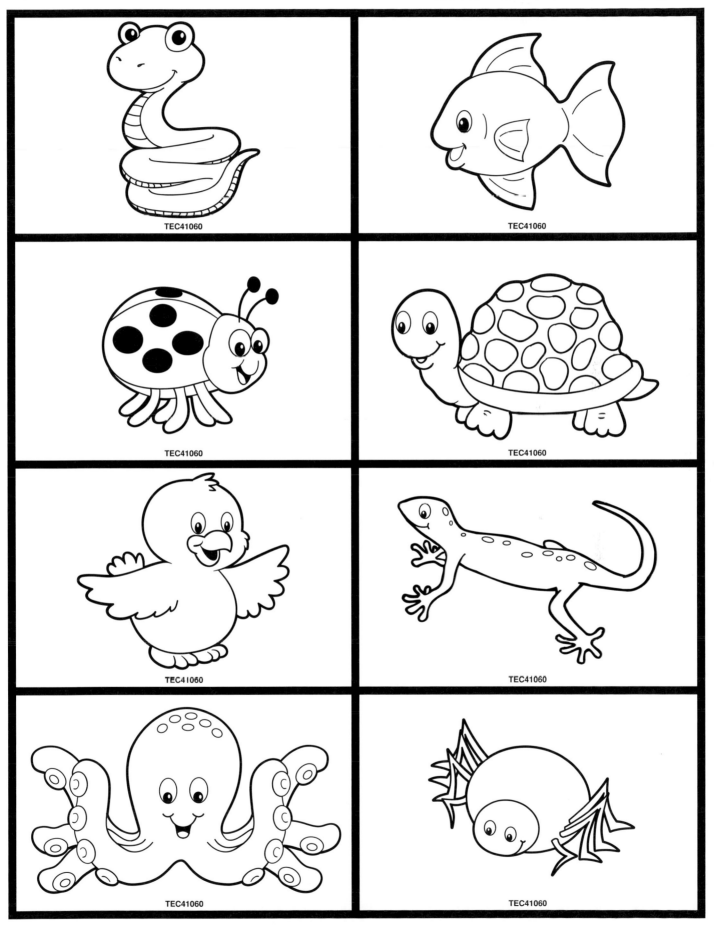

TEC41060

TEC41060

TEC41060

TEC41060

TEC41060

TEC41060

TEC41060

TEC41060

SPLASH!

Written and illustrated by Ann Jonas

A variety of critters splash in and out of a pond in this colorful book that immerses the reader in the wonderful world of addition and subtraction.

ideas contributed by Ada Goren, Winston-Salem, NC, and Margaret Aumen, Emory United Methodist Nursery School, New Oxford, PA

A Busy Pond
Retelling a story

With this activity, youngsters sharpen their counting skills as they retell the story! In advance, copy and cut out the picture cards on page 188, making sure to include two catfish, four goldfish, and three frogs. Also print a photo of each youngster. Place the cards and photos at a center along with a pond-shaped cutout and a copy of the book. Then encourage little ones to "read" the book, placing and removing the picture cards and her photo to retell the story with herself as the main character!

Making a Splash
Responding to a story through art

Set out a class supply of blue construction paper and drinking straws, slightly diluted white paint, and an eyedropper. Invite each child to apply a small amount of paint to a sheet of paper using the eyedropper. Direct him to blow through a straw to spread the paint so it resembles a splash like the ones in the story. After the paint dries, invite him to draw a picture of himself so it looks as if he jumped in a pond and made a big splash.

Proportional Ponds
Estimating size

Revisit several pages in the story, pointing out that the size of the word *splash* changes according to the size of the characters that fall or jump into the pond. Then place small, medium, and large pond-shaped cutouts on the floor. Invite volunteers, in turn, to stand near the ponds. Announce the name of an insect or animal, prompting the youngster to mimic the critter and then jump onto a pond that corresponds to its size. For example, an elephant, a horse, and a cow would make a big splash in the big pond; a rabbit, a beaver, and a duck would make a medium-size splash in the medium-size pond; and a mouse, a cricket, and a butterfly would make a tiny splash in the small pond.

S-P-L-A-S-H Spells *Splash!*
Letter identification

Gather the letter cards *S, P, L, A, S,* and *H* to make a class supply. Place blue yarn in a circle to represent a pond. Then give each child a letter card and have her stand near the pond. To begin, show the cover of the book and say its title aloud. Then have students identify each letter in the title as you point to the letters in order. Next, say, "If you have the letter *S*, jump into the pond!" prompting each child with that letter to jump in the pond. Then continue with each remaining letter in the title.

What's in Your Pond?
Dictating information, counting

Have youngsters create their own personal ponds! Invite each student to attach a fringe-cut green strip to the back of a trimmed sheet of blue construction paper so it resembles a pond and grass. Have her stamp, draw, or attach stickers to show critters in her pond. Encourage her to count the critters in her pond and then dictate information about them.

My pond has 3 ducks, 4 fish, and 1 turtle.

Lina

Picture Cards
Use with "A Busy Pond" on page 186.

TEC41061

TEC41061

TEC41061

TEC41061

TEC41061

TEC41061

TEC41061

TEC41061

CENTER UNITS

Teddy Bear Centers

A "Bear-y" Yummy Snack

Math Center

This adorable activity spotlights counting and presubtraction skills! Provide a stuffed teddy bear, a bowl, pom-poms (berries), and a large die. A child rolls the die, counts the dots aloud, and places that many berries in the bowl. Next, he pretends to feed the bear one berry and then sets that berry aside. He counts the remaining berries to see how many are left; then he continues in the same way until the bowl is empty.

adapted from an idea by Elizabeth Cook, St. Louis, MO

Save the Teddy Bears!

Water Table

Place teddy bear manipulatives in your water table. Gather disposable bowls (rescue boats) that match the colors of the teddy bears; then float the bowls in the water table. Provide slotted spoons. A youngster uses a spoon to pick up each bear and place it in its matching boat. After all the passengers are aboard their appropriate boats, the child gently pushes or blows the boats through the water.

Amber Dingman, Sterling, MI

T Is for Teddy

Literacy Center

Place several stuffed teddy bears and letter *T* cards in your block center. Encourage youngsters to study the letter and then arrange blocks on the floor to make *T*s. Have each student place a teddy bear next to each *T*.

Patches

Art Center

These patched-up teddy bears are simple and sweet! For each child, make a brown construction paper copy of page 192. Provide squares of felt, fabric, scrapbook paper, and tissue paper. A child brushes glue inside the bear outline. Then he presses squares over the glue. When the project is dry, cut out the teddy bear.

Teddy Bear Spa

Dramatic-Play Area

Stock the area with stuffed teddy bears and personal care and spa items, such as a plastic tub, empty body wash bottles, washcloths, towels, receiving blankets (for body wraps), a small table (for massages), hair brushes, and hair accessories. Also provide a toy cash register, play money, a toy phone, an appointment book, and writing tools. A youngster uses the items to engage in pretend spa-related play.

Elizabeth Cook, St. Louis, MO

Teddy Bear Pattern
Use with "Patches" on page 191.

TEC41056

Swish! Crunch! Crackle!

Fabulous Fall Leaf Centers

Shades of Autumn
Art Center

Give youngsters' pincer grasps a workout with this lovely project! Cut leaf shapes from thick white paper towels. (If desired, use the leaf patterns on page 195 to make tracers.) A child uses an eyedropper to drip diluted paint onto the leaf cutouts. When the paint is dry, mount the leaves on contrasting paper.

Margaret Aumen
Emory United Methodist Nursery School
New Oxford, PA

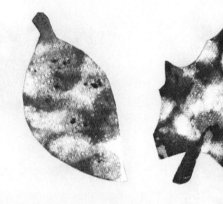

Designer Leaves
Math Center

Cut pairs of leaves (patterns on page 195) from scrapbook paper or old wallpaper books, making each pair of leaves different from the other pairs. Attach one leaf from each pair to a tagboard tree. Mount the tree to a wall and place the remaining leaves nearby with a supply of Sticky-Tac adhesive. A youngster chooses a leaf and puts a small piece of adhesive on the back. Then she attaches the leaf near its match on the tree. She continues until all the leaves are matched.

Vicki Brant
Ravenna, OH

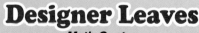

Blowing in the Wind

Game Center

Mark a masking tape start line on the floor and a finish line several feet away. Provide two or more tissue paper leaves. (Use the patterns on page 195 to make tracers.) Youngsters visit the center, and each child kneels behind a different leaf placed on the start line. In unison, they say, "Ready, set, blow!" and then pretend to be the wind blowing the leaves across the ground. Each child blows his leaf until it crosses the finish line.

Free Falling

Fine-Motor Center

Partially fill a plastic tub with real or artificial leaves. Provide a bushel basket and a pair of tweezers. A student uses the tweezers to pick up a leaf and hold it a distance above the basket. Then he drops the leaf, pretending it's gently falling from a tree, and attempts to make it land in the basket. He repeats the process with the remaining leaves.

adapted from an idea by Debbie Ronga
Sunshine Nursery School
Arlington, MA

A Timely Cleanup

Literacy Center

Set out two baskets labeled as shown. Scatter silk or tagboard leaves (patterns on page 195) labeled with either an uppercase *L* or a lowercase *l*. Also provide a simple minute timer. A child turns over the timer and tries to sort the leaves into the basket before the minute passes.

Trudy Tilton
Heartland Learning Center
Olathe, KS

Leaf Patterns
Use with "Shades of Autumn" and
"Designer Leaves" on page
193 and "Blowing in the Wind"
and "A Timely Cleanup"
on page 194.

TEC41057

TEC41057

Yum, Yum, Yum

Scrumptious Bakery Centers

ideas contributed by Margaret Aumen
Emory United Methodist Nursery School, New Oxford, PA

Bakery-Style Cake
Art Center

This cake looks yummy enough to eat! For each child, glue a small gelatin or pudding box (cake) to the center of a large paper plate. A youngster uses markers to decorate the plate. Then she uses a plastic knife to "frost" the cake with a tinted mixture of shaving cream and glue. When she's finished, she presses craft foam decorations into the frosting. Allow the cakes to dry for several days.

"Mmmmini" Cupcakes
Fine-Motor Area

Provide a mini cupcake pan, play dough scented with baking extract, and a variety of random classroom manipulatives. A child pinches off a piece of play dough and rolls it into a ball. Then he places it in a cup and tops it with a manipulative. What fancy mini cupcakes!

Purple Pie
Literacy Center

Youngsters develop phonological awareness skills with this silly center! Cut out a copy of the cards on page 198 and tape a blunt-end toothpick to each one. Then place the cards in a bag. Press purple play dough into a pie tin. A child pulls a card out of the bag. If the picture's name begins with /p/, she pokes the picture in the purple pie. If it does not, she places the picture off to the side. She continues with each remaining picture.

Sweet Sprinkles
Math Center

Little ones practice multiple math skills with this small-group game! Cut out copies of the holiday cookie patterns on page 199. Place the cookies, a supply of colorful pom-poms (sprinkles), and a large foam die at a center. Each player chooses a cookie. Then each youngster, in turn, rolls the die, counts the dots, and decorates his cookie with the matching number of sprinkles. When the decorating is done, students compare the number of sprinkles on their cookies. Then they pretend to "nibble" the sprinkles off their cookies to prepare for another round. **For a more challenging activity**, provide two dice to practice higher counting or pre-addition skills.

Beanbag Batter
Gross-Motor Area

Place beanbags in a plastic mixing bowl near a start line. Place a cookie sheet several feet away. A child picks up a beanbag (cookie batter) and attempts to toss it on the cookie sheet. When the cookie sheet is filled with beanbags, he pretends to eat all the cookies!

Picture Cards
Use with "Purple Pie" on page 197.

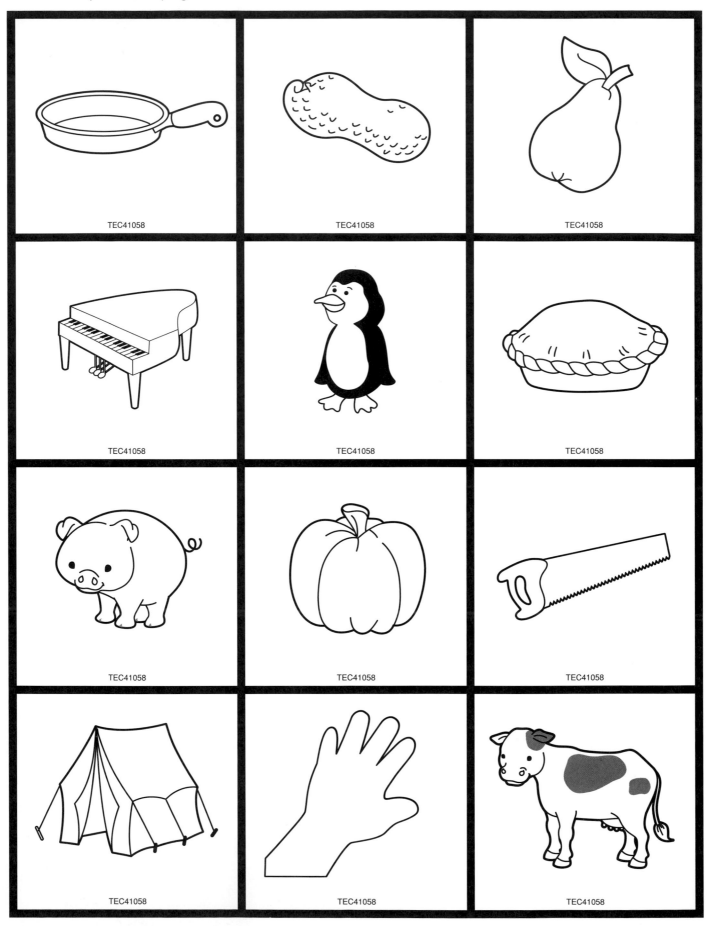

TEC41058

TEC41058

TEC41058

TEC41058

TEC41058

TEC41058

TEC41058

TEC41058

TEC41058

TEC41058

TEC41058

TEC41058

TEC41058

TEC41058

TEC41058

TEC41058

Special Delivery!

Super Post Office Centers

ideas contributed by Roxanne LaBell Dearman
NC Early Intervention for Children Who Are Deaf or Hard of Hearing
Charlotte, NC

Preschool Post Office
Dramatic-Play Area

Turn your dramatic-play area into a mock post office and watch the role-playing begin! Provide light blue button-up shirts (uniforms) and tote bags for mail carriers to use on their routes. Also provide laminated copies of the mailing labels on page 202, wipe-off markers, tape, boxes, assorted envelopes, canceled or promotional stamps, magazines, junk mail, baskets for sorting mail, a scale for weighing letters and packages, and a toy cash register. To make a mail truck, place a chair nearby with a plastic tub behind it. Youngsters use the props to engage in pretend post office play.

For a fun dramatic-play twist, set up a center with an unplugged computer keyboard and monitor (or a drawing of a monitor attached to a wall). Encourage youngsters to visit the center and pretend to send each other email!

name

street

town/city   zip code

Snail Mail
Math Center

Cut out a copy of the stamp cards on page 203 and place the cards facedown at a center. To play, a youngster flips a card. If the card shows a shape, he flips another card. Then, if the shapes match, he sets the pair aside. If they do not, he turns the cards facedown again. If he flips a card that shows a snail, he says, "Uh-oh, snail mail!" Then he turns the card back over and his turn ends. Play continues, in turn, until all the shapes are matched.

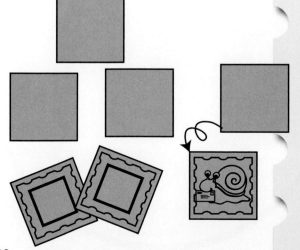

Personal Postcards
Writing Center

Provide sample postcards, large blank index cards, ink pads and rubber stamps, stickers, and markers or crayons. Each child examines the postcards to get inspiration for designing her own. Then she uses the provided materials to create her own personal postcard. When she's finished, she flips the card over and dictates or writes a message. If desired, ask each parent to send in an unused stamp. Help each child add her address and stamp to the postcard and then drop it in the mail!

Textured Packaging
Sensory Center

Place a variety of packing materials in your sensory table. For example, provide packing peanuts, pieces of bubble wrap cushioning material, paper shreds, pieces of foam, and air-filled pouches. A child explores the packing materials. If desired, also provide boxes and items to pack. Encourage little ones to pack the items, making sure to cushion them appropriately with the packing materials.

Stamped Envelopes
Literacy Center

Program each of several large envelopes with a box and an uppercase letter as shown. For each envelope, label a tagboard square (stamp) with the matching lowercase letter. Then tuck inside the envelope a card labeled with the upper and lowercase pair. Provide Sticky-Tac adhesive. A child chooses an envelope and finds the stamp with the matching lowercase letter. Then she uses a small amount of adhesive to attach the stamp to the box. She continues in the same way until each envelope has a stamp. Then she removes the card from each envelope to confirm that the letters match.

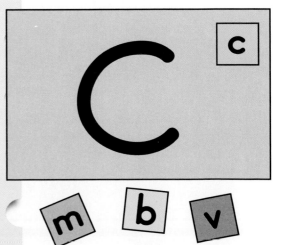

Mailing Labels

Use with "Preschool Post Office" on page 200.

_____

name

_____

street

_____   _____

town/city   zip code

©The Mailbox® • TEC41059 • Feb./Mar. 2012

_____

name

_____

street

_____   _____

town/city   zip code

©The Mailbox® • TEC41059 • Feb./Mar. 2012

TEC41059

TEC41059

TEC41059

TEC41059

TEC41059

TEC41059

TEC41059

TEC41059

TEC41059

TEC41059

TEC41059

TEC41059

Ribbit!

8 Fabulous Frog Centers!

① Speckled Frog
Art Center

For each child, provide a light green frog cutout (pattern on page 207), a sheet of blue construction paper, and a cardboard tube (log). A child glues brown tissue paper to the log; then he glues the log near the bottom of the blue paper as shown. Next, he repeatedly taps a marker on the frog to make speckles; then he glues the frog to the paper above the log. To complete the project, he presses his finger on a black ink pad and then on the paper to make flies around the frog.

Karen Wilson
Copper Creek Preschool
Herriman, UT

② Leap, Frog, Leap!
Math Center

For this partner center, attach a large brown paper log to the floor. Provide a supply of lily pad cutouts (pattern on page 207). One child stands on the log and pretends to be a frog. Her partner calls out "Leap, frog, leap!" Then the frog takes a giant leap off the log. The partner places a lily pad alongside the frog's feet to mark where she landed; then he continues lining up the lily pads until he reaches the log. Finally, the youngsters count aloud to determine how many lily pads long the leap was. Then they switch places and repeat the activity.

Mary Ann Craven
Fallbrook United Methodist Christian School
Fallbrook, CA

Lenny D. Grozier, Endicott, NY

3

Frolicking Frogs
Literacy Center

Program three paper strips with lily pads as shown (pattern on page 207). For each strip, label four frog cutouts (pattern on page 207) to match the lily pads. Put the strips and frogs at a center, spreading the frogs letter-side down. Three children visit the center. Each child turns over a frog and identifies the letter. He "hops" the frog to his strip and says, "Ribbit, ribbit!" Then he places the frog on the corresponding lily pad. If a frog is already on the lily pad, the child returns the frog he is holding to its original position. Play continues until all the frogs are on the lily pads.

Tracy Hora, Magnolia, TX

f r o g

4

Lunch at the Pond
Play Dough Center

Set out blue laminated paper (pond), green play dough, frog cookie cutters, and black play dough. A youngster makes green play dough frogs to put in the pond. Then she makes flies from the black play dough and "feeds" them to the frogs.

adapted from an idea by Shanda Fitte
Precious Cargo Early Learning Center
Salmon, ID

5

Flick!
Game Center

Place five black pom-poms (flies) atop each of several blocks. Provide a personalized party blower (frog tongue) for each child. A child (frog) flicks out his tongue trying to "catch" a fly for lunch. Each time he flicks a fly off the block, he chants, "Ribbit, ribbit, yummy fly!" He continues in the same way until all the flies are eaten.

Shanda Fitte

Hoppin' Along!
Water Table

Label each of several green plastic plates (lily pads) with a different number. (If desired, add a matching dot set below the number.) Then float the lily pads in your water table and place a supply of plastic or craft foam frogs nearby. A child identifies the number on a lily pad and then "hops" the matching number of frogs onto the lily pad. She continues in the same way until all the frogs are on the lily pads.

adapted from ideas by Kyleen Cook, In the Zone, Ocean Springs, MS, and Beth Deki, Chandler, AZ

Squishy Frog
Discovery Center

For each child, place dollops of blue and yellow fingerpaint in opposite corners of a resealable plastic bag. Gently squeeze the air from the bag (trying not to disturb the paint), seal it, and then reinforce the seal with clear packing tape. A student manipulates the bag, blending the paint until it turns green. Then he smoothes out the bag and tapes eye cutouts to it as shown. How unique!

Beth Deki

Leaping Lily Pads
Game Center

Provide a colored copy of the gameboard on page 208 and a large die. Two youngsters each place a toy frog or manipulative on the lily pad with the flower. In turn, each student rolls the die and counts the dots. Then she "hops" her frog along the corresponding number of lily pads. Then her partner takes a turn. Play continues in the same way. When a frog reaches the last lily pad, the player hops her frog onto the log.

Frog Pattern

Use with "Lunch Log" on page 106, "Speckled Frog" on page 204, "Frolicking Frogs" on page 205, and "Jump, Little Frogs!" on page 248.

TEC41060

Lily Pad Pattern

Use with "Leap, Frog, Leap!" on page 204 and "Frolicking Frogs" on page 205.

TEC41060

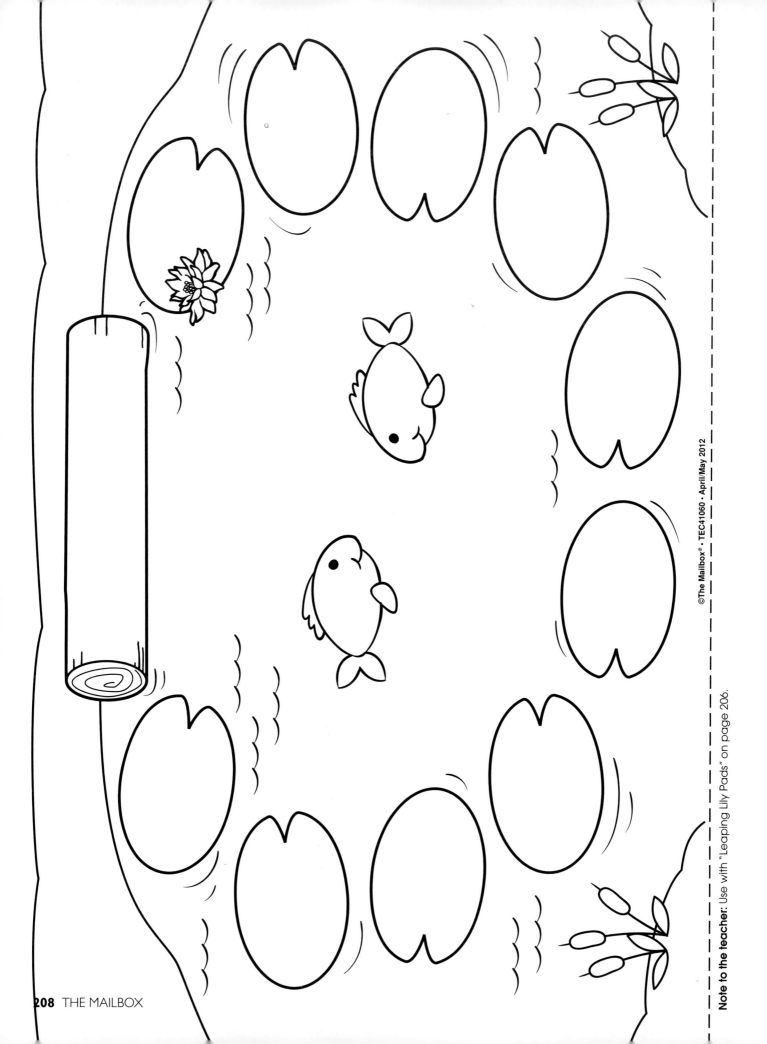

Note to the teacher: Use with "Leaping Lily Pads" on page 206.

Creepy and Crawly!
Bug Centers

Bug Boppers
Literacy Center

Encourage little ones to buzz over to this engaging letter-sound association center! Obtain several flip-flops. Cut out copies of the ant cards on page 62 and label them with different letters. Spread the cards faceup; then give each player a flip-flop. To begin, say a sound associated with one of the letters. The first child to spot an ant with the appropriate letter whacks it with his flip-flop. After confirming that he whacked the correct ant, have him set the card aside. Repeat the process with each remaining ant. Then have each child count his cards.

Cindy Laskowsky
New Adventures Child Development Center
Prescott, AZ

Entomology Lab
Dramatic-Play Area

Stock the area with bug investigation paraphernalia, such as plastic insects, insect boxes, clear plastic jars, tweezers, magnifying glasses, microscopes, standard and nonstandard measurement tools, clipboards, and writing tools for "recording" data. Also provide items like white button-down shirts (lab coats) and nonfiction insect books, magazines, and posters. Youngsters use the props to engage in pretend insect investigation.

Jeanne Hernandez
Risen Savior Lutheran School
Chandler, AZ

Buzzing Along
Math Center

Attach flower stickers to a sheet of tagboard in rows. Then draw a simple beehive at the end of each row. Gather bee manipulatives (found at craft stores) or small bee cutouts. To ready the board, each child places a bee on the first flower in a row. Then each player, in turn, rolls a die, counts the dots, and moves the bee along his row of flowers. Play continues until each bee reaches its hive.

Linda Heavrin, Benton, IL

Spectacular Symmetry!
Discovery Center

Make a copy of page 212 and place it at a center along with an unbreakable mirror. A youngster positions the flat edge of the mirror in a perpendicular position alongside a bug half, discovering that the reflection in the mirror makes the bug appear whole! After making this symmetrical discovery, she repeats the process with each bug half on the page.

Tamara Maijala
Kingdom Kids Christian Preschool
Rochester, MN

Bug Collections
Sensory Center

Youngsters use their sense of sight to search for bugs! Take a photo of a variety of plastic bugs and then print an enlarged copy of the photo. Put the bugs in a plastic jar partially filled with sand and secure the lid with tape. Then place both the jar and the photo at a center. A youngster shakes and moves the jar to find all the bugs he sees in the photo!

Robin Schaeffer
Playmates Preschool
Normal, IL

Swarm of Flies
Art Center

Little ones take aim with this fun art idea! Have a child press her fingertip on a black ink pad and then on a sheet of paper several times to make a swarm of flies. If desired, have her use a black marker to draw wings on each fly. When she's finished, encourage her to press a clean flyswatter in a thin layer of paint and then press it over each fly, adding more paint to the flyswatter as needed. How fun!

Melissa Anderson, J. R. W. Elementary, Somonauk, IL
Christy Anthony, Discovery School, Mansfield, OH

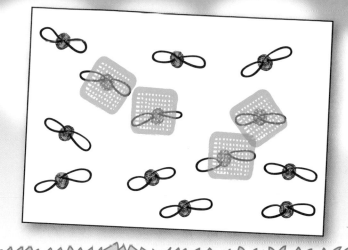

tip → If it's a nice day, take little ones outside and have them actually swat the flies with the paint-covered flyswatter. It's good, messy preschool fun and a memorable experience for little ones!

Interesting Insects
Writing Center

Gather several bug stamps. For each bug, stamp its picture on a blank card and then label the card with the bug's name. Place the cards at a center along with the corresponding bug stamps, ink pads, and paper. A child uses the stamps and stamp pads to make bug prints on a sheet of paper. He labels each print, using the programmed cards as a reference, and then draws additional details on the page.

Renata Balazy
The Sunshine House
Coppell, TX

It can be challenging to incorporate a bug theme into some preschool centers! Linda Heavrin of Benton, Illinois, manages to add bugs to her housekeeping center by using bug-themed dishtowels, paper plates, napkins, napkin rings, and a tablecloth (an inexpensive square of fabric with butterflies on it). There's no doubt that this class is studying bugs!

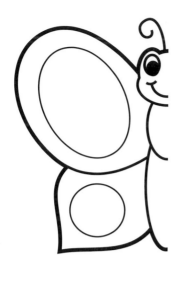

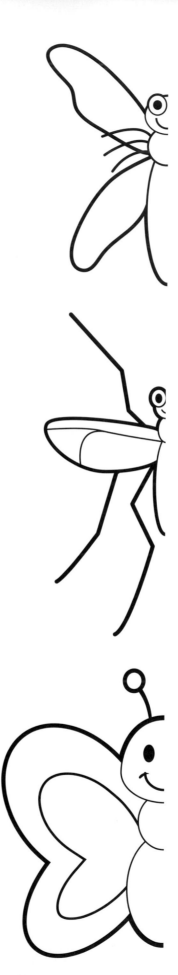

Note to the teacher: Use with "Spectacular Symmetry!" on page 210.

LITERACY UNITS

Time for Nursery Rhymes
Phonological Awareness Fun

ideas contributed by Ada Goren, Winston-Salem, NC

Jump!

Recognizing matching sounds

Recite the nursery rhyme "**Jack Be Nimble**," emphasizing the /j/ sound in *Jack* and *jump*. Then prompt youngsters to name the two words in the rhyme that begin with /j/. After determining that *Jack* and *jump* begin with /j/, give each child a block (candlestick) and have him stand it on the floor. Say a pair of words. If the words begin with /j/, youngsters jump over the candlestick. If the words begin with different sounds, youngsters stand still. Continue with other word pairs.

Dock and Clock

Identifying rhyming words

Lead youngsters in reciting "**Hickory, Dickory, Dock**" and then have them repeat *dock* and *clock* several times to reinforce the rhyming sounds. Next, place the following in a sack: a rock; a sock; a lock; a block; and two distracter items, such as a toy car and a ball. Have a child choose an item from the sack and identify it. Then recite the chant shown, inserting the name of the item. Ask the group to decide whether the word rhymes with *clock*. Then set the item aside and repeat the activity with each remaining item.

Hickory, dickory, dock.
What word rhymes with *clock*?
Oh, let us see.
What can it be?
Does [item's name] rhyme with *clock*?

Syllable Garden
Tapping syllables

Review with youngsters the nursery rhyme "**Mary, Mary, Quite Contrary**." Ask students whether they know the names of any flowers. After they share their thoughts, give each child a bingo dauber and a sheet of white paper. Say, "A tulip is the name of a flower." Have students use their daubers to tap the syllables in the word *tulip*, making prints on the paper. Continue with other flower names. (See suggestions below.) Then have students transform their prints into a garden by adding stems and leaves. How lovely!

Flower suggestions: *rose, tulip, daisy, sunflower, violet, lily, daffodil, carnation, hyacinth*

Hey, 'siddle, siddle,'
the cat played the
'biddle.'

Hey, "Siddle, Siddle"
Manipulating phonemes

After a class recitation of "**Hey, Diddle, Diddle**," switch things up by altering the sounds in the rhyme! Repeat the first two lines of the rhyme. Then say, "*Diddle* begins with /d/. I wonder whether it would sound different if it began with /s/." Lead students in saying the first two lines, changing *diddle* to *siddle*. When the giggling subsides, repeat the activity using other beginning sounds. Once youngsters have the hang of it, change the beginning sound of both *diddle* and *fiddle*, using a different sound for each word.

One-to-One Spiders
Segmenting sentences into words

Gather a small group of youngsters and give each child five spider cards (see the cards on page 216). Familiarize youngsters with the rhyme "**Little Miss Muffet**." Then recite the first line of the rhyme, holding up one finger for each word. Help students identify the number of words in the line. Recite the line again, this time encouraging each child to place in a row one spider for each word you say. To verify that he is correct, have each child recite the line, touching one spider for each word. Have youngsters remove the spiders and continue in the same way with each remaining line.

Little Miss Muffet
Sat on a tuffet,
Eating her curds and whey.
Along came a spider,
Who sat down beside her
And frightened Miss Muffet away.

Spider Cards

Use with "One-to-One Spiders" on page 215.

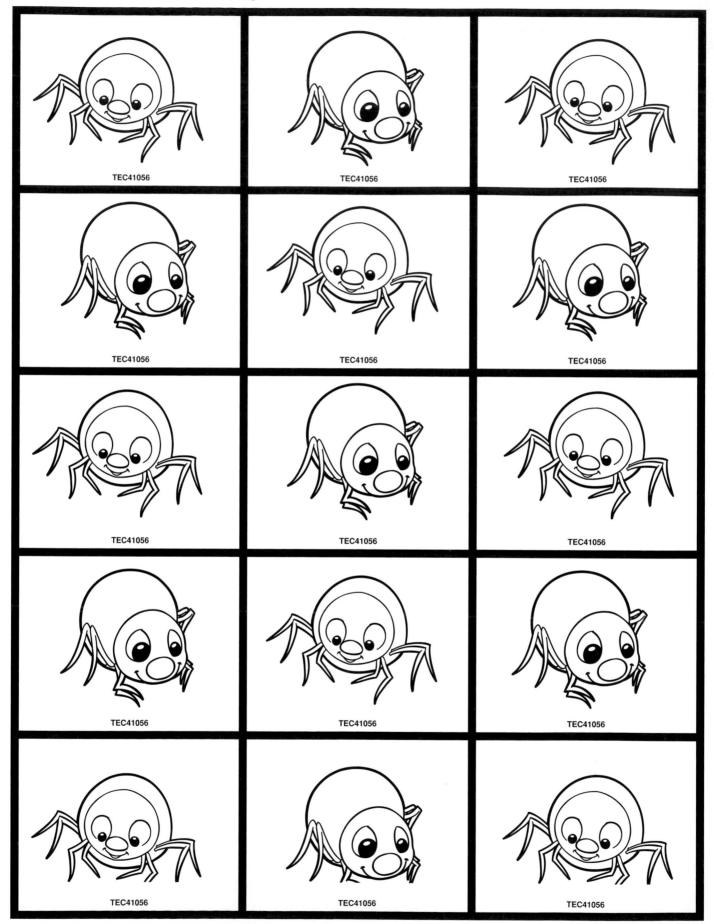

TEC41056

TEC41056

TEC41056

TEC41056

TEC41056

TEC41056

TEC41056

TEC41056

TEC41056

TEC41056

TEC41056

TEC41056

TEC41056

TEC41056

TEC41056

Getting Ready to Read!

Print Concepts

From Left to Right
Understanding text progression

Students' reading and writing will move in the right direction with this catchy tune! Write the words to the song on a sheet of chart paper. Prior to singing, have volunteers follow the text with their fingers as you read it aloud, guiding students to notice that the child is moving his finger from the left side and sweeping it toward the right. Then lead students in singing the song several times.

(sung to the tune of "Mary Had a Little Lamb")

Always go from left to right,
Left to right, left to right.
Always go from left to right
When you read and you write.

Doria Owen, William Paca/Old Post Road Elementary
Abingdon, MD

Snip, snip, snip! That's a sound coming from Penny Brown's classroom at Little Red Schoolhouse in Salem, Oregon! She has her little ones cut coupons at a center, combining environmental print with fine-motor skills! Then she puts the coupons in a tray for parents to look through.

That Doesn't Match!
Recognizing that print has meaning

Gather a set of picture cards and make corresponding word cards. Place the picture cards on the floor and put a word card on top of each one, making sure only some of the word cards match the pictures. Gather youngsters around the cards. Point to a card and say, "This says [word]." Then have a child remove the word card to reveal the picture card. If the picture matches the word, say, "That's right." If the picture doesn't match, say, "That's the wrong word!" Place the cards aside. When all the cards have been revealed, help little ones match the words and pictures correctly.

adapted from an idea by Amber Dingman
Play 'n' Learn Family Child Care and Preschool
Sterling, MI

Good to Eat?
Reading environmental print, sorting
Have parents send in food-related and nonfood-related environmental print. (See parent note on page 219.) Trim the environmental print as needed. Then place two plastic hoops (or circles of yarn) on the floor and label them as shown. Have each child choose a piece of environmental print, identify it, and sort it appropriately.

Jennifer Gemar, Tripp-Delmont Elementary, Tripp, SD

Sticker Search
Writing from left to right
Guide students to begin writing on the left side of the paper with this simple idea. On each child's paper, place a small sticker (or stamp an image) on the left side. Each time a child receives paper, direct her to search for the sticker and begin writing beside it.

Gina Petrassi, Bergen County Special Services, Hackensack, NJ

Who Needs This?
Forms of print
Students pair community helpers with the forms of print they use most often. Gather several print items such as a recipe card, a seed packet, a map, a picture book, a menu, a car manual, and an addressed envelope. Display the items. Then ask, "Which item would a baker need to read?" Discuss the options, leading students to recognize that the baker would need to read a recipe card and a menu. Continue with jobs such as the following: a car dealer, a teacher, a gardener, a postal worker, and a truck driver.

Naomi McCall, Virginia Beach, VA

Dear Family,

    We need pieces of environmental print for an upcoming activity! Environmental print includes product labels and boxes similar to those shown on this page. For this particular activity, we need both food and nonfood related print. Please send in your contributions by _____ .

                Thanks a bunch!

_____

©The Mailbox® • Oct./Nov. 2011

- -

Dear Family,

    We need pieces of environmental print for an upcoming activity! Environmental print includes product labels and boxes similar to those shown on this page. For this particular activity, we need both food and nonfood related print. Please send in your contributions by _____ .

                Thanks a bunch!

_____

©The Mailbox® • Oct./Nov. 2011

Sweet & Soothing!

Hot Chocolate Literacy

Add Some Marshmallows!

Clapping syllables

These mugs of hot chocolate need some marshmallows! Gather three mugs and label them as shown. Also get a supply of white pom-poms (marshmallows). Gather a small group of youngsters and name one of the words below. Help students clap the syllables in the word and identify the number of claps. Then have a child plop a marshmallow in the correct mug.

Suggested words: hot, chocolate, cocoa, marshmallow, toasty, warm, sweet, winter, milk, mix, stir, recipe, snow, snuggle, cold, chilly, yummy, snowflake

Ashley Rives, Lil Sprouts Kids Day Out, Greenwood, MO

Where's the Mix?

Reading environmental print

Gather several clean food boxes and packages, including a hot cocoa mix container. Place the samples of environmental print in a bag. To begin, lead students in reciting the chant shown. Then prompt a child to reach into the bag without looking and remove a piece of environmental print. Encourage him to identify the item. If he finds the hot cocoa mix, congratulate him. If he pulls a different item, say, "Oh no! We'll never find the hot cocoa!" Then continue the game until the hot cocoa is found.

Early in the morning, when I wake up,
I like to have some cocoa in my cup.
I don't want lemonade, soda, or tea.
Where, oh where could the cocoa be?

adapted from an idea by Keely Saunders, Bonney Lake Early Childhood Educational Assistance Program, Bonney Lake, WA

See page 222 for more **print awareness fun!**

Marshmallow Toss
Recognizing beginning sounds

In advance, cut white craft foam into squares so they resemble marshmallows and place the marshmallows in a container. Gather youngsters in a circle around a large brown splotch cutout (hot chocolate). Pull a student card (or stick) and give the child a marshmallow. Name a word. If the word begins with /m/ like *marshmallow*, have the child toss the marshmallow into the hot chocolate while the remaining youngsters say, "Mmmm, mmmm!" Continue in the same way with other little ones until everyone has tossed a marshmallow. Then have students pretend to drink the puddle of hot chocolate!

Suggested words: mail, man, mask, cake, map, mat, mitten, monkey, hop, moon, mop, mouse, tie, mug, mitt, mom, seal, magic, mane, march, pail, market, may, maze, rug, match

Better Than Sand!
Writing

Youngsters are sure to love writing in powdered hot cocoa mix! Place a thin layer of hot cocoa mix in a tray. Then encourage little ones to use a finger, a craft stick, or a chopstick to write and draw in the mix. Prompt them to sniff the chocolaty scent as they play! **For a more advanced option,** provide letter or word cards and encourage little ones to write the letters and words in the mix!

Letter Discovery
Matching letters, identifying letters

Place mini marshmallows and hot cocoa mix in an empty water bottle. Also tuck a few small letter manipulatives in the bottle. Then secure the lid with tape. Write the letters on a sheet of paper and make a class supply. A youngster takes a paper and then shakes and manipulates the bottle, crossing off each letter he finds.

Keely Saunders
Bonney Lake Early Childhood Educational
    Assistance Program
Bonney Lake, WA

P	L	M
S	D	T
A	G	I

Hot Cocoa!

Coca, cocoa,

In a cup,

Warm and toasty.

Drink it up!

©The Mailbox® • TEC41058 • Dec./Jan. 2011–12

Note to the teacher: Give each child a colorful copy of this page and a handful of white pom-poms (marshmallows). Help each youngster point to the words as you read the chant out loud. To reinforce that words are made of groups of letters, have her glue marshmallows to the spaces between the words.

Words, Words, Words!

Engaging Oral Language Activities

Theme Cards
Developing new vocabulary

Eggplants? Pliers? Antelopes? Youngsters will know these vocabulary words—and many others—with this simple activity! Make vocabulary cards to go with your favorite themes. (Use the cards on page 225 or search online for images for a variety of themes, such as transportation, fruits, farm, zoo animals, and tools. You're sure to find lots of options!) Choose a theme and review a few cards with youngsters, encouraging them to notice details about the items. Incorporate action whenever possible, such as moving like an antelope or pretending to squeeze pliers. Review the cards later in the day. The next day, have students name the items and review a few new cards. What a simple way to learn new vocabulary!

Andrea Goodling, Sycamore Tree, Hartford, WI

zebra

baboon

giraffe

ostrich

rhinoceros

hippopotamus

I like waffles!

The Magic Ball
Speaking in complete sentences

Get a colorful ball and tell students that it is a magic ball. Explain that the ball is magic because only the person holding the ball can talk. Everyone else must listen. Roll the ball to a child and then ask a simple question, such as "What do you like to eat for breakfast?" Encourage the child to answer the question using a complete sentence. For example, he might say, "I like to eat waffles for breakfast." Then have him roll the ball back to you so that you can roll it to another child.

Marysue Garren
Middleham and St. Peter's Day School
Lusby, MD

Hello, Who's There?

Speaking to answer questions, developing life skills

Youngsters practice telephone etiquette with this engaging idea! Gather two play phones and give one to a child. Dial a number on your phone and then point to the child, encouraging him to answer the call as a business owner. For example, he might say, "Hello! This is Evan's Cookie Store." Put in an order using full sentences. Then prompt the child to repeat the order and say when it will be ready, adding extra details as desired. Close the phone call encouraging the child to use good manners. Little ones will love this activity!

Lynda Wolfe
John D. Spicer Elementary
Haltom City, TX

Check this out!

Lorie Vanwerven from Blossom Childcare and Learning Center in Bellingham, Washington, develops speaking skills with a streamlined version of "Show-and-Share." Each youngster brings an item from home. Children sit in a circle with their items in their laps. Each child has one minute to talk about his item and then he places it behind his back so he can focus on the next speaker. Now that's quick and easy!

helicopter
car
truck
airplane
highway
motorcycle
bicycle

The Vocabulary Board

Developing new vocabulary

Create a vocabulary board with your youngsters! Add a few details to a bulletin board or wall to match your current theme. For example, for a transportation theme, you might add a road and blue sky or, for an ocean theme, you might add simply a blue background. Write a list of focus vocabulary near the board. Then encourage students to create theme-appropriate artwork to decorate the board. Discuss the progression of the board throughout the theme, incorporating the vocabulary into your discussions! What a simple way to help little ones learn new vocabulary!

Karen Favor, Harold Holliday Montessori
Kansas City, MO

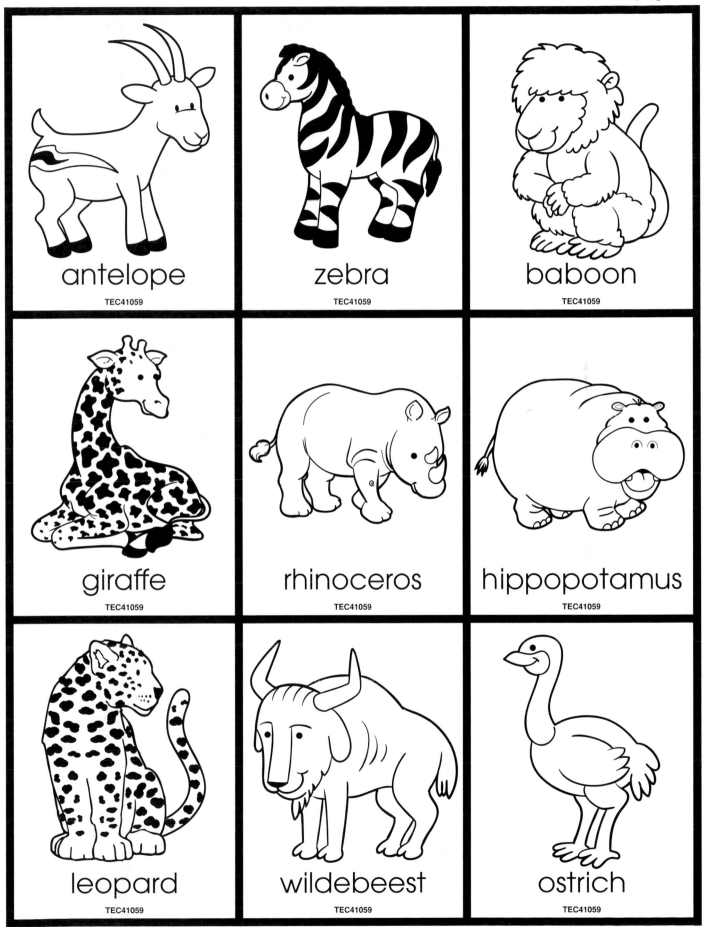

antelope
TEC41059

zebra
TEC41059

baboon
TEC41059

giraffe
TEC41059

rhinoceros
TEC41059

hippopotamus
TEC41059

leopard
TEC41059

wildebeest
TEC41059

ostrich
TEC41059

Learning Letter Sounds

A tiny bird said that these zippy little anytime activities pack some strong letter-sound association skills!

• • • Do You Know? • • •

Here's an adorable whole-group activity that can spotlight any letter sounds of your choosing! Place letter cards in your pocket chart. Then lead youngsters in the first stanza of the song shown. Prompt a child to choose the letter from the pocket chart and hold it up. Then lead students in singing the second stanza. Have the child return the card to the chart. Then play another round!

(sung to the tune of "The Muffin Man")

Oh, do you know the letter [*M*],
The letter [*M*], the letter [*M*]?
Do you know the letter [*M*]?
It makes the sound of [/m/].

Yes, I know the letter [*M*],
The letter [*M*], the letter [*M*].
Yes, I know the letter [*M*].
It makes the sound of [/m/].

Jennifer Gemar, Tripp-Delmont School, Tripp, SD

• • • Sneak in Some Sounds • • •

To help little ones associate words with beginning sounds, print and cut out pictures of items that begin with the letter your youngsters are currently studying. Attach the pictures to the wall where students line up to leave the room and where youngsters wait for the restroom. While students wait, they will naturally touch, talk about, and name the pictures. Then, during circle time, discuss the pictures with youngsters, leading them to notice that their names begin with the same sound—the sound of your focus letter!

Leigh Moran, Glenside, PA

• • • Floating Letters • • •

Label each of several plastic lids with different letters and float the lids in your water table. Name a letter sound and then have a child use a net (or a spatula) to remove the corresponding lid from the water. Continue with the remaining sounds.

Keely Saunders, Bonney Lake Early Childhood Education and Assistance Program, Bonney Lake, WA

• • • Pass and Sing • • •

Place several different letter cards in a gift bag. Have little ones sit in a circle; then hand a child the bag. To begin, play a recording of music and have youngsters pass the bag around the circle. Stop the music and have the child holding the bag remove a card and show it to the group. Then lead students in singing the song shown, inserting the appropriate letter name and sound. At the end of the song, set the card aside and continue in the same way with the remaining cards.

(sung to the tune of "Bingo")

There is a child who has a letter,
And [*B*] is its name-o.
[/b/, /b/, /b/, /b/, /b/],
[/b/, /b/, /b/, /b/, /b/],
[/b/, /b/, /b/, /b/, /b/],
And [*B*] is its name-o!

Jennifer Gemar, Tripp-Delmont School, Tripp, SD

• • • Feely Sack • • •

Hide in a cloth sack three or four familiar objects with different beginning sounds. Place near the sack letter cards that correspond to each sound. A child chooses a card and says the letter name and sound. Then he reaches into the sack without looking and removes an object. If it is the correct item, he places it near the corresponding card. If not, he puts the object back in the sack and tries again. He continues in the same way until each object is paired with the corresponding card.

Suzanne Foote
East Ithaca Preschool
Ithaca, NY

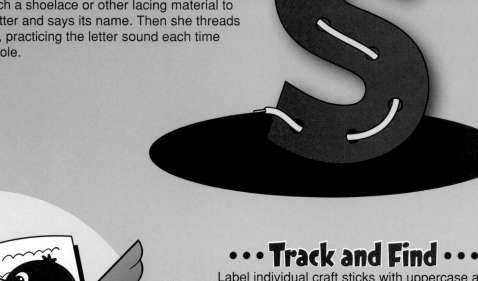

• • • Letter Lacers • • •

Laminate several die-cut letters. Use a hole puncher to punch holes in each letter, as shown; then attach a shoelace or other lacing material to the die-cut. A child chooses a letter and says its name. Then she threads the shoelace through each hole, practicing the letter sound each time she pokes the shoelace into a hole.

Donna Ream
Ms. Donna's Daycare
Plainfield, IL

• • • Track and Find • • •

Label individual craft sticks with uppercase and lowercase letter pairs. Put the sticks in a container and place the container in your reading area. A youngster chooses a letter stick and a book. He turns to the first page and uses the letter stick to track the text in a left-to-right progression. When he sees a letter that matches one on his stick, he pauses to say the letter name and sound. He continues in the same way throughout the book.

Donna Ream

• • • Let's Get Moving! • • •

Youngsters will love this kinesthetic approach to learning letters and sounds! Gather several alphabet cards and have little ones stand with plenty of room between them. Display a card and ask students to identify the letter and its sound. Next, name a familiar exercise that begins with the designated letter (see suggestions shown). Then encourage little ones to perform the exercise while making the letter sound. Repeat the activity with other cards.

Exercise suggestions: *d,* dance; *g,* gallop; *h,* hop; *j,* jump; *k,* kick; *l,* leap; *m,* march; *r,* run; *s,* skip; *t,* tiptoe; *w,* walk

Kelly Tincher
Manson Northwest Webster School
Barnum, IA

Math Units

Big on Sorting and Patterning

These enormously fun ideas are sure to help your youngsters take big steps with their sorting and patterning skills.

That's a Keeper!

Sorting by one attribute

Float a supply of craft foam fish and other craft foam shapes in your water table. Provide a net and a plastic pail. A child puts the net in the water and pulls up her catch. She removes all the fish from her net and drops them into the pail. Then she throws the shapes back into the water. She continues until all the fish have been removed from the water.

Roxanne LaBell Dearman
Western NC Early Intervention Program for Children Who Are Deaf or Hard of Hearing
Charlotte, NC

Taking Turns

Introducing patterning

Visual and auditory repetition make teaching patterning a snap during this partner activity! Prepare two sets of cutouts, each a different shape, and give one set to each partner. In turn, have a child lay down his shape and name it. Continue in this manner until all the cutouts have been used. Then guide the partners to notice the pattern they created.

Karen Eiben
The Learning House Preschool
LaSalle, IL

Triangle.

Stocking Shelves

Sorting by shape

Transform your dramatic-play area into a grocery store to reinforce youngsters' sorting skills. Provide a tub containing two different types of clean, empty grocery items, such as boxes and plastic containers. Place the tub near two empty shelves. (If shelves are not available, designate two areas of the center for the child to use for sorting.) A child sorts the groceries by putting each type of grocery on a different shelf.

Roxanne LaBell Dearman
Western NC Early Intervention Program for Children Who Are
  Deaf or Hard of Hearing
Charlotte, NC

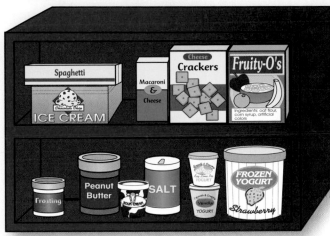

Pasta Patterning

Extending patterns

The many shapes and sizes of pasta make it a must for patterning practice! Purchase a few varieties of pasta and dye each type a different color. When the pasta is dry, place each type of pasta in a separate bowl. Set out the pasta, glue, and tagboard strips. Invite a group of youngsters to join you and give each child a tagboard strip. Place a few pieces of pasta on each child's strip to begin a pattern and have the child glue the pasta to the strip. Then direct him to glue additional pasta pieces to the strip to continue the pattern.

Donna Ream, Ms. Donna's Daycare, Plainfield, IL

Laundry Day!

Sorting by type

To prepare for this center activity, tie a length of string (or a clothesline) between two chairs. Attach a colorful scarf in the middle of the string. Cut out a supply of clothing cards from the patterns on page 232 and place two different types of cards in a basket. (Set the other two types of cards aside.) Provide spring-style clothespins. A center visitor sorts the cards onto opposite sides of the string by clipping them in place. After several days, switch out one or both sets of clothing cards to keep youngsters' interest level high.

Kelly Tincher, Head Start, Fort Dodge, IA

Clothing Cards

Use with "Laundry Day!" on page 231.

TEC41056

TEC41056

TEC41056

TEC41056

Magnificent Math Booklets

Little ones will be eager to make these unique math booklets!

ideas contributed by Ada Goren, Winston-Salem, NC

Buzzing Bees

For each child, accordion-fold a 4" x 18" construction paper strip to make six booklet pages. Label the cover and pages as shown. Set out a yellow stamp pad and a black fine-tip marker. Guide each child in making the appropriate number of yellow fingerprints (bees) on each numbered page. Then encourage him to draw wing and body details on each bee. To complete the booklet, have him glue a construction paper beehive to the last page.

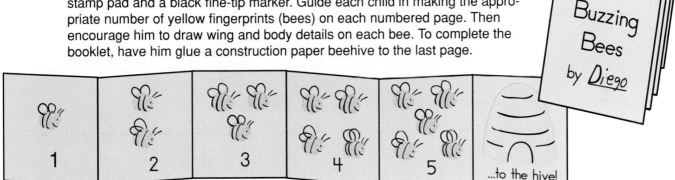

Longer and Shorter

Youngsters compare picture lengths in multiple ways with this unique booklet! To prepare a booklet for each child, staple four sheets of copy paper between construction paper covers programmed as shown. Then cut the copy paper in half lengthwise to make four top pages and four bottom pages. Label each page in the top set with the word *longer* and each page in the bottom set with the word *shorter*. Give each child a copy of the picture strips on page 235 along with a five-inch and a three-inch length of yarn. Then guide her through the steps shown to complete the booklet.

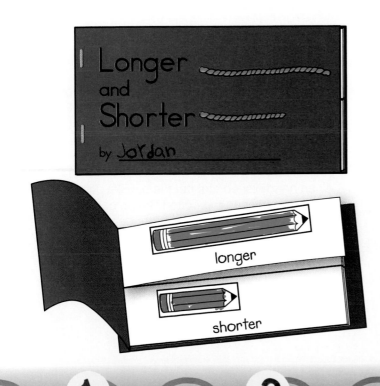

Step 1: Color the picture on each strip; then cut out the strips.
Step 2: Sort the strips into corresponding picture pairs.
Step 3: Glue the strips in each pair above the appropriate labels on corresponding page halves.
Step 4: Glue each length of yarn next to the appropriate word on the cover.

Clouds Float By

To make this adorable booklet that highlights presubtraction skills, trim the corners of seven 4½" x 6" pieces of blue construction paper. Label the cover and pages with the words shown. Have each child glue torn cotton balls (clouds) above the title on the cover. Next, guide her in making the appropriate number of cloud prints on each page using a large pom-pom and white paint. Then have her glue a yellow circle (sun) to the last booklet page. When the paint is dry, help her stack the cover and pages in order and staple them together.

Clouds Float By
by Chloe

5 clouds float by.
1 cloud says, "Goodbye."

4 clouds float by.
1 cloud says, "Goodbye."

3 clouds float by.
1 cloud says, "Goodbye."

2 clouds float by.
1 cloud says, "Goodbye."

1 cloud floats by.
1 cloud says, "Goodbye."

0 clouds float by.
See the sun in the sky!

Where Is Joshua?

Over the rainbow. 1

In front of the house. 2

Behind the tree. 3

Next to the mouse! 4

Where Is Joshua?

Where Is...?

Youngsters are the main characters in their own personalized positional word books! To prepare, trim around a photo of each child. For each student, label a construction paper front cover as shown. Then help him glue a pocket to a construction paper back cover for storing his photo. Next, encourage him to color a copy of the booklet pages (patterns on pages 236 and 237). When he's finished, cut out the booklet pages and then cut along the dotted line on page 3. Help him stack the pages in order between the covers and then staple them together. Read the text aloud, encouraging him to place his photo in the appropriate position on each page. Direct him to slide the photo through the slit on page 3 so it looks as if he's peeking out from behind the tree!

5   6   7   8   9

Picture Strips

Use with "Longer and Shorter" on page 233.

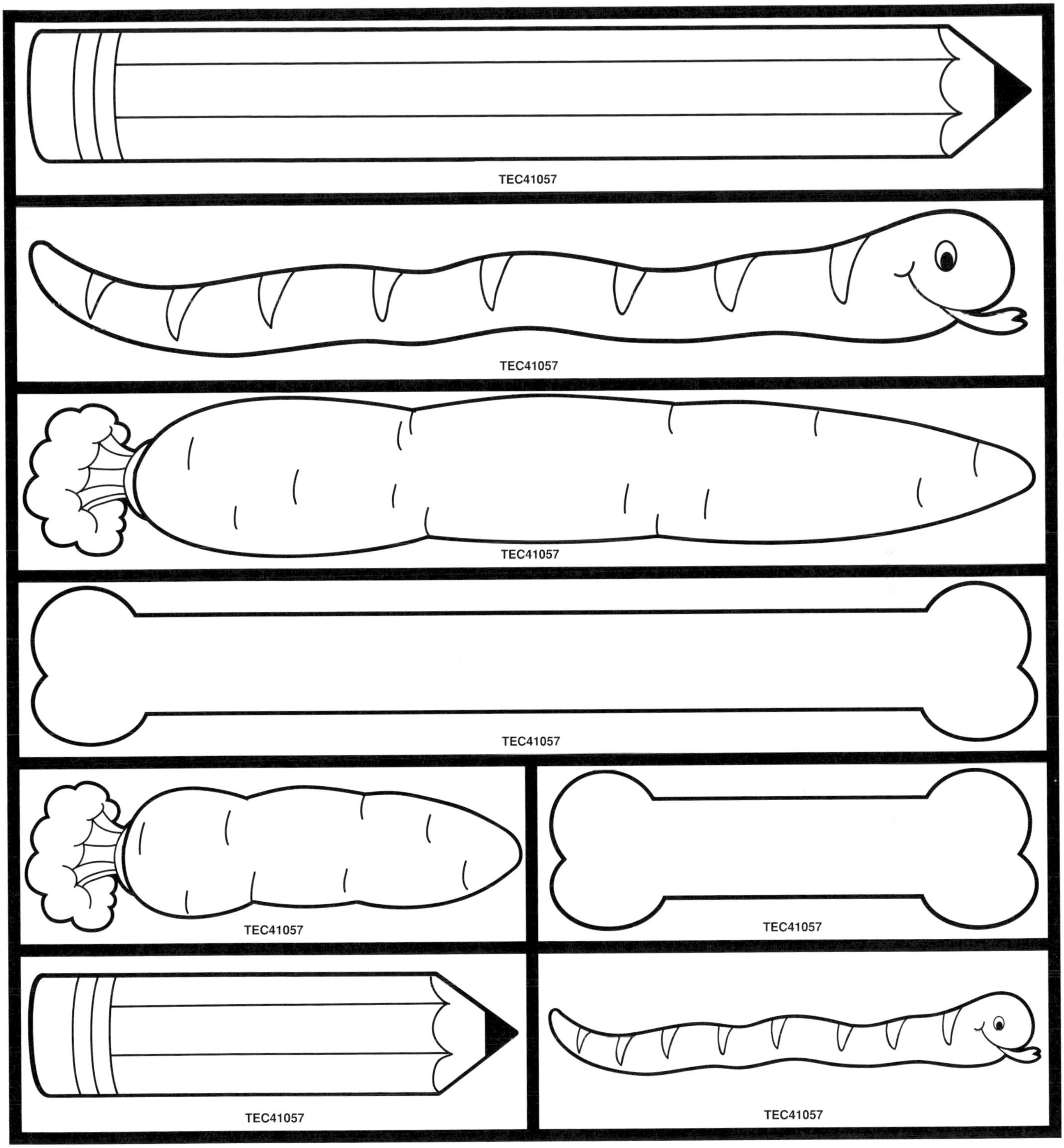
TEC41057
TEC41057
TEC41057
TEC41057
TEC41057
TEC41057
TEC41057
TEC41057

Booklet Pages 1 and 2

Use with "Where Is…?" on page 234.

In front of the house.

2

Over the rainbow.

1

©The Mailbox® • TEC41057 • Oct./Nov. 2011

4

Next to the mouse!

3

Behind the tree.

Math With the Three Little Kittens

Your darling kittens will find their mittens and have some pie with this collection of ideas related to this classic rhyme!

Three little kittens,
They lost their mittens,
And they began to cry,
"Oh, mother dear,
We sadly fear,
Our mittens we have lost."
"What! Lost your mittens,
You naughty kittens!
Then you shall have no pie.
Meow, meow, meow, meow.
You shall have no pie."

Three little kittens,
They found their mittens,
And they began to cry,
"Oh, mother dear,
See here, see here,
Our mittens we have found."
"What! Found your mittens,
You darling kittens!
Then you shall have some pie.
Meow, meow, meow, meow.
You shall have some pie."

tip → This is a terrific rhyme for youngsters to act out! Have little ones pantomime the three little kittens and mother cat as you recite the rhyme.

How Many Kittens?
Identifying numbers, counting

Write the first three lines of the rhyme on sentence strips, writing the numeral for the first word, and place the strips in your pocket chart. Cut out several copies of the kitten cards on page 240. Place number cards in a bag. To begin, recite the lines with youngsters. Then have a child pull a number card. Help her identify the number and place it in the chart over the number 3. Recite the new rhyme with youngsters. Then help a volunteer count out the appropriate number of kittens. Continue with the remaining number cards.

5 | little kittens

They lost their mittens,

And they began to cry,

Paws Aplenty
Organizing information, counting

Three kittens need six mittens! Help little ones decide how many mittens are needed for varying numbers of kittens! Cut out four copies of the kitten cards on page 240 and make a chart with the headings shown. Gather a supply of mittens. Have a child place three kittens on the floor. Write the number 3 on the chart. Then have a child give each kitten a pair of mittens. Prompt youngsters to count the mittens. Say, "Three kittens need six mittens!" Then write the number 6 on the chart. Continue with increasing numbers of kittens.

kittens	mittens
3	6
4	
5	
6	

Lost and Found
Positional words

Youngsters help a little kitten find her lost mittens during this entertaining game. Give one child (kitten) a pair of mittens. While the other little ones cover their eyes, have the kitten hide the mittens in a location where they can be easily found. To signal students to uncover their eyes, have the kitten announce that she has lost her mittens. Then direct her to ask a youngster to look for her mittens. When the youngster finds the mittens, have him use positional words to describe their location. Continue play for several more rounds.

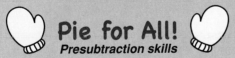

Pie for All!
Presubtraction skills

Place paper pie pieces in a pie pan as shown. Invite youngsters to pretend they are good little kittens who are getting ready to eat some pie. Lead them in counting the number of pie slices in the pan. Then place a paper plate in front of each kitten and yourself. Serve yourself a piece of pie and lead the group in counting the pieces in the pan, guiding them to notice that there is one less piece. Continue in this manner until each kitten has served himself a piece of pie.

Roxanne LaBell Dearman, NC Early Intervention Program for Children Who Are Deaf or Hard of Hearing, Charlotte, NC

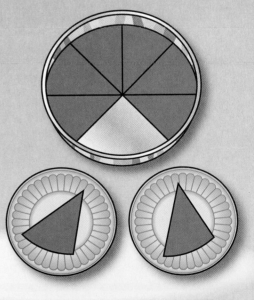

Kitten Cards

Use with "How Many Kittens?" on page 238 and "Paws Aplenty" on page 239.

TEC41058

TEC41058

TEC41058

My Community Math

What happens when you combine social studies with math? Why, you get this adorable collection of community-themed math ideas!

ideas contributed by Ada Goren, Winston-Salem, NC

City Streets
Counting and comparing sets

Which street has more houses: Main Street or Elm Street? Little ones use their number skills to find out! Prepare two street signs like the ones shown and place them in a pocket chart. Then cut apart a few copies of the house cards on page 244 and place them nearby. Gather youngsters near the pocket chart. Put a few houses beside each street sign. Invite a volunteer to count the houses on each street. Then guide the group to determine which street has more houses. Repeat the activity several times.

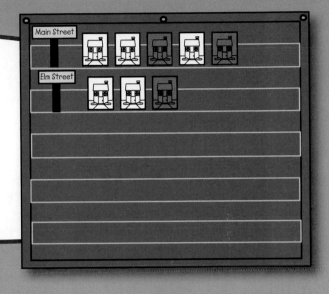

Shopping for Shapes
Color and shape recognition

No doubt your little ones have visited stores in your community. For this activity, have them visit a shape store! Designate an area of the room to be a shape shop. Display a variety of colorful paper shapes. In the center of the circle-time area, place a length of bulletin board paper and a glue stick. Explain to students that you need their help creating a collage. Name a color and shape, such as a blue circle. Then ask a child to visit the store and find that shape. Have him pretend to pay you for his shape. Then have him glue the shape to the paper. Continue with the remaining children to make a lovely shape collage!

Build and Compare
Comparing length and height
Use the materials in your block center to turn your youngsters into road and building engineers. Divide the class into small groups and supply each group with a variety of blocks to use as building materials. Then guide each group to build a community with at least three roads and three buildings. When construction is complete, invite each group to share its community. At each community, lead the youngsters in comparing the lengths of the roads and the heights of the buildings.

Community Jobs
Graphing
Find out students' job preferences with this simple-to-make skyscraper graph. Program a length of bulletin board paper as shown to make a graph. Cut out a copy of the job cards on page 245. Then attach a job card to each column. Have each child write her name on a sticky note and place it above the job she would prefer to have. Discuss the results of the graph. Repeat this activity several times during your community unit using different job cards each time.

Which Job Would You Like Better?

Ellie

Jake

Nadia

firefighter

Lucas

Devin

teacher

Patterned Neighborhoods
Creating and extending patterns
For this partner center, cut apart colorful copies of the house cards on page 244. Place the cards at a center. One child in the pair uses the cards to create a pattern. Then his partner adds cards to the pattern to extend it. The partners switch roles and repeat the activity.

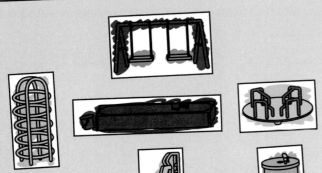

Park Plans
Positional words

Youngsters follow directions to create the perfect community park. Give each child in a small group a copy of the cards on page 246 and a 12" x 18" sheet of construction paper. Have her color and cut apart the cards and set them aside. Read the first instruction shown below and encourage her to follow the direction. Continue until each card is in place, assisting students in locating left and right as needed.

1. Glue the sandbox in the center of the paper.
2. Glue the jungle gym on the left side of the paper.
3. Glue the swings above the sandbox.
4. Glue the merry-go-round on the right side of the paper.
5. Glue the water fountain below the merry-go-round.
6. Glue the slide at the bottom of the paper.

Order Up!
Identifying numbers

This whole-group activity serves up a heaping helping of fun as well as math practice! Arrange the tables in your room so they resemble the dining area of a restaurant. Stand a numbered card at each table. In a location designated as the kitchen, place an adult apron, a number of trays equal to the number of tables, and a supply of toy food. To begin, have little ones sit at the tables. Then put on the apron and invite two youngsters to be the servers. Place a few pieces of toy food on a tray and name a table number, prompting a server to deliver the food to the table. After each table has been served, have the servers clear the tables. Then invite two more youngsters to be the servers.

House Cards

Use with "City Streets" on page 241 and "Patterned Neighborhoods" on page 242.

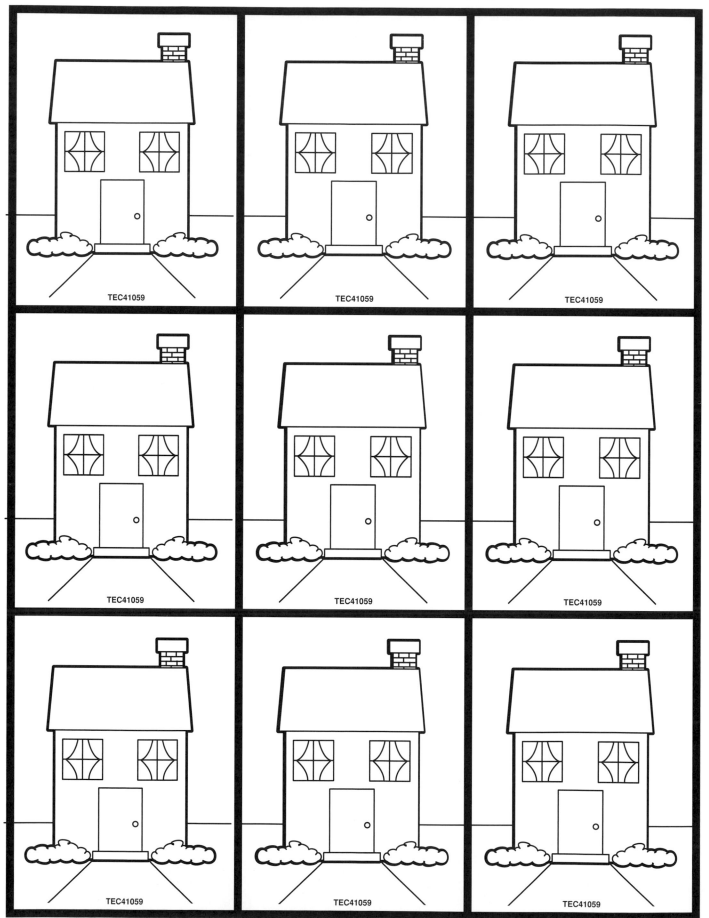

TEC41059

TEC41059

TEC41059

TEC41059

TEC41059

TEC41059

TEC41059

TEC41059

TEC41059

firefighter
TEC41059

police officer
TEC41059

teacher
TEC41059

dentist
TEC41059

doctor
TEC41059

mail carrier
TEC41059

Park Cards
Use with "Park Plans" on page 243.

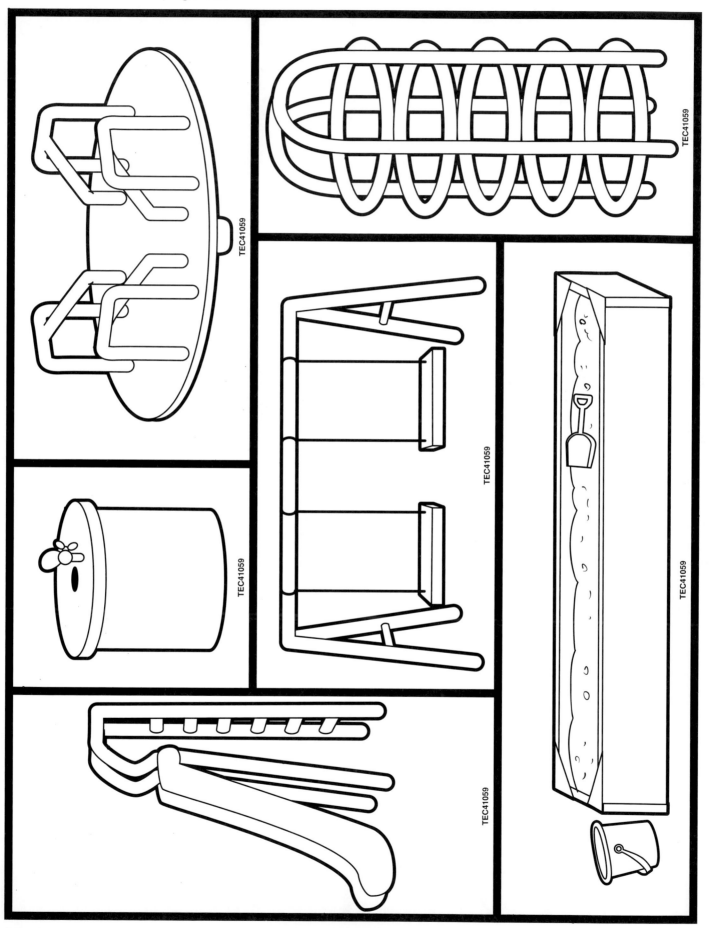

TEC41059

TEC41059

TEC41059

TEC41059

TEC41059

TEC41059

Spring Into Graphing

Little ones' graphing skills are sure to be in full bloom with these engaging ideas!

It's Raining, It's Pouring

Raincoats and boots are not needed when youngsters get caught in this spring shower! Make raindrop cutouts in two different sizes to make a class supply and place the raindrops in an open, upside-down umbrella. Place a floor graph nearby. Lead the group in singing "It's Raining, It's Pouring." As you sing, hold the umbrella up so it "rains" on the students. Direct each child to pick up a raindrop and place it on the correct column. When the graph is complete, lead youngsters in a discussion about the results.

Kari Nielsen
Busy Bee Preschool
Sisseton, SD

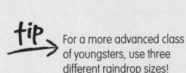 **tip** For a more advanced class of youngsters, use three different raindrop sizes!

Raindrops

small ⬭	big ⬥

The Daily Buzz

To prepare for this daily activity, attach tape to a pocket chart to make several columns. Label a sentence strip with a question and index cards with answer choices and put them in the pocket chart. Then use the patterns on page 249 to create a bee for each child like the ones shown and place them nearby. (You can either attach a head shot photo to each bee or label each bee with a child's name and have the child draw a face.) Read the question-and-answer choices to students. Then invite each child to place his bee on the chart to show his choice. After the graph is complete, guide children as they compare the columns. Choose a different spring-related question for the next day!

Carol Ann Sellers
Williamsburg Head Start
Williamsburg, KY

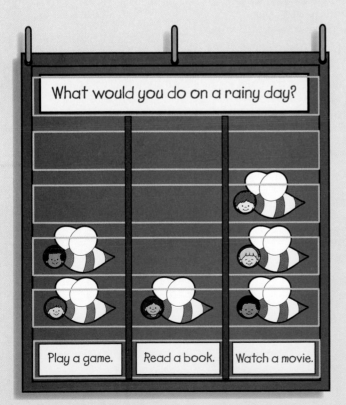

What would you do on a rainy day?

| Play a game. | Read a book. | Watch a movie. |

Stamp, Stamp, Stamp

Provide graph paper labeled as shown, a small butterfly rubber stamp, and an ink pad. Have each child stamp the appropriate number of butterflies above each numeral. Then encourage little ones to note how the larger numbers of butterflies have taller columns.

Susan Pufall, Red Cliff Early Head Start, Bayfield, WI

					🦋
				🦋	🦋
			🦋	🦋	🦋
		🦋	🦋	🦋	🦋
	🦋	🦋	🦋	🦋	🦋
🦋	🦋	🦋	🦋	🦋	🦋
1	2	3	4	5	6

Roll and Graph

Which color of flower will be rolled most often? Students find out by creating a class graph. Color six copies of the flower cards on page 249 as follows: 1 card yellow, 2 cards pink, and 3 cards blue. Then glue the flower cards to a cube-shaped box to make a die. Display a simple graph, as shown. Ask students to look at the cube and predict which color they think will be rolled the most times. Then, in turn, have each child roll the cube and record her color on the graph. Finally, have little ones evaluate their predictions.

adapted from an idea by Norinne Weeks
Carrillo Elementary
Houston, TX

		Seth
	Ann	Kyle
	Joe	Lea
Mia	Sam	Adam
⚘	⚘	⚘

tip → There are many fun ways for youngsters to mark graphs! Consider using sticky notes, themed die-cuts, pom-poms, small photos of the children, or other appropriate-size manipulatives!

Jump, Little Frogs!

Cut out three copies of the frog pattern on page 207 in different colors. Then attach them at regular intervals on the floor along with a start line. Label three columns of a simple graph with corresponding frogs. Have a child stand on the start line and jump to a frog. Have her note which frog she is closest too. After applauding her jumping skills, have her record her jump on the graph. When each child has had a turn, have youngsters evaluate the graph.

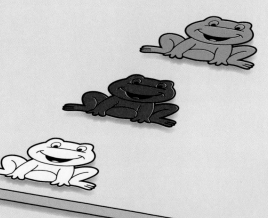

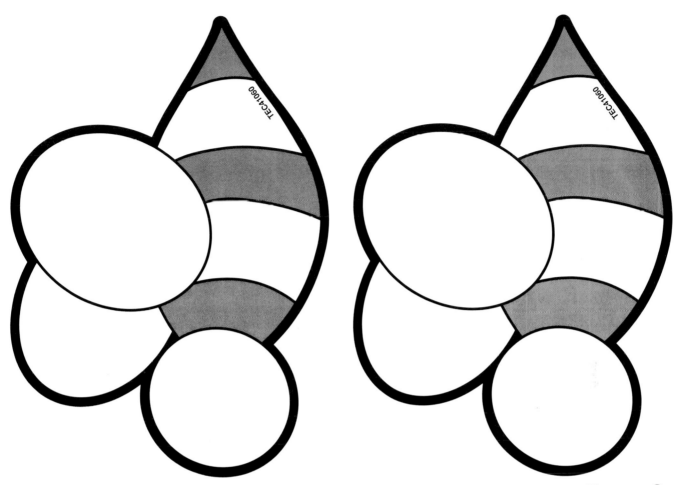

TEC41060

Flower Cards

Use with "Great Gardening!" on page 53 and "Roll and Graph" on page 248.

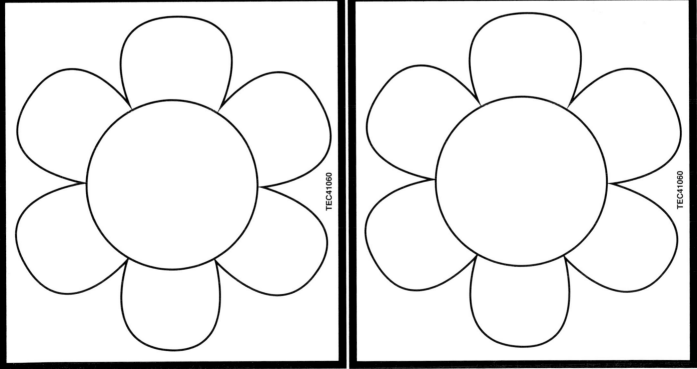

TEC41060

TEC41060

Strawberry Math

Strawberry Study

Exploring measurement

To prepare for this partner center, set out a basket of large strawberries, linking cubes, lengths of yarn, and a balance scale. Each child in the pair chooses a strawberry. Then the youngsters use the cubes to measure the heights of their strawberries and compare the measurements. Next, they use the yarn to measure and compare the distances around their strawberries. They use the scale to compare the weights of their strawberries. Then they wash their strawberries and eat them!

Shelley Hoster
Jack and Jill Early Learning Center
Norcross, GA

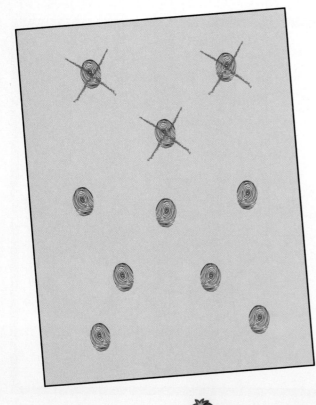

Perfect for Pie

Developing presubtraction skills

A very hungry bear is looking for big, juicy strawberries to use in a yummy pie! Have each child make ten red fingerprints on a sheet of paper to represent ten strawberries. Lead youngsters in reciting the first verse of the rhyme shown, encouraging each child to use a crayon to cross out one strawberry. Continue in the same way nine more times, crossing out another berry each time. Then direct youngsters in saying the last verse.

[Ten] strawberries in a berry patch.
A hungry bear came by.
Yum, yum, yum! I'll take one home
To make a strawberry pie.

Zero strawberries in a berry patch.
A hungry bear came by.
Boohoo-hoo! No berries are left.
I think I'm going to cry!

Roxanne LaBell Dearman
NC Early Intervention Program for Children Who Are Deaf or Hard
    of Hearing
Charlotte, NC

See page 73 for a sassy strawberry display!

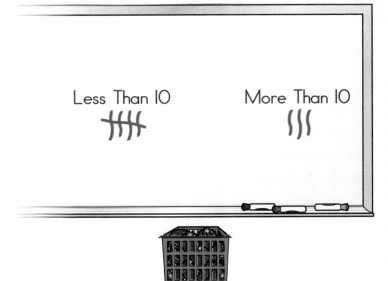

Guess and Check
Estimation, making tally marks, exploring volume
Display a container of strawberries and write on the board the headings shown. Invite each child to predict whether there are fewer than ten or more than ten strawberries in the container and then mark a tally on the board to show his guess. After each child has made his choice, lead the group in counting the strawberries and revisiting the estimates. Next, display three containers, only one of which will hold all the strawberries. Encourage each child to estimate which container will hold all the strawberries. Then have volunteers put strawberries in each container, in turn, to determine which one is the correct choice!

Litsa Jackson
Covington Integrated Arts Academy
Covington, TN

Save the Strawberries!
Counting
Slugs love to eat the farmer's strawberries! Youngsters help the farmer get rid of the slugs in this entertaining game. Roll several pieces of play dough (slugs) and place them on a strawberry cutout (enlarge the pattern on page 252). In turn, each player rolls a die and removes the indicated number of slugs, saying "Slimy slugs!" each time he does so. Play continues until all the slugs have been removed.

Judy Spradlin, Tate's School of Discovery
Knoxville, TN

In Disguise
Comparing sets, one-to-one correspondence
Cut out the patterns on several copies of page 252. Read aloud *The Little Mouse, the Red Ripe Strawberry, and the Big Hungry Bear* by Don and Audrey Wood. Then tell the group that they are going to help the mouse disguise lots of strawberries! Have a child choose a number card and place the corresponding number of strawberries in your pocket chart. Have a second child choose another card and place the appropriate number of disguises on the strawberries. Then have students use the words *more, fewer,* and *equal* to discuss the numbers of strawberries and disguises. Finally, if a strawberry was left undisguised, pretend to be a big, hungry bear and eat it up!

Strawberry Pattern

Use with "Save the Strawberries!"
and "In Disguise" on page 251.

TEC41061

Disguise Pattern

Use with "In Disguise" on page 251.

TEC41061

Cool Stuff!

Making a Simple Glyph

New to glyphs? A glyph is a picture that gives the viewer information.

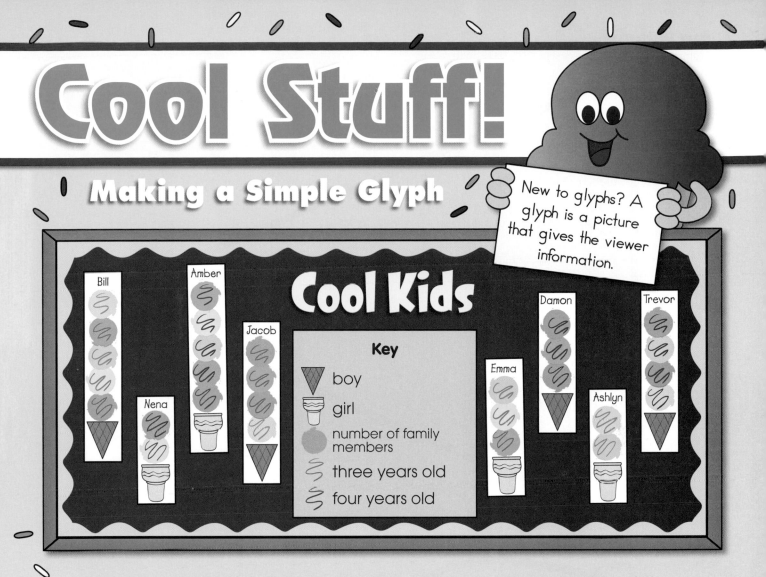

Cool Kids

Key

▽ boy

🍦 girl

⬤ number of family members

〜 three years old

〜 four years old

To prepare for this glyph activity, place the materials at your art table. Then follow the steps to help youngsters construct their glyphs. Finally, display the glyphs along with a key, as shown. That's cool stuff!

Materials:

cone cutouts (patterns on page 254)
class supply of 6" x 18" construction
   paper strips
shallow pans of paint
kitchen scrubber for each pan of paint
squeeze bottle of diluted blue paint
squeeze bottle of diluted pink paint

Steps:

1. Give a child a strip of construction paper. If the child is a boy, have him glue a pointed cone to his paper. If the child is a girl, have her glue a flat-bottomed cone to her paper.
2. Have the student name the number of family members he has. Then encourage him to dip a scrubber in a pan of paint and make a corresponding number of prints (scoops) above the cone.
3. If the child is three years old, have him squeeze blue paint (blueberry sauce) on his scoops. If he is four years old, have him squeeze pink paint (strawberry sauce) on his scoops.
4. Trim the page to match the height of the child's scoops.

Options Aplenty!

For a more complex glyph, consider having youngsters add hole-punch dots in two different colors to represent whether the child has a pet.

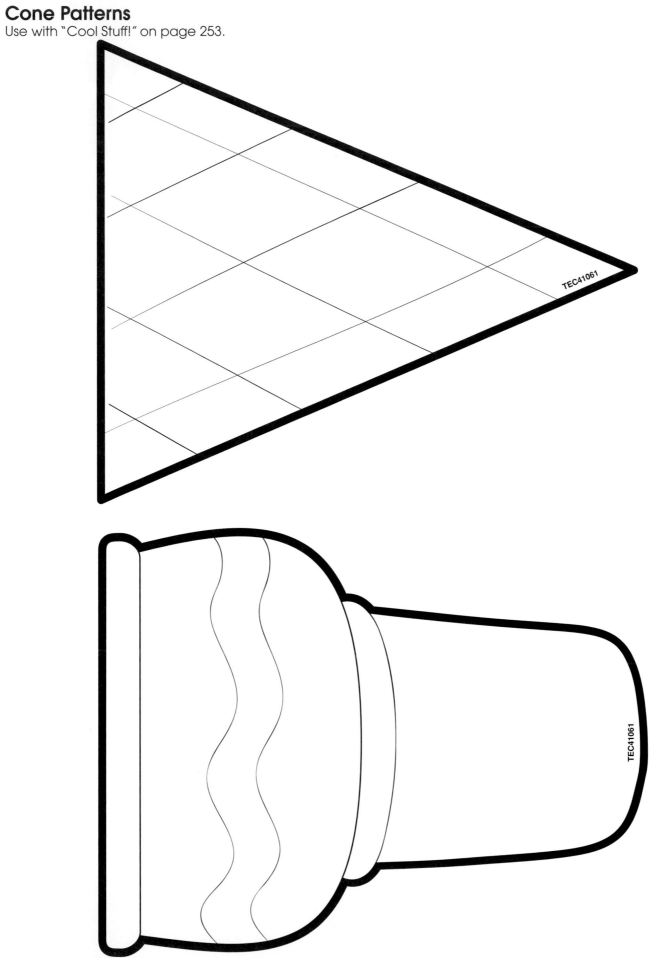

TEC41061

TEC41061

TEACHER RESOURCE UNITS

One, Two, Three— Listen to Me

Little ones learn important listening rules with these fun attention-grabbing tips!

Seasonal Talking Sticks

Reinforce the importance of taking turns listening and speaking with this daily activity. Attach a cute seasonal character cutout to a large craft stick. Each morning, gather students and pass the stick to a child. Invite him to talk about anything for a designated amount of time. Remind his classmates that they are to listen quietly. When the child finishes speaking, direct him to pass the stick to a classmate. Allow a few children to speak each day so all youngsters share at least once throughout the week.

Cathy Wonaitis, St. Anthony Preschool, Frankfort, IL

Mouse Tales

Encourage little ones to be quiet as mice during storytime! Set a small stuffed mouse near the storytime area. Tell youngsters that Miss Mouse loves to listen to stories, but she has small ears. They need to be very quiet during storytime so she can hear the stories too. If youngsters become too loud during storytime, simply remind the group that Miss Mouse can't hear the story.

Mary Lavelle, Richard G. Rosenthal JCC, Cortlandt Manor, NY

Stop or Go

Prepare an octagon-shape sign like the one shown and laminate it for durability. Place the sign in the arms of a stuffed toy critter. When it is time for youngsters to listen during an activity, display the sign so the red side is showing. When it is time for students to actively partic- ipate, turn the sign so the green side is showing. At the end of the activity, have the critter give each child a high five to celebrate students following its directions.

Marianne Cerra, Riverside Elementary, Reading, PA

Who's Listening?

Obtain an owl puppet or create one by gluing an owl cutout to a large craft stick. When youngsters need to listen, hold the owl. Make the owl "fly" around the group and ask students, "'Whoooo' is listening?" Little ones will quickly ready themselves to listen.

Amy Jandebeur, Frogs to Fairy Dust, Yukon, OR

Join In!

Get youngsters' attention with just a whisper! When you need students to listen, whisper, "If you can hear me, touch your nose." The students who hear you join you in doing the action. Continue, substituting different actions, until all the youngsters are paying attention!

Jessie Gilbert, Cesar A. Batalla Elementary, Bridgeport, CT

A Special Spot

Celebrate little ones' listening skills during circle time. At a desired place in your circle-time area, attach a large decorated and laminated star cutout to the floor. At the beginning of circle time, invite a child, who is listening and ready to begin, to sit on the star during the activity. Youngsters will work hard to earn a chance to sit on this special spot.

adapted from an idea by Cheryl Brumbaugh
Tussey Learning Center, Saxton, PA

Jingle, Jingle

Invite students to take control of the noise level in the classroom with this nonverbal cue. For each student center, string a few jumbo jingle bells on a pipe cleaner, twist the ends of the pipe cleaner together, and secure the ends with tape. Place each set of bells at a center and explain to students that they can only shake the bells when they feel that it is too noisy in the room. When youngsters hear the bells, they lower the noise level and continue with center play.

Jean Gentile, Prairieview School, Hainesville, IL

Now, That's Unique!

Art Tips, Solutions, and Activities

Channeling van Gogh

Youngsters get inspiration from a starry night for this engaging art activity. Show students an image of Vincent van Gogh's *Starry Night*. (Hint: An Internet image search of the painting will give you plenty of options.) Ask little ones how Vincent van Gogh painted his sky, leading them to notice that he made little dashes of color. Next, have each student cut a wavy line across a sheet of paper. Have her glue one piece of the paper and a precut black cypress tree cutout to a sheet of construction paper. (Save the scraps for other art projects.) Then encourage her to use chalk or pastels to decorate the sky and hills as desired, prompting her to make dashes of color just as Vincent van Gogh did!

Stephanie Haden
Chestnut Grove Baptist Church Preschool
Earlysville, VA

Looking for a way to keep your easel clean? Try wrapping it with Glad Press 'n Seal wrap before attaching paper to the easel. You'll never have to scrub your easel again! This helpful tip comes from Jennette Harren at North Phoenix Baptist Preschool and Kindergarten in Phoenix, Arizona!

Expanded Easel Space

If you need more easel space or don't have an easel at all, then this tip is for you! Simply attach a vinyl shower curtain to a wall and tape three or more sheets of paper to the shower curtain. Each child stands in front of a sheet of paper and paints. Simply wipe down the shower curtain when he's through or, after a particularly enthusiastic painting session, throw the curtain in the washer to ready it for the next art session.

Melissa Dooley, Discovery Church Preschool, Clayton, NC

Artist of the Day!

Remove the glass from a large, colorful picture frame (or use a tagboard frame cutout) and attach the frame to your wall. Display a title above the frame that says "Artist of the Day!" Then tape a piece of art inside the frame along with a card naming the child who made the artwork. What a simple way to build self-esteem and decorate your classroom!

Linda Tharp, Hickory Child Development Center, Bel Air, MD

Logan Essa

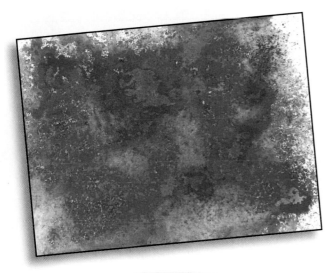

Drip, Drip, Drip!

Is it raining outside? Gather powdered tempera paint, spoons, and a large piece of poster board. Have students put on their rain gear. Then take them outside in a sheltered area and encourage each child to sprinkle a spoonful of tempera paint onto the poster board. Carefully move the poster board out of the sheltered area and encourage youngsters to watch as the rain transforms the powdered paint. Lovely!

Dawne Schmid, Sendcaa Head Start, Fargo, ND

Make paint scrapers like Evonrose Todd of Mid Cities Head Start in Euless, Texas, does! She collects old plastic gift cards and uses scissors to trim one edge into a pattern. Little ones use the cards to scrape paint across paper, making unique designs!

Painting by Ear

Give each child a piece of paper that has been folded in half and unfolded. Play a recording of slow music and encourage each child to draw on only one half of the paper, paying special attention to how the music makes him feel. Repeat the process with fast music and the remaining half. Then display the resulting artwork with music note cutouts and the title "Painting by Ear."

Marianne Cerra, Riverside Elementary, Reading, PA

7 Terrific Transitions and Time Fillers!

1 Teddy Time: Keep youngsters focused and actively engaged as they line up. Hand a stuffed toy bear to a child. Recite the chant, prompting her to quickly pass the bear to a classmate and then line up. Have students continue in the same fashion. Direct the last child to pass the bear to you, signaling you to line up!

> Listen, friends: it's teddy time.
> Please pass the bear and get in line!

Tammy Maijala, Kingdom Kids Christian Preschool, Rochester, MN

2 Lunch Hunch: Here's an idea that's sure to produce lots of gasps and giggles as students transition to lunch or snacktime. To begin, say, "I'm so hungry I could eat an elephant!" Then encourage each child to repeat the sentence, substituting his own bizarre food or nonfood item. What fun!

Susie May, Community Christian School, Orange, TX

3 Perfectly Portable: This transition aid helps kids develop critical-thinking skills and is portable! Write thought-provoking questions on index cards. Store the cards on a metal ring or in a small box. Then read one of the questions aloud during transition time and encourage youngsters to brainstorm answers.

What things are green?

How can you help keep the classroom clean?

Sue Reppert
Widening World Preschool
Mentor, OH

4 **Busy Box:** This transition tool keeps youngsters independently busy in a meaningful way. For each child, fill a plastic pencil case or another container with several items, such as finger puppets, pipe cleaners, a minibook, and a memo pad and crayons. When there's a period of wait time, keep little ones busy with their busy boxes!

Julie Haskins
TLC's Small Blessings Child Care & Preschool
Tulelake, CA

5 **Transition Train:** Help students stay on track to the playground and back! Pretend to be a train conductor. Blow a toy train whistle and then call each student (passenger) to board an imaginary train. Prompt youngsters to perform locomotive motions and sounds as the train travels to its destination. Upon arrival, blow the whistle again, signaling passengers to disembark. Repeat for the return trip.

Michele McDaniel, Michele's House Childcare and Learning Center, Earlham, IA

6 **Sensory Sock:** Conceal a classroom item in a sock. Walk around with the sock and ask each child to feel the hidden object but keep thoughts about its identity to himself. After each child has had a turn, invite youngsters to tell what they think the item is. Then remove the object from the sock to see whether anyone guessed correctly.

Katie Fils, West Point Child Learning Center, Lansdale, PA

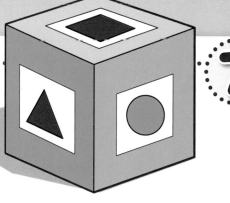

7 **Dandy Die:** Use self-adhesive Velcro fasteners to attach skill builders to each side of a small square box. For example, you could attach cards programmed with colors, shapes, numbers, letters, or pictures. To dismiss a child from the group, roll the die to her and encourage her to identify what lands on top. The Velcro fasteners make it easy to change the cards and extend or switch skills!

Brandy Groves
Shasta Head Start-Enterprise Center
Redding, CA

5 Simple Storage Solutions

1 Perfect Portfolios

Pizza boxes are perfect for storing youngsters' work. Ask the owner of a local pizzeria if he would be willing to donate unused pizza boxes. Label the front edge of each box with a different child's name and then tuck his work inside. Pizza boxes are lightweight and uniform, making them easy to stack and store. *Davan Howe, Julies Storybook Nursery, Westhampton, NY*

2 Recycled Jugs

Here's an earth-friendly storage tip that's great for craft items or for storing student materials on classroom shelves. Simply cut the tops off clean plastic milk containers, leaving the handles intact. Reinforce the cut edges with masking tape, fill each container with desired items, and add a label identifying the contents. *Rexann Roussel, Narrow Acres Preschool, Paulina, LA*

3 Easy Ways With Displays!

To store letters and ideas for displays, snap a photo of a display before taking it down. Place the labeling materials in the pocket of a shoe organizer and attach the photo to the pocket. Repeat with individual pockets for different displays. The organizer takes up minimal space and keeps everything in one convenient location! *Donna Ream, Ms. Donna's Daycare, Plainfield, IL*

4 Terrific Totes

Household cleaning totes are great for storing and transporting center materials. Activity items can be organized in individual totes and placed on shelves or in bookcases. These portable centers can be taken from a shelf to a table, the floor, or even the outdoors! *Karen Smith, Little Tid-Bits, Fresno, CA*

5 Nifty Puzzle Boxes

This storage solution keeps puzzle pieces from getting lost. Cut the picture from a puzzle box and use clear packing tape to attach it to the lid of a plastic pencil box. Then store the puzzle pieces inside. The boxes are sturdy and stackable and youngsters can easily open and close them. *Jessica Pitt, Pittsburgh Banksville PreK–5, Pittsburgh, PA*

Squish, Squeeze, and Create!

Play Dough Possibilities

Tropical Treasure Dough

Enjoy a soothing tropical scent while making and playing with this dough! Mix the ingredients in a large saucepan. Cook the mixture over medium heat, stirring continually, until a ball forms. Cool the dough on a hard surface; then knead it until it's smooth. For added fun, mix in gold glitter or sequins during the kneading process!

3 c. flour
3 c. salt
3 c. water
3 tsp. cream of tartar
3 tsp. vegetable oil
2 to 3 tsp. coconut extract
yellow food coloring

Mary Keyes, Bears Preschool, Columbus, OH

Joyful Dough

For a timesaving, great smelling, noncook play dough, try this recipe! In a large bowl, mix the ingredients shown. (Hint: Add more water for a desired consistency.) Store in an airtight container or a resealable plastic bag.

5 c. flour
1 c. salt
1 c. Joy dish detergent
   (ultra concentrated)
1¼ c. water
3 tsp. vegetable oil
food coloring

Lidia Toledo
Small Blessings
Tampa, FL

Paper Pulp Dough

What a clever way to recycle construction paper scraps! Put the paper scraps and water in a blender. Grate the mixture for 30 seconds, liquefy it for 45 seconds, and then pour it into a large bowl. Mix in the gelatin and salt; then slowly add the flour until the dough reaches a desired consistency. Store the dough in a refrigerator.

1½ c. water
1 c. torn construction
   paper scraps
2 c. flour
1 c. salt
1 small package
   sugar-free gelatin

Evonrose Todd
Mid Cities Head Start
Euless, TX

Squeeze Dough

To make this squeezable dough, mix together one cup of flour, a half cup of salt, food coloring, and water to create a toothpaste-like consistency. Put the mixture in a wide-tip squeeze bottle. Make several colors, if desired. Youngsters can squeeze the dough onto a paper plate and manipulate it. Or they can squeeze it onto a tagboard shape and then add craft materials, such as pom-poms, sequins, buttons, and feathers. Allow several days for the dough to dry.

Amy D'Agostino, Syracuse, NY

5 Playful Pom-pom Possibilities

Looking for creative ways to use pom-poms? Try these nifty ideas for those fuzzy craft companions!

1 Put a supply of colorful pom-poms in a bag. Spill the pom-poms onto the floor and chant, "Fuzzy pom-poms all around. Pick the [color name] ones off the ground!" Prompt youngsters to put the designated-color pom-poms in the bag. *Donna Ream, Ms. Donna's Daycare, Plainfield, IL*

2 Hot-glue small magnets to pom-poms. Place the pom-poms near a magnetic board along with letter, number, or shape cards. Encourage a youngster to choose a card and make a three-dimensional copy of the symbol on the card by attaching pom-poms to the magnetic board. *Donna Ream*

3 Invite each child to glue a brown craft foam circle (pancake) to a paper plate. Have her squeeze pancake syrup (or brown-tinted glue) onto the pancake and then press red and blue pom-poms (berries) in the syrup. Finally, have her glue a plastic fork to the plate. *Janella Mehmen, First Kids Preschool and Child Care, Cedar Falls, IA*

4 Stack number cards from one suit of a deck of playing cards facedown along with the joker cards. Place a large supply of red pom-poms (cherries) on a tree cutout. Gather two or three youngsters. In turn, each student flips a card, identifies the number, and "picks" that many cherries from the tree. Then he sets the card aside. When a joker is picked, the player must put two cherries back on the tree. When all the cards have been played, the player with the most cherries wins! *Jennifer Gemar, Tripp-Delmont School District, Tripp, SD*

5 Trace a different shape on each of several index cards; then glue mini pom-poms to each shape outline as shown. Instruct a student to close her eyes as you place a card in front of her. Then have her feel the tactile shape and guess what it is! *Marianne Cerra, St. Ignatius R. C. School, Sinking Spring, PA*

THEMATIC UNITS

Welcome to PRESCHOOL

Apples Aplenty!

This fabulous welcome unit focuses on that well-known educational symbol—the apple!

ideas contributed by Margaret Aumen, Emory United Methodist Nursery School, New Oxford, PA

Jada

Lorenzo

Emma

Where's My Apple?

Getting acquainted

Label apple cutouts (see the large apple pattern on page 268) with youngsters' names and scatter the apples on the floor. Get a basket. Gather youngsters around the apples and recite the couplet below, inserting a student's name. Prompt students to reply with the couplet shown. Then encourage the child to find her apple and put it in the basket. Continue in the same way with other students' names.

Teacher: All these apples fell from the tree.
Where can [child's name]'s apple be?
Students: [Child's name], [child's name], look around.
Find your apple on the ground.

Who's Here?

Attendance

This adorable display won't take up a lot of valuable wall space! Personalize a jumbo craft stick for each child and draw a smile on each stick, as shown, so the stick resembles a worm. (If desired, spray-paint the sticks green before labeling.) Attach the loop side of a Velcro fastener piece to the back of each worm. Make a large poster board apple cutout and securely attach it to your wall. Then attach the hook side of the Velcro fastener pieces to the apple cutout. Before youngsters arrive each day, place the worms on a table. Each child finds his worm and attaches it to the apple. If you want youngsters to transition to using a sign-in sheet, have them use their worms as guides to help them write their names.

Anita

Tameka

Justin

Ben

Juan

Caroline

Suna

Apple Stack

Storytime

In advance, cut out ten copies of the apple cards on page 268 and attach each apple to a block. Read aloud *Ten Apples Up on Top!* by Theo. LeSieg. In this story, three friends compete with each other to see how many apples they can balance on their heads. Next, hold up a number card and identify the number. Then say, "Stack [number] apples up on top." Have a child stack the appropriate number of apple blocks. Then say, "Let the apples drop!" prompting the child to knock down the stack. Continue with other numbers.

 **See page 269 for a fun reproducible activity!**

On the Tree, on the Ground

Fingerplay

Lead youngsters in reciting this adorable action rhyme!

I went to an apple orchard—what did I see?	*Point to self. Put hand above eyes.*
Apples high up in a tree!	*Point up.*
I went to an apple orchard—guess what I found!	*Point to self. Place hands out with palms up.*
Apples down low on the ground.	*Point down.*
Reach up high.	*Stand on tiptoes and put hands in air.*
Bend down low.	*Touch toes.*
Gather the apples.	*Clap to the beat.*
Then home we go!	

Seeing Double!

Process art

To make this project, fold a sheet of white construction paper in half and then unfold it. Tint water dark red and then place a coffee filter in the water. Soak it for several seconds to let it absorb the color. Then remove the filter and let it drip over the container for a few seconds. Place it on one half of the prefolded paper. Then refold the paper and smooth it with your hands. Unfold the paper and remove the coffee filter to reveal the project. When the paper is dry, add stem and leaf cutouts.

Marie E. Cecchini, West Dundee, IL

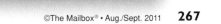

Large Apple Pattern
Use with "Where's My Apple?"
on page 266.

TEC41056

Apple Cards
Use with "Apple Stack" on page 267.

TEC41056

TEC41056

©The Mailbox® • TEC41056 • Aug./Sept. 2011

Apples Aplenty!

Note to the teacher: Have a child place a dot of glue above the cat's head. Then have her press a pom-pom (apple) in the glue. Encourage her to continue until the cat has a stack of apples above her head. (Crumpled red tissue paper can be glued or bingo dauber marks can be used instead of gluing pom-poms.)

Above My Head, Below My Feet

Excellent Earth Science Explorations

Plink!

Counting

With this activity, youngsters make marvelous rain sounds! Get a metal bucket and blue linking cubes (or small blocks) to represent raindrops. Say, "It is so rainy today! I heard five raindrops fall." Prompt a child to count five raindrops and drop them in the bucket one by one, listening to the sound they make as they hit the bottom. Continue with several youngsters. Then pick up the bucket, recognizing with great dramatic flair the heavy rain they've collected!

Bonnie C. Krum, St. Matthew's Early Education Center, Bowie, MD

What Do You See?

Writing

To begin, explain that people long ago would look at the sky and think that the stars looked like animals or people, forming constellations. Have each child attach star stickers to a sheet of black construction paper. Then encourage her to use a white crayon to connect the stars as desired. (For extra flair, have her trace the lines with glue and shake silver glitter on the glue.) Next, prompt her to rotate her paper until she decides what her constellation looks like. Write her words on the page.

Gail Farmer, Kiddie Kampus of Medford, Medford, NY

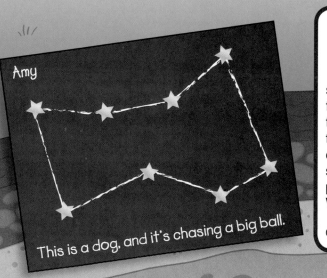

Amy

This is a dog, and it's chasing a big ball.

Do your youngsters love glitter? Try sprinkling some in the sand in your sand table to make moon sand! Simply add a variety of random manipulatives and encourage youngsters to explore. (idea contributed by Carissa Stricklen, Discover Kids, Maple Plain, MN)

Lots of Drops!

Exploring science through art

Youngsters investigate water with this rain-themed process art! Provide diluted tempera paint and a variety of objects that can make drops, such as toothpicks, drinking straws, paintbrushes, eyedroppers, teaspoons, and craft sticks. A child dips one of the objects in the paint and then allows the paint to drip on her paper. She continues with other objects, noting that the items produce drops of different sizes and shapes.

Marie E. Cecchini, West Dundee, IL

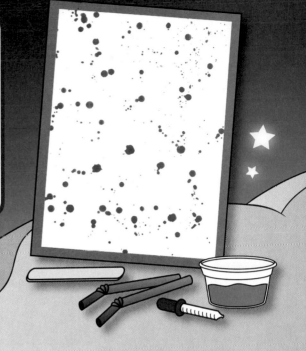

Rock Excavation

Developing fine-motor skills

In advance, place play dough in separate trays and then bury rocks in the play dough. Provide craft sticks, tweezers, tongs, and magnifying glasses. Encourage youngsters to use the tools to dig through the play dough and remove the rocks. Then prompt them to use the magnifying glass to view their finds.

Roxanne LaBell Dearman, Western NC Early Intervention Program for Children Who Are Deaf or Hard of Hearing, Charlotte, NC

The Scoop on Dirt

Making comparisons

Does all dirt look alike? Little ones find out with this fun activity! Send home with each youngster a copy of a parent letter on page 273 along with a small resealable plastic bag and a plastic spoon. When youngsters bring their soil samples back, gather a small group of students and prompt each child to empty his soil on a white sheet of paper. Encourage him to use a magnifying glass and tweezers to explore his soil. Then prompt him to look at his classmates' samples, leading him to notice that the samples look different!

Suzanne Moore, Tucson, AZ

Munching the Moon

Responding to a story

Read aloud *Mooncake* by Frank Asch. In the story, a bear wants to taste the moon. He falls asleep in his rocket ship and wakes up during wintertime. He thinks he is on the moon, tastes the snow, and decides the moon is delicious! Give each child a sheet of black paper with a circle drawn on it in white crayon. Encourage each student to paint the circle with a mixture of white paint and flour. Then have him press a bottle cap in the mixture several times to make craters. If desired, have him press star stickers on the paper. Then have him glue a spoon to the project. Encourage him to dictate what he believes the moon would taste like.

Evan

I think the moon tastes like macaroni and cheese.

Weather Report

Participating in a rhyme, observing

For your morning weather report, encourage students to look out the window. Then lead them in reciting this rhyme, inserting a child's name in the final line. Encourage the named student to discuss the current weather!

We've been looking out the window for a long, long time,
Checking out the weather as we say this rhyme.
Do you see the sun shine?
Is there rain or snow?
[Child's name], won't you tell us
How our day will go?

Deb Solan, Wesley Hall Nursery School, Westfield, NJ

No-Grow Garden

Creating a sense of pride and responsibility

Designate a small outdoor area (around the size of a bathmat) for a rock garden. Fill the area with white rocks from a garden center. Then ask each child to bring a rock from home to add to the rock garden. Encourage students to visit the rock garden during outdoor play, pulling any weeds and rearranging the rocks as desired. Emphasize that any rocks brought in throughout the year can be added to the rock garden.

Marie E. Cecchini,
   West Dundee, IL
Erin McGinness,
   Great New Beginnings, Bear, DE

tip For another option, partially fill a plastic tub with soil to use as an indoor rock garden!

Preschool Rock Garden

Dear Family,

We're studying earth science! Please have your child place three spoonfuls of dirt in this plastic bag and return the bag to school by _____.
date

We are going to compare and contrast our samples!

All the best,

_____

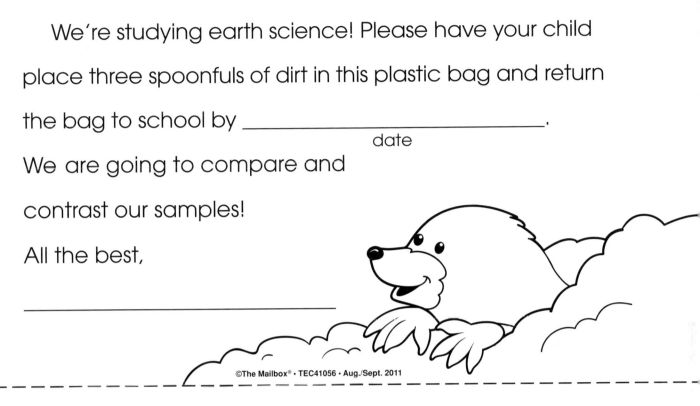

©The Mailbox® • TEC41056 • Aug./Sept. 2011

Dear Family,

We're studying earth science! Please have your child place three spoonfuls of dirt in this plastic bag and return the bag to school by _____.
date

We are going to compare and contrast our samples!

All the best,

_____

©The Mailbox® • TEC41056 • Aug./Sept. 2011

Note to the teacher: Use with "The Scoop on Dirt" on page 271.

Sensational Spiders!

These wondrous web makers are sure to fascinate your little ones.

Legs, Eyes, and Flies!

Tracking print from left to right, investigating living things

Here's an adorable booklet that reminds little ones of important spider facts! Give each youngster a copy of pages 276 and 277. Guide each student through the steps below. Then help her cut out the booklet pages and bind them together with a cover titled "Super Spiders!" Give each child a spider ring and encourage her to place it on an index finger. Then read the booklet pages aloud as she follows the text from left to right with her spider!

Page 1: Draw eight legs on the spider. Color the page.
Page 2: Draw eight eyes on your spider (or glue eight mini wiggly eyes on the spider). Color the page.
Page 3: Trace the dotted line. Color the page.
Page 4: Make fingerprints on the web. Draw wings on the fingerprints. Color the page.

A spider has eight legs. 1

It can also have eight eyes. 2

It spins a web so it can catch 3

Some tasty juicy flies. 4

Webs and Blocks

Developing spatial skills

Place fake spiderwebs and plastic spiders in your block center. Then encourage little ones to visit the center and build block structures, stretching the webs over their structures and placing plastic spiders on the webs.

Carissa Dwyer
Discovery Kids Preschool
Maple Plain, MN

Black Spider, Orange Spider
Patterning

This oversize patterning activity is perfect for a Halloween celebration or a fall festival! Place separate mesh scrubbers (or bath puffs) next to two shallow containers of paint. Gather two or three youngsters and give each child a large strip of bulletin board paper or newsprint. The child makes prints with the scrubbers in an *AB* pattern. When the paint is dry, she adds eight legs and eye stickers or cutouts to each print. These patterning projects make lovely classroom decorations!

That's Silly!
Participating in a song

Make a simple spider stick puppet. Then lead students in singing the song shown, inserting the name of a child and manipulating the stick puppet appropriately so it rests on the child's head, wiggles down her shoulder, and jumps to the floor. Repeat the song several times with different volunteers.

(sung to the tune of "The Itsy-Bitsy Spider")

The silly-willy spider
Crawls up on [child's name]'s head!
It crawls all around
And makes a nice soft bed.
It wiggles down [her] shoulder
And jumps down to the floor.
Then the silly-willy spider
Crawls off to play some more!

Norinne Weeks, Carrillo Elementary, Houston, TX

Spool Spiders
Developing fine-motor skills

These crafts look adorable perched on classroom shelves. Gather a wooden spool for each youngster. (Packs of wooden spools are available at craft stores and through online retailers.) A child paints a spool black. When the paint is dry, he threads four pipe cleaner pieces through the hole in the spool. Then he bends the pipe cleaners so they resemble legs. Finally, he glues mini wiggle eyes or eye stickers to the spool.

Darci Henning, Grinnell Full Day Head Start, Grinnell, IA

Looking for an excellent nonfiction book about spiders that's preschool friendly? Try *Are You a Spider?* by Judy Allen. You're sure to love the engaging text and fabulous illustrations!

2

It can also have eight eyes.

1

A spider has eight legs.

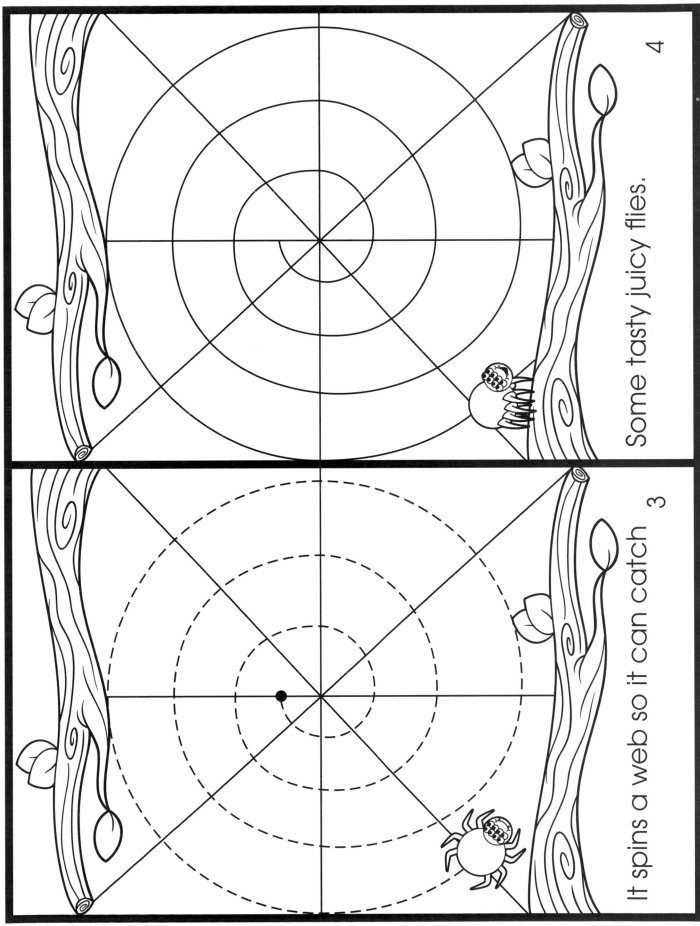

4

Some tasty juicy flies.

It spins a web so it can catch 3

It's Time to Harvest!

Apples, corn, pumpkins! These engaging harvest-themed activities will have your little ones feeling particularly pleased with fabulous fall produce!

Write a Recipe
Writing

Your little chefs will love to make tasty fall recipes with these fabulous harvest foods! Place at a center typical fall fruits and vegetables, such as a pumpkin, a squash, an apple, a potato, a yam, and an ear of corn. Cut out copies of the recipe cards on page 281 and place them at the table along with writing utensils. Also provide plastic mixing bowls, baking pans, aprons, empty seasoning shakers, food magazines, and kitchen utensils. Little ones "write" recipes that have the harvest foods as ingredients and then pretend to make the foods. Mmmm, tasty!

adapted from an idea by Ann Miller
Ann's Bright Beginnings Preschool
Paulding, OH

Be the Scarecrow
Participating in dramatic play, fine-motor skills

Provide scarecrow dress-up clothing, such as overalls, large jeans with rope belts, plaid shirts, and straw hats. Decorate a center with pumpkins, gourds, and crow cutouts (pattern on page 281). Also provide a mirror. Youngsters dress themselves as scarecrows. Then they admire themselves in the mirror, making their scariest faces to scare crows away from the fall produce!

Darci Henning
Grinnell Full Day Head Start
Grinnell, IA

Colorful Produce

Responding to a story through art

Read aloud the book *Red Are the Apples* by Marc Harshman and Cheryl Ryan. In this story, a child explores fall on the farm, highlighting everything from orange pumpkins and purple eggplants to yellow corn and white beans. Have youngsters make artwork that resembles a bird's-eye view of all these fabulous fruits and vegetables. Provide several shallow containers of paint in colors found in the story. Place a piece of sponge by each container. Have each child sponge-paint a piece of Bubble Wrap cushioning material with several colors of paint. Then have her press a brown sheet of construction paper on the painted surface and remove the paper to reveal the print. How lovely!

adapted from an idea by Keely Saunders
Bonney Lake Early Childhood Educational Assistance Program
Bonney Lake, WA

Pumpkins on the Move!

Positional words, listening

This adorable action chant will produce lots of giggles in your classroom! Give each child a miniature pumpkin or a pumpkin cutout and have her sit in a chair. Then guide youngsters in performing this chant, moving their pumpkins as described in each line.

I have a pumpkin in front of me.
I think I'll put it on my knee!
Then I'll hide it under my chair.
Can you see it under there?

I'll take it out so I can put
That pretty pumpkin on my foot.
Then off my foot and in my hair.
My, it looks so nice up there!

Out to the side! Up in the air!
Is that a pumpkin way up there?
Down to the ground my pumpkin lands.
I pull it up with my two hands.

Behind my back my pumpkin goes.
Where can it be? Nobody knows!
Here it is for all to see.
It's right back here in front of me!

Kathryn Badger
P. I. Dunbar Elementary
Laurel, DE

tip This rhyme works for other seasons and props! Repeat this activity in the winter with a snowman cutout, in the spring with a flower, and in the summer with an unused flip-flop or a beach ball cutout!

Corn Comparison
Measurement

In advance, get three ears of corn. Then gather youngsters around and give each ear of corn to a different child. Set a timer for several seconds and encourage each child to find something that is shorter than the ear of corn before the timer rings. Have students hold up the objects for all to see. Then give the ears of corn to three different youngsters. If desired, have students find objects that are longer than the ears of corn.

Harvest Moon
Arts and crafts

These nifty harvest moons make an excellent room decoration for the fall season. Explain to little ones that a harvest moon is a big round moon that we see in the sky near the first day of fall. To make this fall moon art, give each child a piece of waxed paper with a circle drawn on it. Have students dip lengths of white yarn in diluted white glue and then lay the yarn on the circle, overlapping the pieces whenever possible. When several lengths of yarn have been placed, press a black bat on the moist yarn. Then sprinkle iridescent glitter on the yarn. After the glue is dry, remove the waxed paper.

Keely Saunders
Bonney Lake Early Childhood Educational Assistance Program
Bonney Lake, WA

tip → Display these sparkly moons on a wall with the title "Shine On, Harvest Moon!"

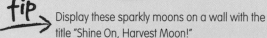

Digging Taters!
Counting

Little ones harvest a pail full of potatoes at this easy-to-prepare center! Bury potatoes in your sand table and provide a pail, garden gloves, and a trowel. Youngsters put on the garden gloves and dig through the sand to find the potatoes. They put each potato they find into the pail. When they've collected them all, they count the potatoes!

Roxanne LaBell Dearman
NC Early Intervention Program for Children Who Are
   Deaf or Hard of Hearing
Charlotte, NC

TEC41057

Crow Pattern
Use with "Be the Scarecrow" on page 278.

Trees, Candles, AND Garland!

Little ones are sure to love this collection of fun seasonal decor-themed activities!

Adorable Ornaments
Developing fine-motor skills

These supersize ornaments will shine brightly in your classroom! Have each child tear and glue pieces of aluminum foil to a small disposable plate. Have her attach colorful strips of paper to the foil. Then trim any foil and paper overlapping the edges. Encourage her to make dots of glue on the project and sprinkle glitter over the glue. Finally, add a pipe cleaner hanger. Then attach these ornaments to your wall or to a simple holiday tree mural such as the one described on page 284.

Keely Saunders, Bonney Lake Early Childhood Educational Assistance Program, Bonney Lake, WA

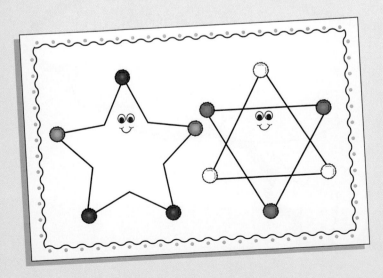

So Many Stars
Counting

Little ones are sure to have seen ornaments and decorations with stars! Have little ones notice the differences between a Christmas tree star and the Star of David with this simple activity. Give students a copy of page 285 and explain that the star usually seen on a Christmas tree has five points. Have each child touch and count each point on the Christmas star, noticing that there are five points. Then explain that the Star of David is a traditional Hanukkah symbol and is seen on many decorations and ornaments. Have students touch and count the points on the Star of David, noticing that there are six. Finally, have little ones glue red and green pom-poms to the points of the Christmas star and blue and white pom-poms to the Star of David. How lovely!

"Tree-mendous" Treetop!
Recalling story events

In advance, make a large evergreen tree cutout. Read aloud *Mr. Willowby's Christmas Tree* by Robert Barry. In this story, Mr. Willowby unknowingly spreads lots of holiday cheer when the top of his oversize Christmas tree is cut off. Next, cut off the top of your tree, just as Mr. Willowby did! Ask students who received the tree top, using the book as a reference if needed. When youngsters identify that it was the maid, cut off the top of the maid's tree. Ask, "Who received the top of the maid's tree?" Continue in the same way, cutting off portions of the tree to show that the gardener, the bear, the fox, the rabbits, and the mice all received portions of the tree.

Dancing Garland
Developing gross-motor and listening skills

For each child, use heavy-duty tape to attach a paper doily (snowflake) to a length of white or silver tinsel garland. Play a recording of soothing music and encourage youngsters to move and sway, gently manipulating the snowflakes as if they are drifting in the air. Stop the music, signaling youngsters to stand still. Then call out, "Snowstorm!" prompting little ones to vigorously shimmy and shake their snowflakes. Restart the music and play several more rounds of this fun game!

Keely Saunders
Bonney Lake Early Childhood Educational Assistance
    Program
Bonney Lake, WA

Candle Count
Identifying numbers, counting, sense of smell

Provide a variety of votive candles and a large muffin tin. A youngster rolls a die, counts out the corresponding number of candles, and smells each one as he places it in a muffin cup. He removes the candles and repeats the process. **For a more challenging option,** provide more candles, a larger muffin tin, and two dice.

Roxanne LaBell Dearman
NC Early Intervention Program for Children
    Who Are Deaf or Hard of Hearing
Charlotte, NC

Tree Mural
Arts and crafts

To make this simple mural, have students sponge-paint a length of bulletin board paper green. When the paint is dry, trim a tree shape from the paper and display it on a wall. Place a variety of collage items in your art center. Then encourage students to visit the center and make things to attach to the tree. You're sure to see a variety of creative and unique ornaments!

Noel Kuhn
Vermont Hills Family Life Center
Portland, OR

Twinkle, Twinkle
Participating in a song

Encourage little ones to "twinkle" their fingers as you lead them in singing this cute holiday song!

(sung to the tune of "Twinkle, Twinkle, Little Star")

Twinkle, twinkle, Christmas lights
Lighting up December nights.
Red and yellow, green and blue,
Making such a lovely view.
Twinkle, twinkle, Christmas lights
Lighting up December nights.

Jennifer Gemar
Tripp-Delmont Schools
Tripp, SD

Where Does It Belong?
Sorting

This splendid sort will have youngsters ready for the holidays! Gather a variety of holiday decorations, including some that go on a tree and some that do not. Label two hoops as shown. Then help youngsters sort the items into the correct hoop. (Keep in mind that some youngsters' families may have traditional tree decorations displayed on a tabletop.)

on the tree

not on the tree

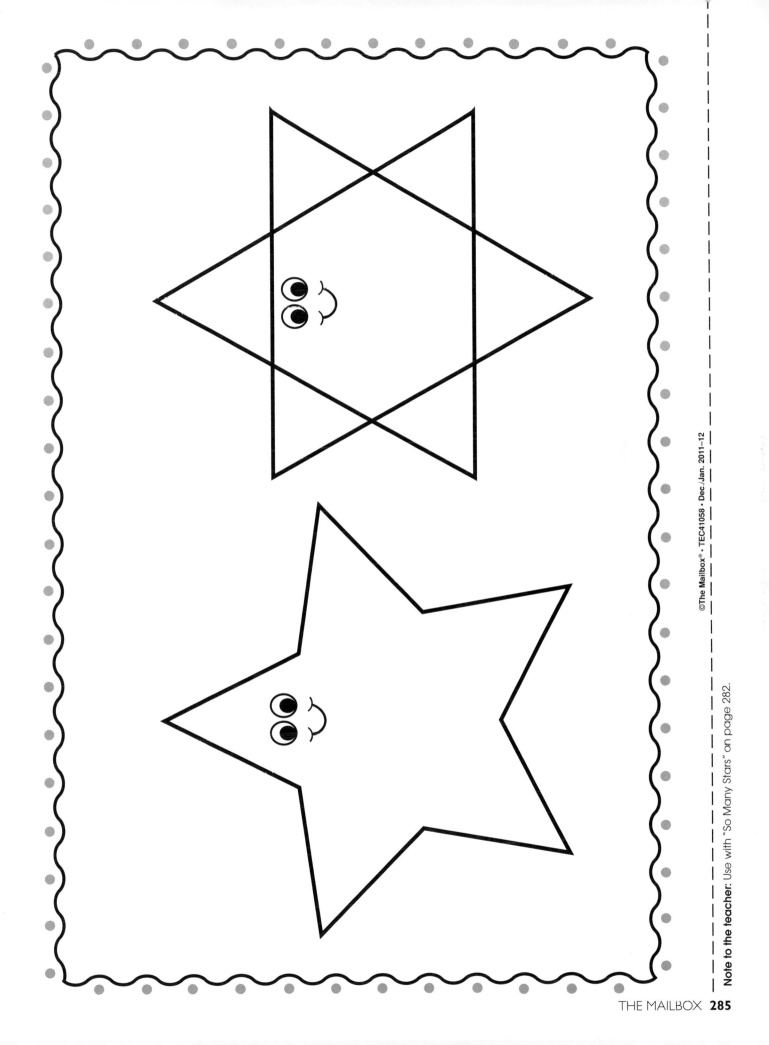

©The Mailbox® • TEC41058 • Dec./Jan. 2011–12

Note to the teacher: Use with "So Many Stars" on page 282.

Wild and Woolly!

Thematic Fun With Lions and Lambs

Watching the Weather
Observing, organizing data, sorting

Youngsters identify lion and lamb weather throughout the month of March! Cut out a supply of the cards on page 288 and place them near a calendar as shown. Briefly explain the adage "March comes in like a lion and goes out like a lamb," meaning that March begins with ferocious weather and ends with gentle weather. Next, have youngsters make a simple two-sided lion and lamb puppet from a small paper plate. Each day throughout the month of March, have students hold up their puppets to reflect the weather and then place an appropriate card on the calendar. At the end of March, have students determine if the saying is true. Then have them remove the cards and sort them, comparing numbers of lion and lamb days.

Jennifer Gemar, Tripp Elementary, Tripp, SD
Janice Minton, Little Husky Childcare & Preschool, Oelwein, IA

So Different!
Opposites, making comparisons

Discuss with youngsters how lions are loud and active, while lambs are quiet and gentle. Next, divide youngsters into two groups: a lion group and a lamb group. Have the lion group complete an active activity, such as tossing beanbags or rolling a ball. Encourage them to growl enthusiastically! Have the lamb group complete a quiet activity with an adult helper, such as manipulating play dough or drawing. Prompt them to baa quietly. Then have youngsters switch groups!

Keely Saunders
Bonney Lake Early Childhood Education and Assistance Program
Bonney Lake, WA

According to the *Farmer's Almanac*, March is a popular month for weather-related sayings. Other sayings used in the past are "A dry March and a wet May? Fill barns and bays with corn and hay" and "As it rains in March so it rains in June."

One or Two?
Counting syllables

Lions and lambs help little ones with this syllable-counting comparison! Draw a simple lion and lamb as shown (or enlarge a lion and lamb from the cards on page 288). Cut out the cards from pages 289 and 290. Place the lion and lamb on the floor and put the cards in a bag. Have a child draw a card from the bag and say the name of the picture. Prompt students to clap the name. If it has two syllables like *lion*, have the child place the card on the lion and then roar. If it has one syllable like *lamb*, have him place it on the lamb and baa. Continue with each remaining card.

tip → The cards show common February and March symbols. As an additional activity, discuss the meanings with your little ones!

Let's Get Moving!
Gross-motor skills

This activity is a great way to get the wiggles out as well as a terrific time filler between activities! Get lion and lamb puppets. (You can also use cutouts or toy figures.) Hold up the lion puppet and encourage students to prowl around the room roaring loudly. Then hold up the lamb puppet and prompt little ones to tiptoe about the room baaing quietly. Continue for several rounds.

Katie Dimitrijevich, YMCA Preschool, Beaver Dam, WI

More Lions? More Lambs?
Comparing sets

Place a mixture of yellow pom-poms (lions) and white pom-poms (lambs) in a container. Gather a small group of youngsters and give each child a sheet of green paper (meadow). Have each child take a handful of pom-poms and place them on her meadow. Encourage her to count her lions and her lambs and then name whether she has more lions or more lambs. **For a more challenging version,** give each child a laminated meadow. When she counts her lions and lambs, encourage her to use a dry-erase marker to write the numbers on her meadow. Then have her erase the numbers and play another round.

Lion and Lamb Cards

Use with "Watching the Weather" on page 286 and "One or Two?" on page 287.

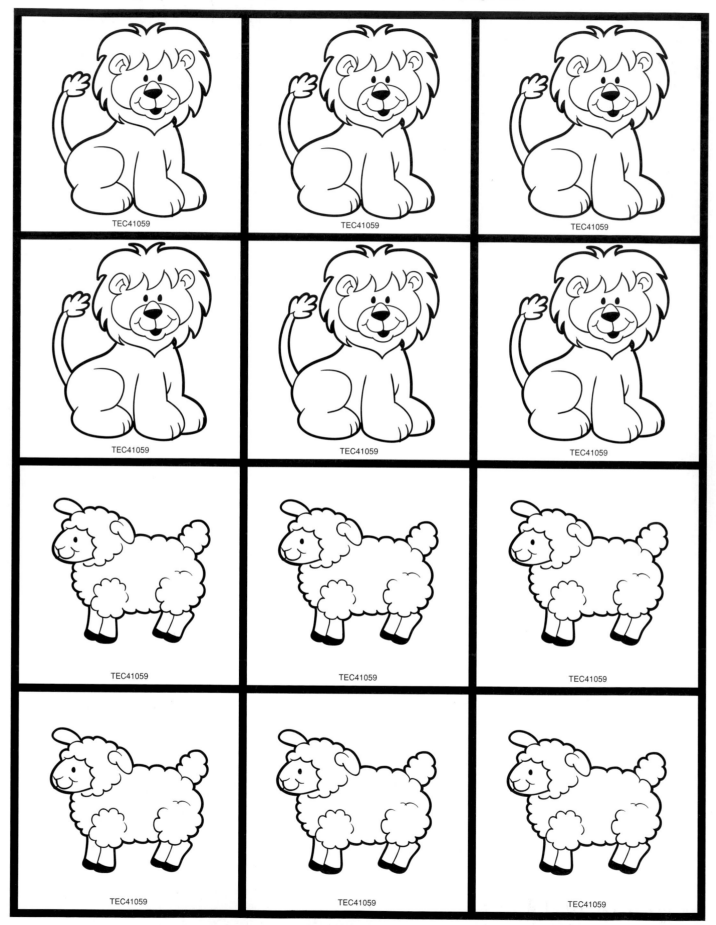

TEC41059
TEC41059
TEC41059
TEC41059
TEC41059
TEC41059
TEC41059
TEC41059
TEC41059
TEC41059
TEC41059
TEC41059

TEC41059

TEC41059

TEC41059

TEC41059

TEC41059

TEC41059

TEC41059

TEC41059

USA FIRST-CLASS FOREVER

Picture Cards

Use with "One or Two?" on page 287.

TEC41059

TEC41059

TEC41059

TEC41059

TEC41059

TEC41059

TEC41059

TEC41059

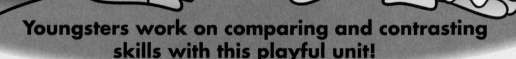

Are They the Same?

Are They Different?

Youngsters work on comparing and contrasting skills with this playful unit!

Two Towers

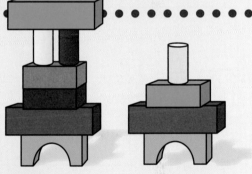

Little ones modify block towers to show their knowledge of same and different! Have little ones observe as you build two identical block towers. Ask, "Are these towers the same?" After students confirm that they are, encourage a child to modify your constructions to make the towers different. After several rounds of this game, place the blocks at a center and encourage pairs of children to repeat the activity.

Suzanne Moore, Tuscan, AZ

They're All Oranges!

Lead students in singing this catchy little ditty! Then display several oranges. Have students identify how the oranges are the same. Then prompt them to notice the subtle differences between the oranges.

(sung to the tune of "My Bonnie Lies Over the Ocean")

My mother brought home lots of oranges
For my hungry family to eat.
She told me to find one that's different,
But they're all the same type of treat!
Oranges, oranges—the oranges are orange, you see, you see!
Oranges, oranges—the oranges are orange, you see!

But then I stopped thinking of color.
Which orange was the biggest of all?
I sorted them by different sizes.
Some oranges were big; some were small!
Oranges, oranges—the oranges were different, you see, you see!
Oranges, oranges—the oranges were different, you see!

Suzanne Moore

Pick Two!

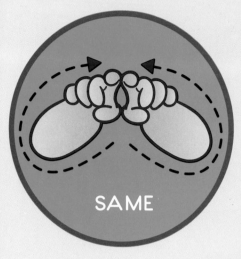

SAME

Here's an idea that combines the concepts of same and different with American Sign Language! Place small items in a container, making sure that several of the items are the same. Have a youngster choose two items that are different. Have him hold up the items. Then ask the remaining youngsters, "Are they the same or different?" using the signs as you speak. Prompt students to answer the question using the appropriate sign. Repeat the process, having a student choose two items that are the same!

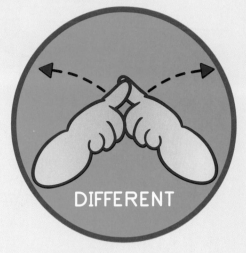

DIFFERENT

Alyson Flanagan, Riverton School, Riverton, NJ
Kelly Tincher, Manson Northwest Webster School, Barnum, IA

That One Is Different!

different

same

Place a set of manipulatives at a table along with a paper labeled as shown. A child places the same manipulatives in the area on the paper labeled "same" and then he chooses a different manipulative to place in the circle. Finally, he points to the paper and says, "These are the same, and this one is different." Then he repeats the activity with other manipulatives.

Donna Ream
Ms. Donna's Daycare
Plainfield, IL

Here's a twist on the idea!
Consider giving students individual programmed papers and having them make prints with rubber stamps to identify same and different!

Old Ladies

Have little ones compare old ladies with odd eating habits! Get two different copies of the traditional tale *There Was an Old Lady Who Swallowed a Fly*, such as the two shown. Read aloud each version and then place the books on the floor. Name a detail from one of the books that is *different* from the other. Then have a child swat the book that contains that detail. Then name a detail that is the *same* in both books, prompting a child to swat both of the books. Continue in the same way with other story details.

Michelle Gwinn, Wood County Schools, Parkersburg, WV

How Are They Different?

Note to the teacher: Give each child a copy of this page and discuss how the two dragons are the same and how they are different. If desired, have students color their dragons.

Once Upon a Time...

Fantastic Fairy Tales and Folktales

ideas contributed by Roxanne LaBell Dearman
NC Early Intervention Program for Children Who Are Deaf or Hard of Hearing
Charlotte, NC

B Is for *Beanstalk*

Identifying letter B and its sound

Help little ones identify letter *B* with this small-group activity. After a read-aloud of *Jack and the Beanstalk*, give each child a copy of page 297. Gather letter cards, including several *B*s. Then present a container of craft foam bean cutouts and explain that they are magic beans just like the ones that Jack was given. Hold up a letter card. If the card shows a letter *B*, have each child place a bean on the beanstalk. If not, have youngsters do nothing with the beans. Continue for several rounds.

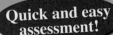

Quick and easy assessment!

Small, Medium, and Large

Ordering by size

After a storytime session featuring *Goldilocks and the Three Bears*, gather a small group of youngsters around a supply of brown play dough and wiggle eyes in three different sizes. Have each child make balls of play dough in three different sizes to represent the three bears. Then have her attach appropriately sized eyes to the bears. Finally, have her order her bears from small to large and identify them by size. After the assessment, store the wiggle eyes for safekeeping.

Linda Utley
Little Pals Preschool
Herriman, UT

Who Will Help?
Rhyming
Cut out the cards on pages 298 and 299, and attach each one to a simple bread slice cutout. Gather paper plates. Read aloud a version of *The Little Red Hen.* Then place a few of the bread slices on the floor and place the matching slices near you. Hold up a slice of bread and say, "Who will help me make a sandwich?" Call on a youngster and have him identify the picture, find the slice of bread that shows the rhyme, and then put them together on a paper plate. Continue until all the sandwiches have been made. Then repeat the activity with a different set of bread slices.

Aiming Acorns
Developing gross-motor skills
With this active center idea, little ones pretend to be oak trees! Enlarge the Chicken Little pattern on page 300 and make several copies. Cut out the copies and place them on your floor. Provide a container of brown pom-poms (acorns). A student picks up an acorn and stands near a Chicken Little cutout. Then he attempts to drop the acorn from a standing position, hitting Chicken Little on the head. He continues with each Chicken Little cutout.

For simple acorn-themed process art, have a student spread a thick layer of tinted glue on a sheet of paper. Then have her drop brown pom-poms (acorns) onto the glue. The sky is falling!

The Sky Is Falling!
Participating in a group song
After a read-aloud of *Chicken Little,* gather little ones in a circle to review the plot of the story with this quick and engaging activity!

(sung to the tune of "Ring Around the Rosie")

An acorn falls from a tree;	*Hold hands and walk in a circle.*
The animals are worried!	*Walk in the opposite direction.*
Tell King!	*Stop and drop hands.*
Tell King!	
The sky's falling down!	*Fall to the floor.*

Fairy Tale Fun!
Developing fine-motor skills

Spotlight your fairy tale theme with these whimsical wind-socks! For each child, cut a window and notches from a sheet of gray construction paper so it resembles a crenellated tower. (Depending on the child's fine-motor skills, you may want him to cut out the notches himself.) Encourage him to drizzle or brush glue on the paper and then shake glitter over the glue. Then encourage him to glue streamers to the bottom edge of the paper. Glue a photo of the child wearing a crown to the paper so it shows through the window. Then roll the paper, staple it in place, and add a yarn handle. Too cute!

Bonnie Brandt, Beginnings Learning Center, Santa Monica, CA

Listen Up
Developing listening skills

Enlarge the house pattern on page 300 and make a copy for each child. Then give each young-ster a bingo dauber. During a second reading of *The Three Little Pigs*, have each child make a mark (brick) on her house every time she hears the word *house*. What a fun way to encourage critical-listening skills!

Trip, Trap, Trip, Trap!

These adorable activities go with that classic tale *The Three Billy Goats Gruff*!

- Give youngsters rhythm sticks. Read the story and encourage youngsters to play the sticks each time the goats cross the bridge. ***Taking part in an interactive reading***
- Attach two lines of tape to your floor to repre-sent a bridge. Have students pretend to be goats as they tiptoe, stomp, skip, crawl, march, and gallop across the bridge. ***Developing gross-motor skills***
- Have students dip the feet of plastic animal toys in paint and then walk them across a paper bridge as they say, "Trip, trap, trip, trap." ***Responding to a story through art***

©The Mailbox® • TEC41060 • April/May 2012

Note to the teacher: Use with "*B* Is for *Beanstalk*" on page 294.

THE MAILBOX **297**

TEC41060

TEC41060

TEC41060

TEC41060

TEC41060

TEC41060

TEC41060

TEC41060

TEC41060

TEC41060

TEC41060

TEC41060

TEC41060

TEC41060

TEC41060

Chicken Little Pattern
Use with "Aiming Acorns" on page 295.

TEC41060

House Pattern
Use with "Listen Up" on page 296.

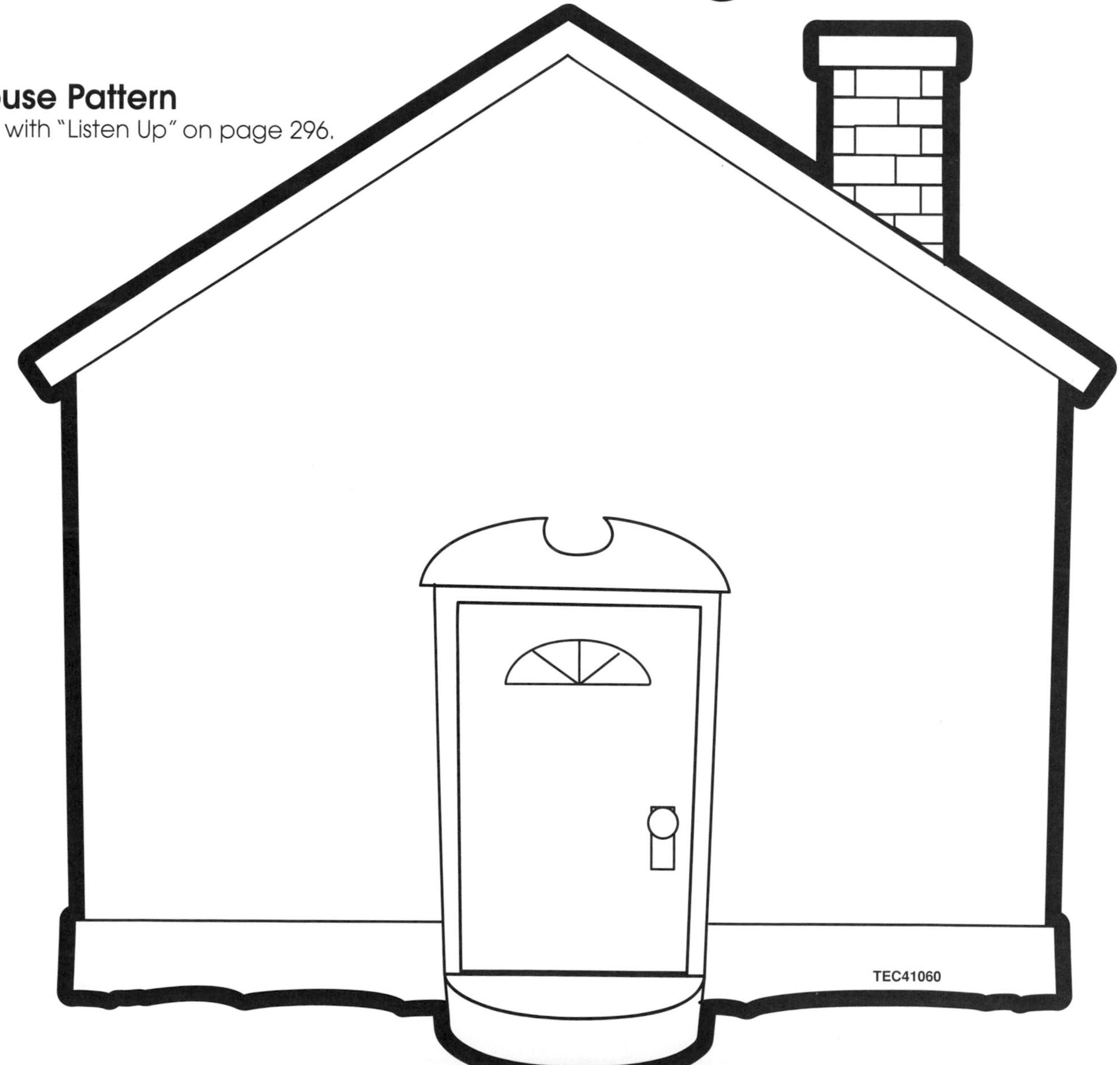

TEC41060

Wiggly, Slimy, Squirmy!

Wonderful Worms

Compost Critters
Investigating living things, developing earth-friendly habits

Put youngsters in charge of this wormy wonderland! Place moist soil and earthworms in a plastic tub. Then have students put small pieces of vegetable and fruit scraps on the soil surface, emphasizing to youngsters that the worms will eat the food and make the soil better for plants. Cover the food with newspaper shreds. (The worms like the dark, and they will eat the newspaper as well!) Place a spray bottle of water near the tub. Have little ones occasionally spray the environment to keep it moist. Little ones will love to observe the workings of these happy worms!

Tena Reynolds, South Heights Head Start, Henderson, KY

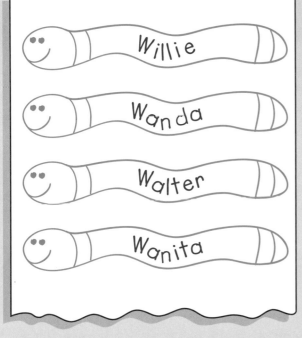

Willie

Wanda

Walter

Wanita

Name That Worm!
Identifying the letter W and its sound

Draw several worms on your chart paper. Say, "Which worm do you think has the name "Willie"? Have a volunteer point to a worm. Then write "Willie" on the worm and lead students in a round of the song shown. Continue with the remaining worms and names. Then have students recite the names, leading them to notice that all the names begin with the letter *W* and the /w/ sound just like the word *worm*. If desired, draw a few more worms and have students make up worm names that begin with /w/.

(sung to the tune of "Are You Sleeping?")

Where is [Willie] Worm? Where is [Willie] Worm?
Here he is! Here he is!
What do you say, [Willie]? What do you say, [Willie]?
/w/, /w/, /w/, /w/, /w/, /w/.

Continue with the following: *Wanda, Walter, Wanita, Wally, Wesley*

Jennifer Gemar, Tripp-Delmont School, Tripp, SD

Observation Deck
Investigating living things

Little ones will love observing earthworms with this simple setup! Use a sheet of Plexiglas material to form a bridge between two chairs; then secure it in place with duct tape or packing tape. Place earthworms on the Plexiglas sheet to crawl around. Then encourage youngsters to lie beneath the Plexiglas sheet to observe the wandering worms. Be sure to have youngsters place the worms back in a moist soil environment after observation.

Patti Chase, Noah's Ark Nursery School
Quarryville, PA

Worms do not like the light. They are long and slimy. Evan

A Long Story
Dictating information, expressing oneself through art

To make this class book, have each child fringe-cut a green paper strip and glue it to the top of a 12" x 18" sheet of white construction paper. Next, direct her to use a foam brush to spread brown paint below the grass, leaving strips of white (worm tunnels) visible. Then have her dip a finger in pink paint and drag it along the tunnels to make worms. Encourage her to dictate information about worms. Write or print her dictation and attach it to the artwork. Bind the finished projects together with a cover titled "Earthworms: A Long Story!"

Cheryl Cicioni, St. Anne Preschool at St. John Neumann, Lancaster, PA
Jo Carol Hebert, ABC Dual Language Learning Center, Bryan, TX

A Not-So-Slimy Snack
Following directions

You won't believe how simple and satisfying this snack is! Get a tube of breadsticks from your grocery's refrigerator section. Then have each child roll out a breadstick (worm) on a strip of foil. Encourage her to sprinkle cinnamon and sugar on her worm and then press on raisin eyes. Bake the worms according to package directions. After they cool slightly, have students nibble on these squirmy snacks!

Margaret Cromwell, Grace Episcopal Preschool
Georgetown, TX

For the Birds
Identifying numbers, counting

Cut out several colorful copies of the bird pattern on page 304 and label each bird with a different number. Snip brown pipe cleaners to make worms and then bury them in sand in your sand table. Explain to youngsters that many birds eat worms. A child searches through the sand to find the worms. Then he places the appropriate number of worms on each bird.

Lori Dworsky, Middletown, DE

Light and Dark
Developing gross-motor skills, investigating living things

Explain that a worm moves across the floor by using its muscles to stretch out long and thin, reaching as far as possible. Then it bunches up, short and fat. Have students practice wiggling like worms. Then tell them that worms like the dark. Turn off the light and prompt students to wiggle like worms. Then turn on the lights and prompt your little worms to freeze. Continue this game for several rounds.

Betty Silkunas, Lower Gwynedd Elementary, Ambler, PA

Wiggly Warbling
Participating in a song

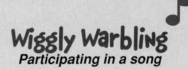

Your little worms will get their wiggles out with this neat performance!

(sung to the tune of the chorus of "Jingle Bells")

Wiggle worm,
Wiggle worm,
Wiggle your way down   *Wiggle to the floor.*
In the soil deep and dark   *Continue wiggling.*
You wiggle underground.
Wiggle worm,
Wiggle worm,
Wiggle your way up.   *Wiggle up to a standing position.*
To the surface, you must go.   *Continue wiggling.*
It's raining way too much!

Roxanne LaBell Dearman, NC Early Intervention Program for Children Who Are Deaf or Hard of Hearing, Charlotte, NC

TEC41060

It's a JUNGLE In Here!

These rain forest-themed activities will be tops with your little explorers—and that's no monkey business!

Caiman Clip

Counting, developing fine-motor skills

Youngsters develop vocabulary and get to know rain forest animals with simple clip-on caimans! Spray-paint spring-style clothespins green and then draw eyes on each clothespin so it resembles a caiman. Make several blue construction paper swamps or lakes and then label each one with a different number. To begin, explain to little ones that a caiman looks a lot like an alligator and lives in a jungle or rain forest. Arrange youngsters in small groups and give each group a swamp and a bunch of caimans. Have each group work together to identify the number and attach that number of caimans to the swamp. Check each group's work. Then have students switch swamps and repeat the activity.

Carissa Stricklen, Discovery Kids Preschool, Maple Plain, MN

11

A Fragrant Forest!

Exploring rain forest products, investigating the sense of smell

Gather cocoa, loose-leaf tea, and ground coffee or coffee beans. Give each child a cutout copy of the monkey pattern (see page 308) and encourage children to color it as desired. Explain that monkeys live in the jungle. Also explain that we get many things that people like from the jungle. Show youngsters the items and allow them to touch and smell them. Then prompt little ones to identify the items and discuss how people use them. Finally, have students brush glue on the monkey and then sprinkle the items over the glue to make a jungle collage.

Sharon Whitfield, Davidson United Methodist Church Preschool, Davidson, NC

Coffee

TEA

COCOA

What other items come from a rain forest?

Black pepper, sugar, papayas, mangos, ginger, allspice, nutmeg, bananas, and avocados to name a few! For extra rain forest fun, place these items in your discovery center for little ones to explore.

Everybody In!
Dramatizing a story, reinforcing sequencing skills

Little ones will love dramatizing the events of Jan Brett's *The Umbrella*! In this story, a boy takes his umbrella into the cloud forest to look for animals. When he leaves his umbrella on the forest floor, all the animals decide it's the perfect place to rest! Place a circle of yarn (or a blanket) on the floor and designate it as the umbrella. Before a second reading of the story, assign the story characters. As you read, prompt little ones to "climb" into the umbrella when indicated. Then have them all fall out appropriately at the end.

Kelsea Wright, Seal Elementary, Douglass, KS

Bonus Fun Stuff!

See page 309 for cards depicting common rain forest animals. Youngsters can identify them, sort them, or use them along with an umbrella prop to create their own version of this story. Also, get fabulous full-page patterns of these animals online!

Macaw Mix
Following directions

This tropical rain forest mix is sure to be pleasing to preschoolers' palates! Slice tropical dried fruit bits into small, thin pieces. Then place the fruits, sesame sticks, and coconut flakes in separate bowls. (Check for tree nut allergies if using coconut.) Have each child take a large spoonful of each treat and place it in a resealable plastic bag. Help her seal and shake her bag. Then encourage her to eat her tasty tropical treat!

A Jungle Adventure!
Exploring through dramatic play

Decorate a large box as shown to make a jungle jeep. Place the jeep at a center along with backpacks and pretend binoculars (cardboard tubes taped together). Place mosquito netting (found online or at outdoor recreation stores) over tables and attach leaf cutouts to the netting. Drape crepe paper streamer vines around the area and provide appropriate stuffed toys for a jungle adventure!

Melissa Anderson, James R. Wood Elementary, Somonauk, IL
Margaret Cromwell, Grace Episcopal Preschool, Georgetown, TX

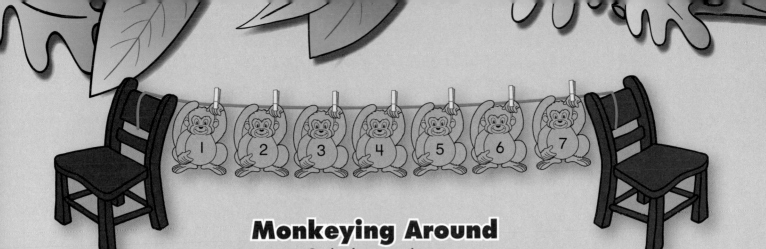

Monkeying Around
Ordering numbers

Cut out several copies of the monkey pattern on page 308 and number them consecutively. Suspend a length of thick green yarn between two chairs and provide clothespins. Scatter the monkeys on the floor and gather youngsters around. Have a child find the first monkey and make monkey noises as he attaches it to the vine. Continue in the same way, having students attach the monkeys in numerical order. **For a more challenging option**, have students complete the activity independently at a center.

Melissa Anderson, James R. Wood Elementary, Somonauk, IL

That's interesting! Monkeys peel bananas from the opposite end that people peel bananas, and the monkeys know what they're doing because their way is easier! Give each child a banana and encourage her to pinch the bottom of her banana. The bottom will split open and then it can be peeled in two or three pieces. Little ones will probably note that the stem makes a handy handle! *Mickey Miller, Cradle to Crayons Learning Center, Little Chute, WI*

Deep in the Jungle!
Investigating living things, participating in a rhyming chant

Cut out a copy of the cards on page 309 and place them facedown on the floor. Lead youngsters in reciting the chant shown, speaking very quietly on lines five and six. Before the final line, have a child turn over a card. Then guide youngsters to chant the final line, naming the animal when appropriate. For extra fun, if a child turns over the jaguar card, prompt little ones to run in place as if they're leaving the jungle quickly!

kinkajou

Deep in the jungle
Where the kapoks grow
And the green vines drape
Both high and low,
I think that something
Must be looking at me.
What oh what could that
something be?
Why, it's a [kinkajou], yes sirree!

Monkey Pattern

Use with "A Fragrant Forest!" on page 305 and "Monkeying Around" on page 307.

TEC41061

toucan
TEC41061

boa constrictor
TEC41061

sloth
TEC41061

jaguar
TEC41061

quetzal
TEC41061

kinkajou
TEC41061

tree frog
TEC41061

tapir
TEC41061

squirrel monkey
TEC41061

Ice Cream, Beach Trips, and Watermelon!

Super Signs of Summer

A Marvelous Mural
Collecting data, dictating information

Little ones identify signs of summer with a sassy display! Draw a large sun in the middle of a length of bulletin board paper. Have students color and decorate the sun. Then display the paper. Ask, "How do you know when it's summer?" and write youngsters' thoughts on the mural. Consider adding sketches as well, if desired! Have little ones add things—such as photos, magazine pictures, and drawings of summer signs—to the mural throughout the week.

Amy Compton, Brainy Bunch Home Daycare/Preschool, Roseville, CA

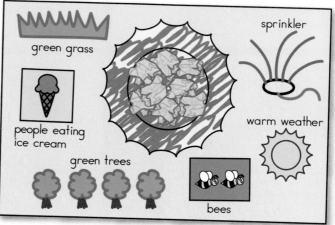

green grass

people eating ice cream

green trees

sprinkler

warm weather

bees

Going to the Beach!
Developing memory skills, participating in a group game

Give each child a paper plate steering wheel and have students form a line. Lead your little drivers around the room as they recite the chant shown. Prompt students to stop their cars and then encourage a youngster to name something he might see on the way to a beach, such as a gas station, a park, or a stop sign. Encourage students to "drive" farther. Then stop again to have a different child recite the last child's suggestion and then name his own. Continue in the same way, helping youngsters remember each suggestion before naming their own.

> We're going to the beach!
> We're going to the beach!
> We're in the car—it's not that far.
> We're going to the beach.

Donna Olp, St. Gregory the Great Preschool, South Euclid, OH

Summer Smells

Writing letters and words, developing fine-motor skills

For fun summer writing practice, place lemonade drink mix in the bottom of a tray. Provide colorful drinking straws and letter or word cards, depending on your little ones' skill levels. Have a child choose a card and use a straw to trace the letter or word in the drink mix, sniffing its lovely lemony aroma as she works.

Janet Boyce, Cokato, MN

Seasonal Song

Participating in a song

Lead little ones in singing this active summer song!

(sung to the tune of "The Farmer in the Dell")

[It's getting kind of hot]!	*Fan self with hand.*
[It's getting kind of hot]!	*Fan self with hand.*
Heigh-ho, it's summer so	
[It's getting kind of hot]!	*Fan self with hand.*

Continue with the following:

You see the lightning bugs. *(Open and close hands to represent flashing.)*
It's time to swim and splash. *(Pantomime swimming.)*
You hear the ice cream truck. *(Cup hand to ear.)*
You have a picnic lunch. *(Rub tummy.)*

Roxanne LaBell Dearman, NC Early Intervention Program for Children Who Are Deaf or Hard of Hearing, Charlotte, NC

Picnic Pests

Investigating living things

Here's an activity that allows youngsters to investigate ant behavior! Take students outside for a snack. While students are eating, prompt them to leave behind a few crumbs. Take a picture of the area prior to leaving. Then go back indoors. An hour later, return to the area with your little ones and have students check to see if there are any ants. Encourage students to observe and discuss the ants' behavior. Then take another photo and display both photos in your classroom.

Litsa Jackson, Covington Integrated Arts Academy, Covington, TN

Sprinkle Toss!
Counting, comparing sets, gross-motor skills
For this fun activity, make a simple supersize ice cream cone cutout and place it on the floor. Put a container of pom-poms (sprinkles) and a small plastic shovel (or cup) nearby. Have a child stand in a designated location and toss a shovel full of sprinkles at the cone. Say, "Oh my goodness! Sprinkles are everywhere!" with great drama. Then help students count the number of sprinkles on the cone and off the cone and compare the amounts.

adapted from an idea by Kelly Davis, Country Bumpkin Childcare, Clifton, ME

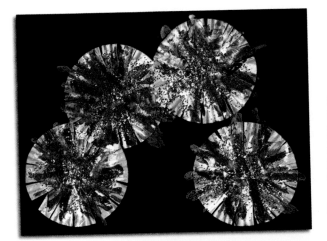

Bang! Pop! Boom!
Reinforcing holiday symbols
To make this fun firework craft, have each student flatten cupcake liners and then snip a fringe around the edges. Have her glue the liners to a black sheet of construction paper and add red, blue, and white paint as desired. Finally, prompt the student to sprinkle glitter on the wet paint. What a lovely fireworks show!

Donna Ream, Ms. Donna's Daycare, Plainfield, IL

Fun Stuff!
The Fourth of July is a favorite holiday for grilling out! To set up some play grilling fun, glue red and orange scraps of paper beneath a wire grill grate and then place the grate on a table along with dowel pieces painted brownish red (hot dogs) and tongs! *Kathleen McGannon, Grand Avenue Preschool/Day Care, Western Spring, IL*

Watermelon Spin
Speaking to share an opinion
Place a watermelon in your circle-time area and gather youngsters around it. Have a child spin the melon and, when it stops, identify the child the melon is pointing to, using the end where the stem was attached as a guide. Prompt that child to name a favorite characteristic of summer before taking the next turn spinning the melon.

Doris Sligh, YMCA Child Development Center at Colonial Williamsburg, Williamsburg, VA